ESSAYS IN HONOR
of
CLAUDE M. WISE

ESSAYS IN HONOR

of

CLAUDE M. WISE

EDITED BY

ARTHUR J. BRONSTEIN
*Herbert H. Lehman College
of the City University of New York*

CLAUDE L. SHAVER
Louisiana State University

Cj STEVENS
*Herbert H. Lehman College
of the City University of New York*

«»

A PROJECT SPONSORED BY THE
SPEECH ASSOCIATION OF AMERICA

«»

THE STANDARD PRINTING COMPANY
Hannibal, Missouri

LIMITED PRINTING

Library of Congress Catalogue Card Number:
74-121235

Printed in the United States of America
by
The Standard Printing Company
Hannibal, Missouri

TO THE MEMORY OF

SHIRLEY GORRELL WISE

TO WHOM SO MANY OF CLAUDE M. WISE'S BOOKS WERE DEDICATED

The Editors gratefully acknowledge the support of the Sponsors of this volume, those friends of C. M. Wise who made this undertaking practical.

THE SPONSORS

James W. Abel	A. Donald George
Johnnye Akin	Giles Wilkeson Gray
Bower Aly	Samuel I. Hayakawa
John W. Black	Sara M. Ivey
Waldo W. Braden	T. Earle Johnson
Cameron Garbutt	Lucia C. Morgan
Elizabeth B. Carr	John B. Newman
Richard Corson	Loren Reid
Frank B. Davis	Cecil Taylor
Richard P. Douthit	Jesse J. Villareal
Ilene Fife	Karl R. Wallace
Hilda B. Fisher	Eugene E. White

Wesley Wiksell

PREFACE

The names in this volume—those of the contributors, the sponsors, and the editors—are clear reason and justification for this published memorial to C. M. Wise. It was a quality of the man that he inspired: he inspired years of students in their day-to-day work; he inspired scholarly research and writings; he inspired respect, admiration, and friendship.

All of these facets of the quality of the man are evident in this volume. It is a labor of love, undertaken in part and in whole by virtue of continuing respect, admiration, friendship, and a sense of enduring obligation. The essays herein are indicative of the broad range of C. M. Wise's research and writing, and the genesis of some can be traced directly to his influence. Former students, as well as colleagues, are represented in these pages.

The contributors and those others who have made this volume possible do not represent any single geographic area. Neither were the interests and influence of C. M. Wise confined by geographic boundaries. Nor are they confined by time.

ACKNOWLEDGMENTS

The editors are indebted to many who have helped make this volume possible. Foremost among them are the sponsors (whose names appear elsewhere) and the contributors whose essays are the reason for this volume. Mr. Heath Meriwether, the publisher, gave his time, money, and extensive skill in typesetting the volume, organizing the flow of galleys and following our directions to our utmost satisfaction. We are sincerely grateful to him. The Speech Association of America, through the recommendations of its Committee on Publications, is a sponsor of this volume, thus making available to the editors the assistance of the SAA office and the considerable skill and support of the Executive Secretary of the Association, Dr. William Work. The Speech Association of America office has helped advertise the volume, is handling the publication orders, and has supported us with advice and skill whenever asked.

Three assistants have seen us through the mass of correspondence—keeping the files straight, answering our letters, taking our calls, easing our schedules. Miss Carolyn Herzog of Queens College, Mrs. Angela Schwimmer, and Miss Miriam Ramos of Lehman College have been delightful and efficient. What sense of humor is left to us, we thank them for. Queens College, Lehman College, and Louisiana State University have helped defray office and postal expenses. And our wives Elsa Bronstein, Ruth Shaver, and Edith Stevens have been patient, understanding and encouraging.

We owe a special thanks to Cheryl Judith Stevens for the design and execution of the dustjacket. She counted it a privilege, for she has known Claude Wise most of her life.

The students and colleagues of Claude Wise will remember the man without this volume. If its contents remind those many friends somewhat more often, the efforts of the many persons we've noted above will have been worth the doing and noting.

THE EDITORS

Arthur J. Bronstein
Claude L. Shaver
Cj Stevens

CONTENTS

C. M. WISE

A Biographical Note

In this age of social- and self-evaluation one of the great imponderables is the future of the deprived child, the starved child, the disadvantaged child. By current standards Claude Wise was such a child. In the last few weeks of his life, he puzzled anew a matter which his children repeatedly questioned; Where did the drive to succeed, which motivated his life, originate?

Just before the War Between the States, in the panhandle of Virginia that was soon to be West Virginia, one of a dozen boys was born to a slave-hating mountain clan. Being a younger son, as he reached his early teens, his patriarchal father decided he was to be a blacksmith; he wanted to be a teacher. In the post-war years his father apprenticed him to a smith; after two years of apprenticeship, he ran away down the Ohio to Missouri. He farmed, clerked in a store, studied, and in time went to a one-man seminary (college) in Edina, Missouri. In two years he was graduated with a Diploma in Arts and married a girl from a slave-holding family who also had a diploma. From her family he received a dowry of a few acres of bottom land, near forty acres of scrub-oak hill farm which he owned. Of their seven or eight children only two survived infancy. Of these Claude was the eldest. Because of the dangers in getting to school (even then there was a safety problem for school children) his mother did not allow him to go until age eight, teaching him to read and cipher at home. By age twelve he had completed all of the schooling available to him at the little one-room school house across the hills from home, perhaps the equivalent of an eighth grade education.

On a forty-acre hill farm there was little way to earn money; food consisted of what could be raised and what could be hunted. Cash consisted of his father's intermittent teaching stipend of a few dollars per pupil per year and in summer his mother's "egg and butter" money. In Claude's latter years he often spoke of "winter hunger" and the eagerness with which he and his family watched for the dandelion and Canadian thistle "greens" of the early spring; nobody then knew about vitamin deficiency or the mental blunting of hunger.

His father's library consisted of fifteen or twenty textbooks he had bought from other students, including three volumes of Ridpath's *History of the World*. His mother was determined that Claude would go to college. At age nineteen his father gave him the "tie" timber on half of the forty-acre farm. He was allowed to cut, trim, and sell ties to the railroads for whatever money the oak logs would bring. By so doing, he earned enough money, a little over one-hundred dollars, to go to Kirksville Normal School. There he completed his four-year high school education and obtained a three-year college teaching certificate by age 21. He also met a young art student-teacher, Shirley Gorrell, who later became his wife.

Under the stimulus of Professor John R. Kirk, President of the College, he was imbued with the idea of the educated man and the "responsibility of ability" so eloquently espoused many years later by John F. Kennedy and his brothers. The historian E. M. Violette reinforced his sense of history and man's debt to society. Mr. A. P. Settle, his professor of English, created in him a love for literature and writing and gave him his start as a college teacher, dramatist, and advisor. Over the years these influences were reflected in his drive to publication, his interest in teaching students, and his "ethic by example" which is best exemplified in a quotation from his own writing in an early issue of the *Southern Speech Journal*.

> I believe in accessibility to students and companionship with them. I believe in promoting attitudes of professional ethics in them, habits of professional participation in state and regional associations and the SAA. . . . I believe in treating graduate students as fellow student scholars; in giving them hard tasks to do —in friendliness; in conducting severe master's and doctor's examinations with dignity and kindliness . . . I believe the department of speech should be a place of graciousness and gentility; a place of learned and learning people; a place for the forming of lifelong personal friendships and for the building of lifelong scholarly associations; a place not so much to prepare for living as to live fully and richly some of the best years of a good life.[1]

This is the man to whom this volume is dedicated. This is the man who was pioneer, dramatist, writer, phonetician, linguist, experimenter, traveler, and above all, master teacher. This is the man who proved that all rules have exceptions, even the rule of the underprivileged child. For, except for his mother's unswerving belief that he must go to college and his father's legacy of "tie" oaks and a small library, he had none of the material advantages of childhood which would make one expect him to attain in a competitive society the stature which he reached.

---

[1] C. M. Wise, "Department of Speech—A Point of View," *Southern Speech Journal*, Fall, 1954, pp. 1-6.

THE UNITS OF PHONOLOGY*

GORDON E. PETERSON† AND JUNE E. SHOUP
Speech Communications Research Laboratory
Santa Barbara, California

To those interested in the phonological description of languages there are two dominant and enduring questions. (1) What are the essential units with which such descriptions may be constructed? (2) How can the parameters of the speech wave, which are generally continuous over short intervals of time, be associated in an unambiguous way with basic discrete phonological units? These questions are much more important than the one of whether a description should be formulated in generative or analytical terms, and they are much more important than the question of the particular format selected for a phonological description.

The term "phonological theory" is used in this paper to refer to the general properties of spoken dialects and spoken languages, and not to refer to the statement of the phonological structure of an individual language, which will simply be called a "phonological description." To consider the description of a specific language as a theory is much like considering the description of some physical object as a theory, disregarding the fact that there are more general theories of chemistry and physics. It would seem that the enduring interest and the basic problems in linguistic science must be primarily concerned with the general properties of languages. There are a few basic assumptions which should be reviewed at this time.

ASSUMPTIONS

1. *There are various types of related units in spoken languages.* To deny the existence of linguistic units is to deny that languages have structure and that there are language universals. If no units are specifiable, then one is free to construct the description of a dialect with any arbitrary units. There is, of course, no well defined relation between such arbitrary and variable units and actual speech production. There is then no basis for evaluating various descriptions of a dialect or for comparing the descriptions of different dialects. It seems necessary to conclude that there are basic linguistic units, and this paper will be concerned with such units in phonology.

* The preparation of this paper was supported by the Directorate of Information Sciences of the United States Air Force Office of Scientific Research under Grant AF-AFOSR-1252-67 and Contract F44620-69-C-0078.
† Deceased.

2. *The dialects of a language differ phonologically and require different phonological descriptions.* It is assumed that all dialects differ at least phonetically and prosodically whether or not they differ phonemically and prosodemically. It is, therefore, as a minimum necessary to indicate these phonological variations in the respective phonological descriptions.

3. *The phonological description of a dialect must be closely related to actual conversational speech.* A serious phonological description must provide for the production and the analysis of speech as it actually occurs. To account for what might have been said, what should have been said, or what was intended according to some idealized simplification accomplishes little. In science one seeks models that account for actual events and data, not potential data which are hoped for or imagined. In a generative system a phonetic and prosodic array must specify a behavior of the vocal mechanism which results in fully intelligible and natural speech within the dialect. This relation must be biunique. That is, if speech is produced from a given phonetic and prosodic array and that speech is then analyzed phonetically, it must result in the same phonetic and prosodic array. The terms "phonetic" and "prosodic" here refer to lower level units than phonemes or prosodemes. At higher levels of phonological structure, biuniqueness is a futile simplification. At the phonetic level, however, it is a necessity to rigor. If a phonetic and prosodic transcription can be pronounced in ways which are significantly different or if a single utterance can be transcribed in different ways, then the transcription does not meet the criterion of being phonetic. Thus an effective phonetic system is absolutely essential to a phonological description. Without a reasonably complete system there is no possibility of developing a coherent and complete phonological description of a dialect.

4. *The physiology of speech production provides the most effective basis for describing the elements of descriptive phonetics.* The elements of phonetics are normally described in terms of the control of the breath stream and the positions and movements of the various anatomical structures of the vocal mechanism. Since there has been substantially more progress in the investigation of the acoustical characteristics of speech than in the experimental description of the physiology of speech production, many investigators have attempted to specify the elements of phonetics in acoustical terms. This appears to be an unrealistic and futile goal. It is now generally accepted by a wide range of specialists that the physiology of speech production provides the most appropriate basis for the description of speech.

To assume that the physiology of speech production provides the basis for an organized description of the phonetic elements of speech is not nearly as general as assuming that there is a motor process in speech perception. In the former case the structure of the signal is described in physiological dynamics and parameter values, and there are no implications about the neural mechanisms employed in the perception of the dynamics and parameter values. In the latter case, there is the added implication that the motor mechanism is somehow involved in the perceptual process. These two hypotheses are thus very different and it appears that there is only justification for the former. The latter hypothesis seems to imply that there is an interaction between the motor and sensory pathways at neurological levels of a magnitude which has not yet been demonstrated. To follow this approach to its logical conclusion, it would be necessary that we have an internal motor mechanism equivalent to every device whose signals we can perceive. According to this theory, since the human has a speech mechanism he is able to interpret speech signals. How, then, is he able to interpret the sound of an automobile horn, the noise of a freight train, or the roar of a waterfall?

5. *An utterance is a single instance.* Two independent actions of the vocal mechanism which seem to be identical, which sound alike, and which may be interpreted in the same way, are two different utterances. An utterance is thus a token in the terminology of semantics, and any element within an utterance is also a token. An utterance and its parts are each different tokens of particular types. The token-type distinction is extremely important in phonology and in other components of language theory as well. Failure to observe this distinction has resulted in many of the confusions that have been generated about language structure.

PHONETIC THEORY

Under the above assumptions it is quite obvious that a carefully formulated phonetic theory is essential to any successful phonological description. Phonetics is a much more complicated subject than it is generally considered to be and yet requires extensive theoretical and empirical research.

Even though a suitable basis for phonetic theory and phonetic notation was developed long ago, phonetics has generally had great weaknesses. These weaknesses result more from a lack of specificity and adequate experimental knowledge than from an inappropriate orientation. Although the theory of distinctive features (2) was originally proposed as a phonemic theory, it has sometimes been viewed as a phonetic theory. Actually the theory of distinctive features has relatively few of the properties required of a phonetic theory. Only very recently have there been serious attempts to construct more rigorous and more relevant formulations of various aspects of phonetic theory.

PHYSIOLOGICAL PHONETIC PARAMETER VALUES

If a particular distinction in speech production is significant in a given dialect, then it should be possible to denote that distinction by means of phonetic notation. There are a number of different parameters within which distinctions are made in speech. Any one of these distinctions will result in a different meaning between utterances in some language.

One phonetic theory (3) suggests three primary physiological phonetic parameters and twelve secondary phonetic parameters. Three additional prosodic parameters are also designated. With the exception of cases of multiple articulation, at any particular instant during speech production there is present one and only one value of each of the fifteen phonetic parameters. Multiple articulations have at least one value of each parameter at any particular instant but some parameters may be multi-valued. In constructing the theory it was the objective to include as many categories or values within each parameter as was necessary to specify the distinctions found in languages.

Most of the parameters could not reasonably be separated into binary divisions. For example, there are a minimum of three basic air mechanisms with which speech is produced, specifically: pulmonic, glottic, and velic. Various combinations of these are also employed as when both a velic and pulmonic mechanism are employed in the production of a nasalized click. There are, of course, more than two different manners of articulation, for example: nasal, stop, flap, trill, sibilant, fricative, sonorant, and vowel. Likewise there are a number of different laryngeal actions observed in spoken languages, including voiceless, whispered, breathy, voiced, laryngealized, and others.

A phonetic system must provide the basis for describing all of the various physiological formations which are distinct or potentially distinct in any spoken natural language. The notion of "distinctive features" as presently defined appears to be much too limited for phonetics. If the feature is equated to parameter value, then the more general categories according to which related features may be grouped are lacking. Alternatively, the features may be considered as the general categories, but then the subdivisions are lacking. Without an adequate number of parameter values it is hopeless to expect to specify rules which will convert from phonetic elements to natural speech or to achieve an unambiguous phonetic transcription of an utterance.

A basic diagram as shown in Figure 1 may be constructed with the

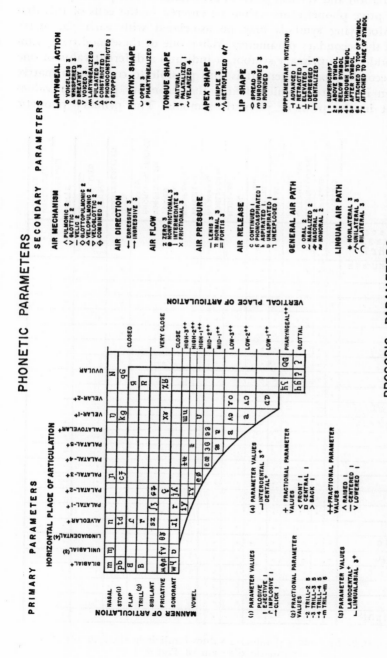

Figure 1. The physiological speech parameters.

three primary parameters: manner of articulation, horizontal place of articulation and vertical place of articulation. The primary symbols of descriptive phonetics may then be entered in the cells of this diagram. Modifying symbols may be associated with each parameter value of the secondary parameters. When one of these modifying symbols is added to a primary symbol, it indicates a different value of one of the secondary parameters. It is thus possible to construct a matrix as shown in Figure 2 which defines the secondary parameter values inherent in the primary phonetic symbols. The primary phonetic

Symbol	PULMONIC	EGRESSIVE	NONFRICTIONAL / INTERMEDIATE / FRICTIONAL	NORMAL	CONTINUED / UNASPIRATED	ORAL / NONORAL	NONLATERAL / BILATERAL	VOICELESS / WHISPERED / BREATHY / VOICED / CONSTRICTED / PHONOCONSTRICTED / STOPPED	OPEN / PHARYNGEALIZED	NATURAL / PALATALIZED / VELARIZED	SIMPLE / RETROFLEXED	UNROUNDED / ROUNDED
iɨɯɪɪɛɜɘə æɐɐʌɑʌɑ/ ʙʀR/ʙɾʀ	•	•	•	•	•	•	•	•	•	•	•	•
yʉuɤʊʊœɵɞə ɔoɔɒ	•	•	•	•	•	•	•	•	•	•	•	•
w	•	•	•	•	•	•	•	•	•	• •	•	•
ɥ	•	•	•	•	•	•	•	•	•	• •	•	•
ʋ ɹ	•	•	•	•	•	•	•	•	•	•	•	•
l	•	•	•	•	•	•	•	•	•	•	•	•
ɾ	•	•	•	•	•	•	•	•	•	•	• •	•
j	•	•	•	•	•	•	•	•	•	•	•	•
ʎ	•	•	•	•	•	•	•	•	•	•	•	•
ʍ	•	•	•	•	•	•	•	•	•	• •	•	•
ɸf θç xχ/sʃ	•	•	•	•	•	•	•	•	•	•	•	•
βv ðδ ʁ/zʒ	•	•	•	•	•	•	•	•	•	•	•	•
ħ	•	•	•	•	•	•	•	•	• •	•	•	•
ʕ	•	•	•	•	•	•	•	•	• •	•	•	•
h	•	•	•	•	•	•	•	• •	•	•	•	•
ɦ	•	•	•	•	•	•	•	• •	•	•	•	•
ɕ	•	•	•	•	•	•	•	•	•	•	• •	•
ʑ	•	•	•	•	•	•	•	•	•	•	• •	•
ʔ	•	•	•	•	•	•	•	•	• •	•	•	•
ptckq	•	•	•	•	• •	•	•	•	•	•	•	•
bdɟgɢ	•	•	•	•	• •	•	•	•	•	•	•	•
Q	•	•	•	•	• •	•	•	•	•	• •	•	•
ɢ	•	•	•	•	• •	•	•	•	•	• •	•	•
ʔ	•	•	•	•	• •	•	•	•	• •	•	•	•
mɱ ŋɲŋN	•	•	•	•	• •	•	• •	•	•	•	•	•

FIGURE 2. Secondary parameter values implicit in the symbols of the phonetic diagram of Figure 1.

symbols may be used to define the rows of the matrix, and the various secondary parameter values which are inherent in the notation of the primary symbols may be used to define the columns.

When the prosodic parameters are also adequately specified, such a phonetic theory will provide a symbolization for the phonetic and prosodic description of any normal utterance.

PHONES

The most difficult and challenging part of phonetic theory is to specify the dynamic aspects of speech production. The various physiological parameters undergo almost continuous change during speech production. The interpretation of the continuous parameters of speech as discrete elements is an essential and major problem of phonetic theory. There are many complexities in the interpretation of the variations that occur. Steady-state conditions, controlled movements, oscillations, and transitions must all be properly treated. To date there has been no attempt at a phonetic theory, other than that mentioned above, which even considers this problem. It is customary to associate a sequence of phonetic elements with an utterance, but how are these elements selected? The vocal mechanism passes through many conditions, that is, through many different complete sets of phonetic parameter values, which are not indicated in a phonetic transcription, or if one prefers, indicated with distinctive features. A phonetic theory must show which sets of phonetic parameter values are to be denoted and which sets are to be excluded in a phonetic transcription.

Before the development of the sound spectrograph it seemed to be generally assumed that speech consisted of a sequence of relatively discrete and static sounds connected together to form utterances. The extensive amount of variation with time observed in sound spectrograms introduced considerable chaos into previously simple conceptions of speech production. It has sometimes been overlooked, however, that the changes observed in sound spectrograms are changes in the total acoustic output and may result from concurrent changes in the positions of various articulators. The transformation from the physiology of speech production to the acoustic parameters of speech is highly complex. In phonetic specifications it is thus essential to observe directly the positions and movements of the organs of the vocal mechanism. There appear to be essentially four different rates of movement found among the articulators.

1. An *articulatory steady-state* may be characterized as a minimum in the absolute magnitude of the average rate of change of the position and shape of an articulator as it forms successive constrictions and

closures, and during which the articulator is not engaged in an oscillation or tap.

2. A *controlled articulatory movement* may be characterized as a movement of an articulator which is slow relative to most of the movements of the articulator and in which the average change in the position and shape of the articulator is relatively constant and regular throughout.

3. An *articulatory oscillation* may be characterized as a sequence of one or more consecutive vibrations of an articulator which is caused by the tension and position of the articulator, the pressure difference between the two sides of the articulator, and the airflow past the articulator.

4. An *articulatory transition* may be characterized as a relatively rapid movement of an articulator between successive articulatory steady-states, controlled articulatory movements, and/or articulatory oscillations.

It should be emphasized that the above statements are simply explanations, not definitions. A more detailed and systematic development is required actually to specify these terms. The above four concepts, however, are among those basic to the concept of phone. In a phonetic transcription there is one symbol for each phone. During articulatory transitions, however, the vocal mechanism normally passes through a sequence of many complete sets of phonetic parameter values. It is thus utterly meaningless to attempt to provide a phonetic representation in terms of the sequence of all complete sets of phonetic parameter values which occur, or in terms of the sequence of all sets of distinctive features. Only certain of the complete sets of parameter values are significant and are associated with phones. Specifying which complete sets are relevant is a very challenging and interesting part of phonetic theory.

Even when the appropriate sets are identified, however, there is no reason whatever to list each individual parameter value in the phonetic transcription. The individual symbols of phonetics provide a complete summary of the parameter values and thus form a very simple and efficient code for phonetic transcription. Although the code has not been adequately specified in the past, it has been used effectively for a long time and it is not likely that anything of greater convenience will soon replace it. When the code is made exact, it becomes a very efficient device for denoting the basic phonetic properties of utterance.

It should thus be obvious that parameter values are not the ultimate units of phonology or phonetics. They are, however, the ultimate significant properties of the units or elements of phonetics. One cannot discard the problem of segmentation with a sophisticated set of parameter values or of distinctive features. The basic units of phonetics are phones and they must be specified in terms of complete sets of parameter values. Thus both parameter values and phones are indispensible concepts in phonetics. Even if one thinks in terms of distinctive features, both distinctive features and some type of segment are required.

PHONETIC EQUIVALENCE

According to the above discussion a phone is one of a sequence of elements which constitute the phonetic part of an utterance. A phone is thus a single instance or token. It occurs only once in only one utterance. Two different utterances may contain phones of the same type but the two phones are different tokens. Unless a phonetic symbol is subscripted, it denotes a set of phones which are all of the same type. Note that phones of the same type may occur in many different languages.

In order to specify the units of phonology, it is necessary to describe the way in which phones, not phone types, are organized into higher ordered sets. A phone type contains all the phones of that type which have occurred or will occur in all of the utterances of all of the languages of the earth. It is phones, not phone types, which occur in utterances. The assignment of a phone of a particular type to a higher ordered set depends upon the dialect and the language in which it is found.

The above discussion has been concerned primarily with phones and phone types. A related formal system must be developed for the prosodies. A complete phonetic theory would thus specify an unambiguous relation between the elements of phonetic and prosodic transcriptions and the physiology of speech production. Slight variations in speech production would be expected in different utterances produced according to the same phonetic and prosodic transcription. Thus a particular phonetic and prosodic transcription does not uniquely specify the speech wave of an utterance. Variations would be allowable, however, only within the values of the parameters of the various phone types and prosodies indicated by the transcription. In no instance should a variation exceed the boundaries of a particular physiological parameter value. There is thus a unique relation between the elements of a phonetic transcription and the physiological parameter values involved in producing an utterance according to that transcription.

One might speculate that with such a unique relation, higher ordered units are not required in phonology but rather that the lexical items could be specified directly in phone types. Such a speculation is, of course, exceedingly naive. First, the speech of any given dialect involves phones of a very large number of different phone types. A single lexical item may usually be pronounced normally with various sequences of phones of different phone types, although some sequences may be more common than others within a particular dialect. More importantly, when lexical items are embedded in a larger syntax, phonetic intereffects may radically influence the types of the initial and final phones, and frequently the types of medial phones within lexical items will also be influenced. To introduce all of these phonetic variations into the lexicon or syntax of a language description obviously achieves nothing but confusion. The relation between phonology and grammar need not be so involved, and can be described much more simply with intermediate phonological units, traditionally referred to as phonemes. If an attempt is made in such a system to by-pass or exclude the phonemic concept, the system either will not have a reasonable relation to actual speech production or the generative and analytical rules will be so hopelessly complicated that the entire system will be exceedingly awkward.

We may now consider the organization of phones and prosodies into higher ordered phonological units. Although it is recognized that the term "phoneme" has certain associations owing to the general use it has had in the linguistic field during the last few decades, this term for the higher-ordered phonological sets is preferred by the present authors to more general terms such as "phonological representations." Certain concepts which are basic to the phoneme include phonetic similarity between phones, semantic equivalence between utterances, phonetic and/or prosodic equivalence between utterances, minimal utterance, functionally equivalent phones, contrasting phones, functionally related sets of phones, and allophones.

1. *Phonetic similarity between phones* indicates a closeness in physiological parameter value measures which contributes to the native speaker's intuitive feeling that certain phones are not substantially different from one another.

2. *Semantic equivalence between utterances* indicates that the utterances denote the same set of objects, properties, relationships, and/or events.

3. *Phonetic and/or prosodic equivalence between utterances* indicates that the utterances contain the same number of phones and prosodies and that the phones of the one utterance are respectively phonetically equivalent to the corresponding phones of the other and that the prosodies of the one utterance are respectively prosodically equivalent to the corresponding prosodies of the other.

4. A *minimal utterance* is one which cannot be separated into a sequence of two or more utterances.

5. *Functionally equivalent phones* occur in corresponding positions in semantically equivalent utterances which are either phonetically equivalent or are phonetically equivalent except for one pair of phones which occur in corresponding positions in the two utterances.

6. *Contrastive phones* occur in the same position in minimal utterances which are not semantically equivalent, but which are prosodically equivalent and phonetically equivalent except for the phones in question.

7. *Functionally related sets of phones* are sets of phones obtained by taking the union of all phones of a given phone type in a dialect with all the phones which are functionally equivalent to any of these phones.

8. *Allophones* are the intersections of relevant functionally related sets of the dialect with the phone types.

The above statements are not definitions, but rather brief explanations of some of the concepts most crucial to the definition of the term "phoneme." In essence then a *phoneme* is a collection of allophones which meet certain specifiable criteria involving phonetic similarity and functional relatedness.

It is exceedingly important to note that in general there are no unique complete sets of physiological phonetic parameter values for phonemes. An allophone has a unique set of parameter values or a sequence of unique sets of parameter values according to the type of its phones. Many different complete sets of phonetic parameter values may be associated with a phoneme, however, according to its allophones, and some of the sets may not be unique to a single phoneme. It is thus meaningless to attempt to classify phonemes in a matrix of parameter values or distinctive features. The classification will not apply to many allophones of the phonemes and it will not be unique for all phonemes. The use of parameter value or distinctive features is obviously even more inappropriate for the classification of morphophonemes.

In the development of a forthcoming phonemic theory (4), certain observations have been made. Two utterances which are phonetically equivalent are usually semantically equivalent. When such utterances are embedded in different contexts, however, they may not be semantically equivalent. There are usually numerous examples of this circumstance which can be found in almost any language. The result is that two phones of the same phone type within two different utterances may be associated with different phonological elements. A very common example is the flap-r when used in both "latter" and "ladder." If the context indicates that "latter" is intended, then the flap-r may be associated with /t/. If the context indicates that "ladder" is intended, then the flap-r may be associated with /d/. Thus it is that phones of the same phone type may be associated with different higher level phonological units, depending upon the semantics of the context in which they are embedded. This possibility was described in detail long ago by Y. R. Chao (1) but has often been rejected, if not in publication, at least operationally by those working with languages. It is only during the past few years that the lack of biuniqueness among higher level phonological units has been sufficiently emphasized that it is now generally recognized.

For some strange reason this seems to have generated a great deal of confusion in the field of phonology. Many seem ready to abandon the notion of higher ordered units beyond the phone type in phonology. Actually, the non-uniqueness of the function of phones of the same type in speech production and speech perception should in no way be surprising. There is no question but that most processes of human perception function in this way. In most aspects of human perception the same physical object or event may be interpreted differently depending upon the environment or background in which it is observed. In the case of speech, one might say that redundancy in the language clarifies the otherwise ambiguous instances.

The essential units of the phonemic part of a phonological theory include phones, phone types, allophones, allophone types, and phonemes. We have less knowledge about the prosodic parts of phonology, and so at this time the specification of the prosodic units is more difficult but seems realizable. Once the units of phonology have been specified, one is then in a position to describe the properties of the phonological description of dialect. Without the specification of phonological units which are universally applicable, it is difficult if not impossible to compare phonological descriptions of different dialects and different languages. The task of defining the units of phonology is one of the most interesting and challenging aspects of the study of spoken language.

REFERENCES

1. Y.-R. Chao, "The Non-Uniqueness of Phonemic Solutions of Phonetic Systems," *Bulletin of the Institute of History and Philology Academia Sinica*, Volume IV, Part 4, pages 363-397, 1934.
2. R. Jakobson, C. G. M. Fant, and M. Halle, "Preliminaries to Speech Analysis." *Technical Report No. 13*, Acoustics Laboratory, Massachusetts Institute of Technology, May, 1952.
3. G. E. Peterson and J. E. Shoup, "A Physiological Theory of Phonetics," *Journal of Speech and Hearing Research*, Volume 9, Number 1, pages 5-67, March, 1966.
4. J. E. Shoup, J. R. Hanne, and G. E. Peterson, A Formalization of Phonemic Theory (forthcoming).

RESEARCH IN DEVELOPMENTAL PHONOLOGY

HILDA B. FISHER

Northwestern University

In 1943, Irwin and Chen criticized early research in developmental phonology in terms essentially repeated by McCarthy in 1954: (1) researchers inadequately trained in phonetics; (2) inadequate sampling; (3) failure to establish reliability of observations; (4) neglect of data analysis. The seat of the problem, according to Leopold 1961, is that considerably more of the research in developmental phonology has been done by psychologists and educators than by linguists.

A number of survey-studies, conducted to investigate the chronology of maturation in the articulation of English phonemes, were structured to avoid such criticisms. The most comprehensive of these investigations, by Mildred Templin, drew data from a large sample (about 1500 children), at successive ages between 3 and 8, so that statistical handling of data would yield a normal profile of articulatory competence by age. Test material comprised a large list of words chosen to contain all of a "standard" set of English phonemes occurring in various phonemic contexts and positions in words. Utterances were elicited from a child as responses to presented pictures or printed words. When the child said a word containing a particular phoneme (or combination of phonemes) being tested, the investigator (trained in the use of IPA phonemic symbols) made a judgment whether the child articulated the phoneme "correctly" (meeting his adult standards), omitted it, "distorted" it, or substituted another phoneme for it. Data consisted of a count of the number of a child's correct productions, converted to a percentage by comparison with the total number of expected occurrences of that phoneme.

Templin's conclusions, like those of other surveys with comparable research design, reveal a striking maturation in articulation skills between the ages of 3 and 6 years. Her data (as rearranged somewhat by Carroll) show that at age 3 there were 90% "correct" articulations of /p, b, t, d, k, g, m, n, w, h/, 70-80% "correct" articulations of /f, s, ŋ, l, j/, 50-60% "correct" articulations of /v, ʃ, tʃ, dʒ, r/, and 10-40% "correct" articulations of /θ, ð, z, ʍ/, while at age 6 the only phonemes having less than 90% "correct" articulations were /s, z, ʃ, ʒ, tʃ, ð, ʍ/. She concluded, additionally, that boys lag approximately a year behind girls in articulation accuracy, and that children from a lower socio-economic class are about a year behind children from a higher socio-economic class.

Various investigations of articulatory maturation in children have reached different conclusions as to the order of mastery of English phonemes. There is general agreement that a child can "correctly" produce all of a "standard" set of phonemes somewhere between the ages of 5 and 7, but the chronology of phoneme articulatory competency has not been clearly established, as the reviews by McCarthy and Powers have demonstrated.

Early studies by Leopold 1939 and others employed a research method familiar to field research in dialect geography. Observations of the child's utterances were made during a specified time period or performance period (a specified number of consecutive respiratory cycles) at periodic intervals. Their data, in varying degrees of "closeness" of transcription, represented the actual utterances of the child, rather than a judgment of his articulation accuracy in producing expected phonemes.

Methods used in the analysis of data varied. Krehbiel simply counted the number of different sounds produced by each infant. Irwin and Curry computed the frequency of occurrence of vowel elements by place of articulation (front, central, back), and later Irwin displayed his data in histograms showing frequency of use of each sound type, arranged as profiles by age. Chen's data were reported in terms of a vowel ratio, a consonant ratio, a vowel-consonant ratio, and a type-token ratio. Leopold 1939, whose study of his bilingual daughter extended to the age of 2, presented his observations chronologically with ample descriptive notes, revealing the emergence of phonemic discriminations.

The first researcher to apply phonemic analysis to the study of children's phonology was Roman Jacobson 1941. Unfortunately, his influence was not immediately reflected in American research because the publication was in German. Jacobson's confidence in an orderly chronology of phonological development, at least by phoneme types if not by specific phonemes, and not simply in one language but in all languages, is shared by later researchers. Yet the concept of universals in developmental phonology remains to be substantiated in large-scale investigations.

The most cogent theories on developmental phonology have been based on investigations in which the child's actual utterances were transcribed and evaluated, not by judging the child's competence in producing an idealized set of English phonemes according to adult standards. The method of the linguist is to research the child's idiolect as if it were an unknown language, and to derive from the phonetic data an analysis of the child's phonological system.

Research of the articulation survey type tacitly defines phonological maturation in the child in terms of increasing accuracy in phoneme production, thereby inferring that the child's phonological system is identical to that of adults in his environment, or to an idealized speaker of his language. The evidence of linguistic research supports the view that the distinctiveness of phonemes grows out of the child's *communication need.* Early emergence of certain phonemic distinctions is generally credited to the heavy *information load* those phonemes carry, while Fry believes that certain phonemes (e.g. /ʒ/) appear late because of their meager use in the language. The child's developing phonemic structure is facilitated by the occurrence of *minimal pairs* in his own vocabulary. Conversely, phonemic distinctions for which few minimal pairs can be found, such as /ʍ, w/, /ʒ, z/ and /ʊ, u/ would be expected to attain distinctiveness later. Leopold 1961 warns that an isolated occurrence of correct articulation of a phoneme is not proof of the child's having acquired that phoneme in his phonological system. The phoneme exists for the child when he makes an articulatory and perceptual distinction between that sound and another, and when that distinction is *critical* for meaning.

Developmental phonology, then, is not simply an increasing accuracy in producing the sounds of a language, but the gradual acquisition of a *phonological system.* In the capable definition of D. B. Fry, the evolving of a phonological system embraces three distinct but interrelated functions: (1) facility for the necessary articulatory discriminations; (2) facility for the necessary perceptual discriminations; and (3) knowledge of the distribution of phonemes.

The child's ability to articulate speech sounds greatly affects his phonological system. At an age when his articulatory gestures are still only grossly differentiated, his repertory of phonemes will be seriously limited. It has been repeatedly observed that an infant produces stop consonants earlier than fricatives. House believes this order of phonemic emergence to be related to the greater ease of producing a stop, which involves an actual touching together of articulators in a rapid ballistic motion, while the production of a fricative requires *almost* touching the articulators, involving a more delicate muscular control. Jacobson and Halle explain that the syllable /bɑ/ occurs earliest in an infant's vocalization because it involves the greatest articulatory *extremes,* /b/ being labial and /ɑ/ velar, and that the order of phonemic emergence thereafter involves increasing specification and refinement of articulatory adjustments. Fry believes that the child's use of phonemic categories is closely dependent on his articulatory ability, and that while his articulation is in a phase of rapid change his phonemic classes will be less well defined.

Fry argues for the close association between perception and articulation in the acquisition of phonemes. It is possible that a phoneme evolves in the child's perceptual discrimination even before he acquires facility in articulating the sound. The inter-dependence of the two facilities is illustrated by Wier's recordings of sequences of experimentation with words by her small son, in which he tried first one articulation and another until apparently satisfied with the result.

Perceptual identification of phonemes requires the utilization of a complex set of acoustic cues in the sorting of incoming speech segments, first into phoneme classes and thence into specific phonemes. Jacobson, Fant, and Halle have postulated that speech sounds are composed of bundles of features, having both acoustic and articulatory parameters. The concept of distinctive features relies on a binary sorting of the incoming signal. Phonemic discrimination, then, is not an absolute identification but a differential function, a process of sorting by a series of binary choices of distinctive features. When one hears a /t/, for instance, he does not perceive specifically that it is a /t/, but rather perceives that it is a consonant, not a vowel; an oral, not a nasal; a stop, not a continuant; an alveolar, not a velar; an alveolar, not a labial; voiceless, not voiced.

The phonemic structure of a particular language or dialect determines the distinctive features and their underlying acoustic cues necessary to the identification of any phoneme. Similarly, the developmental stage of the child's phonology determines the acoustic cues which he must employ. Jacobson and Halle describe the development of perception as a gradual refinement from sounds involving maximal feature distinctions to those requiring minimal distinctions. The infant's babbling /ba/ combines the greatest *extremes* in acoustic properties, the stop /b/ representing the closest approach to silence, and the vowel /a/ representing maximal concentration of vocal energy, while /b/ represents an extreme limitation in the time domain but essentially limitless spectral frequency, and /a/ represents essentially no limitation in time but marked limitation in spectral frequency. Then, as the phonological system evolves, the child learns to perceive distinctions based on fewer differences in acoustic cues. Support of this theory is found in Menyuk's study, which showed that phonemes differing by fewest distinctive features, e.g. /f/-/θ/, tended to be distinguished by children latest.

A crucial aspect of developmental phonology is the child's learning the distribution of phonemes in his native language. This includes the learning of limitations and prohibitions governing the occurrence of phonemes. If he is learning English, for instance, he must learn that certain vowels occur exclusively in closed syllables, that /r, j, w, h/

must be contiguous to a vowel, that /ŋ/ and /ʒ/ do not initiate a word, that initial /s/ occurs in the predictable clusters /st, sp, sk, sw, sl, sn/ but never preceding a voiced stop or a fricative, and so on.

More specifically, the child learns the phonology of his dialect rather than an abstract set of English phonemes. The dialect has geographical boundaries and cultural or class boundaries. It may differ not only with place but also with socio-economic class, foreign language influence, or ethnic group. As a child in Baton Rouge, Louisiana, for instance, I learned that post-vocalic /r/ became /ə/ except after /ɑ/, where a prolongation of the vowel served as the /r/ allophone. In the same geographic area, children of a different cultural environment learned that /r/ had a zero allophone after the vowel /o/ as in *pork*, and that /r/ in *car* was signalled by /ə/ plus lip-rounding of the preceding vowel, to give [kɒə]. In my native dialect, also, /ŋ/ and /n/ were distinguished in root-final position, as in *sing-sin*, but were non-distinctive in the participial suffix, as in *doing*. If articulatory proficiency of such children were evaluated out of dialectal context, the percentage of "correct" productions of /r/ or /ŋ/ would be quite low. One wonders if poor performance on the phonemes /ʍ/ and /ð/ reported by Templin 1957 might, in reality, reflect non-distinctiveness of these sounds in the dialect native to the particular children studied. Phonemic analysis reveals phonemic distinctions actually made by the child. Realistic measures of phonological maturity depend on comparing the child's phonemic structure with the phonology of the dialect of his environment.

Ideal data for phonemic analysis would provide minimal pairs for all phonemic distinctions. Additionally, data should include various allophones of each phoneme, so that phoneme boundaries could be established and the conditions governing the occurence of particular combinatory variants could be described. Carroll urges that the researcher of children's language differentiate between phonemics and phonetics in order to observe the child's acquisition of allophones in normal distribution.

It should be remembered that a phoneme is not a discrete motoric or perceptual entity but a composite of articulatory and acoustic features belonging to its various allophones. The child learns to perceive and to articulate the numerous combinatory variants of a phoneme, each in its appropriate phonetic context. For example, he is confronted with the task not simply of producing and perceiving a /t/. His articulatory adjustments and perception of acoustic cues must be programmed to accommodate such allophones as the aspirate [tʰ] in initial position, an unaspirated variety in an /st/ cluster, the lax [d̥] or [ɾ] in intervocalic position, a dentalized [t̪] before /θ/ or /ð/, a /t/

with nasal release before a nasal consonant or lateral release before /l/, often an unreleased [tᶜ] in absolute final position, in some dialects a retroflex /t/ acoustically near a palatal [c] before /r/, or possibly a glottal [ʔ] in *that was* or *little* (depending again on the dialect). And as demonstrated by adult perception, he learns to sort each of these phonetic segments into the phoneme /t/ without awareness of perceiving any distinction among the various combinatory forms. *Phonetic* transcription is tedious and time-consuming, but it is basic to phonemic analysis.

The primary data, therefore, will be in phonetic symbols representing *phone types*. According to the definition of Peterson and Shoup, a *phone* is the representation of a set of phonetic parameters occurring in an interval of time (p. 38), while a *phone type* is the set of all phones which are phonetically equivalent (p. 41). A single phonetic (not phonemic) symbol represents a phone type. Any classification of phone types into a phoneme must be based on their demonstrated occurrence as non-distinctive variants of that phoneme. Description of the phonetic parameters of a phoneme must derive from description of its allophones and conditions governing their occurrence. As Fischer-Jørgensen has said (p. 140), phonetic description begins with the allophone, for "only when distinctive features have been phonetically defined for various positions separately can we attempt to find a common denominator."

The transcriber's perception and symbolization appear to be chiefly related to articulatory parameters, with correlative acoustic cues. IPA is a symbolic system devised primarily in reference to articulatory features, to represent phonemes of various known languages of the world. A methodological weakness of much of the research in developmental phonology is the collection of data exclusively in English phonemes. However, even the complete IPA symbolization fails to include all phonetic parameters of all possible languages and of possible non-verbal utterances, as Pike has demonstrated. A symbolic system meeting Pike's criteria is required for transcription of children's phone types. One such system, which Peterson and Shoup have presented as a new phonetic theory of physiological speech parameters, rectifies many of the inadequacies of IPA. Whatever the perceptual-articulatory symbolism, it must provide for unambiguous, specific representation of all phonetic parameters of any phone type actually produced.

The validity of phonetic data depends on the acuity of the investigator's perception. First-hand observations, providing visual cues to the place of articulation should be confirmed by re-play of high-fidelity recordings on magnetic tape.

The accuracy of the investigator's transcriptions will be determined by the rigor of his phonetic training, which should include a correlation of his transcription reliability in comparison with experienced phoneticians. Also, periodic determination of an individual researcher's reliability should be established, on the basis of his agreement with his own transcription of sample utterances on different occasions. Reliability between different investigators will depend on the compatability of their training and the comparable care of their observations. Validity of data is not necessarily insured by high interinvestigator reliability. Significant conclusions must depend on *valid* phonetic data.

Phonemic analysis of phonetic data reveals the articulatory distinctions the child makes, the distribution of phonemes in his language, and the conditions governing the occurrence of each phoneme's allophones. Only a few studies, involving small populations, have applied this research method to developmental phonology in children. From those studies reasonable theories of developmental phonology have been postulated, but they require corroboration in research with larger samples.

An area of research in phonological development which has been sorely neglected is the investigation of the child's capacity for making *perceptual* distinctions. Jacobson's theory of increasingly fine discrimination in children was based largely on adult judgments of children's articulatory competence and application of phonological rules. Agreement with the Jacobson description of speech perception development by Leopold 1939 and Velten was also based on observed speech production in their children. Menyuk's distinctive feature analysis of phonemes correctly produced by young children of various ages, of two language environments, led her to confirm Jacobson's theory that the chronological order of maintaining feature distinctions is a linguistic universal. None of these studies investigated the child's developing perceptual capacity by testing his ability to utilize acoustic cues for phonemic discrimination.

Templin's 1943 study of speech sound perception of preschool children revealed improvement in gross discrimination at each successive age level from three to four-and-a-half. However, the method of preparing test material and organizing the data in this study prevents any specific interpretation regarding particular phonemic discriminations or the acoustic cues subtending perceptual distinctions.

A pilot study of consonant discrimination in three-year-olds was conducted by Koenigsknecht and Lee. Test material comprised monosyllabic CVC words common to the vocabulary of their subjects.

Every consonant occurred in initial and final position (within the restrictions of English phonology). The tape recorded listening test contrasted each consonant with every other consonant, by means of multiple presentations of sequences of 3 to 6 minimal pairs (including some nonsense syllables). As the child heard the sequence of productions including a test word, he indicated which production of the word he accepted by showing the picture representing that word to a cardboard clown in front of him. Evaluation of perceptual capacity involved distinctive feature analysis of the error identifications, using the distinctive feature system Miller and Nicely used in studying adult consonant identifications. The percentage of error identifications was found to vary inversely with the number of feature distinctions belonging to the phonemic discrimination. The feature best observed was the nasal-oral distinction, while the highest percentage of error identifications involved voicing distinction; and more error identifications were based on distinction in place of articulation than on the stop-continuant distinction.

Application of the Koenigsknecht and Lee research method to a wider range of ages is needed, in order to establish the developmental sequence of feature distinctions in children. Feature distinctions subtending children's perception of vowel phonemes should also be investigated.

The advent of electronic instrumentation for speech analysis and synthesis has facilitated intensive research during the last twenty years in the acoustic properties of the speech signal and the acoustic features significant to phonetic distinctions. Two types of acoustic cues which contribute to distinctive features have been identified: spectral cues and temporal cues. Vowel identifications are based primarily on spectral cues, or the concentration of energy at particular formant frequencies. Spectral cues provide the basis for the nasal-oral distinction. Spectral cues convey information about the place of consonant articulation along the vocal tract. The acoustic distinction between a stop, a fricative, and an affricate (with like place of articulation) is based on temporal cues. The voiced-voiceless distinction depends on both spectral and temporal cues.

Research in the utilization of acoustic cues for phonemic distinctions has been limited to adult perception, until quite recently. Inferences about children's perception were drawn from research in adult perception, implying that the utilization of acoustic cues in children and adults was identical. In the Koenigsknecht study, the perceptual capacity of three-year-olds, six-year-olds, and adults were compared. The test material consisted of minimal pairs contrasting consonant phonemes. The pairs chiefly comprised recorded real speech which had been mechanically altered so that only one acoustic cue (temporal or spectral) would remain to provide information for distinguishing between members of a pair, plus some samples which were electronically synthesized for the same purpose. Unaltered real speech pairs were randomly distributed through the stimulus tape. Subjects hearing the tape were required, in methods suiting their age, to indicate whether the members of each pair were same or differnt. The data disclosed that adults experience essentially no difficulty in phonetic distinction when only one acoustic cue is provided, indicating a redundancy in acoustic cues of normal speech for normal adult perception. The three-year-old children showed considerably greater dependence on spectral cues than on temporal cues for phonemic distinctions, but six-year-olds were found to utilize temporal cues almost as well as the adults. Such research probes the capacity of the child to utilize specific subphonemic acoustic components of the speech signal. Further application of this research method should contribute to increased understanding of the functioning of perception in developmental phonology and possibly elucidate some of the problems of children with retarded phonemic mastery.

Previous research in developmental phonology has focused largely on the evolving articulatory competency of the child. The large-scale longitudinal surveys of articulation revealed increasing mastery of English phonemes in essential maturity at about six years of age, but failed to agree on the order of phonemic acquisition, largely because of errors in methodology. Phonemic analysis of children's speech has served as the basis for theories regarding the order of mastery of phoneme types and an awareness that phonological maturation involves not only articulatory capacity but also perceptual capacity and competence in the application of phonological rules. These theories remain to be proved in investigations of larger samples, with the rigorous standards of transcription and data analysis appropriate to any linguistic research. Finally, the role of perception in developmental phonology should not be inferred from articulation competency but should be directly investigated by tests of perception, preferably by the acoustic phonetician.

LIST OF WORKS CITED

Albright, Robert W., and Joy Buck Albright. "The Phonology of a Two-Year-Old Child," *WORD*, XII (December, 1956).

Carroll, John B. "Language Development in Children," in *Psycholinguistics: A Book of Readings*: ed. Sol Saporta. New York, 1961.

Chen, Han Piao. *Speech Sounds of Infants: The Newborn Period*. Unpublished Master's thesis, State University of Iowa, 1942.

Fischer-Jørgensen, Eli., "What can the New Techniques of Acoustic Phonetics Contribute to Linguistics," in *Psycholinguistics: A Book of Readings*: ed. Sol Saporta. New York, 1961.

Fry, D. B., "The Development of the Phonological System in the Normal and the Deaf Child," in *The Genesis of Language: A Psycholinguistic Approach*, eds. Frank Smith and George A. Miller. Cambridge, Mass., 1966.

House, Arthur S., comments following Templin, Mildred. "The Study of Articulation and Language Development During the Early School Years," in *The Genesis of Language: A Psycholinguistic* Approach. eds. Frank Smith and George A. Miller. Cambridge, Mass., 1966.

Irwin, Orvis, C. "The Profile as a Visual Device for Indicating Central Tendencies in Speech Data," *Child Developm.* XII (1941), 111-120.

Irwin, Orvis C. and Thayer Curry. "Vowel Elements in the Crying Vocalization of Infants Under Ten Days of Age," *Child Developm.*, XII, (1941), 99-109.

Irwin, Orvis, C. and Han Piao Chen. "Speech Sound Elements During the First Year of Life: A Review of the Literature," *JSD*, VIII (June 1943).

Jacobson, Roman. *Kindersprache, Aphasia, und allgemeine Lantgesetze.* Uppsala, 1941.

Jacobson, Roman, G., Gunnar M. Fant, and Morris Halle. *Preliminaries to Speech Analysis: The Distinctive Features and their Correlates,* Cambridge, Mass., 1965 (6th ed.).

Jacobson, Roman and Morris Halle. "Phonemic Patterning," in *Psycholinguistics: A Book of Readings.* ed.: Sol Saporta, New York, 1961.

Koenigsknecht, Roy A., *An Investigation of the Discrimination of Certain Spectral and Temporal Acoustic Cues for Speech Sounds in Three-Year-Old Children, Six-Year-Old Children, and Adults.* Unpublished Ph.D. Thesis, Northwestern University, 1968.

Koenigsknecht, Roy A., and Laura L. Lee. *Distinctive Feature Analysis of Speech Sound Discrimination in Three Year Old Children.* Unpublished paper presented at ASHA convention, 1968.

Krehbiel, T. E. *Speech Sounds of Infants: The Fourth, Fifth, and Sixth Months.* Unpublished Master's thesis, State University of Iowa, 1941.

Leopold, Werner F. "Patterning in Children's Language Learning," in *Psycholinguistics: A Book of Readings.* ed. Sol Saporta. New York, 1961.

Leopold, Werner, F. *Speech Development of a Bilingual Child: Vocabulary Growth in the First Two Years of Life.* Evanston, Northwestern University, 1939.

McCarthy, Dorothea. "Language Development in Children" in *Manual of Child Psychology,* ed. Leonard Carmichael, New York, 1954.

Menyuk, Paula. "The Role of Distinctive Features in Children's Acquisition of Phonology," *JSHR*, XI (March, 1968), 138-146.

Miller, George A. and P. E. Nicely. "An analysis of perceptual confusions among some English consonants," *JASA*, XXVII (1955), 338-352.

Peterson, Gordon E., and June E. Shoup. "A Physiological Theory of Phonetics," *JSHR*, IX (March, 1966), 5-67.

Pike, Kenneth L. *Phonetics: A Critical Analysis of Phonetic Theory and a Technic for the Practical Description of Sounds,* Ann Arbor, 1943.

Powers, Margaret Hall. "Functional Disorders of Articulation," in *Handbook of Speech Pathology,* ed. Lee Edward Travis. New York, 1957.

Templin, Mildred. "A Study of Sound Discrimination Ability of Elementary School Pupils," *JSHD*, VIII (March, 1943), 127-132.

Templin, Mildred. *Certain Language Skills in Children, Their Development and Interrelationships.* Minneapolis, 1957.

Velten, H. V., "The Growth of Phonemic and Lexical Patterns in Infant Language," *Language*, XIX (1943), 281-292.

Weir, Ruth H., *Language in the Crib.* The Hague, 1962.

THE QUEST FOR PHONETIC REALITY

ILSE LEHISTE

The Ohio State University

INTRODUCTION

This essay brings together some thoughts that have occupied me over a number of years in connection with the question of phonetic reality. A more technical treatment, with a full bibliography, is offered elsewhere;[1] what is presented on these pages is mostly a series of reflections. Although slightly rambling in nature, the essay does follow an inner logic which will become apparent as it progresses.

I should like to begin with the recollection of an experience I had when I taught my first class in acoustic phonetics at The University of Michigan in 1958. I wanted to demonstrate the amplitude difference that I expected to be associated with a difference in stress in such word pairs as *con*vict (noun) —con*vict* (verb). To my great dismay, the oscilloscope registered greater amplitude on the first syllable in both productions, although in the verb 'to convict' the stress was clearly on the second syllable. Puzzlement over the contradiction between linguistic expectations and acoustic manifestation led directly to the research published in the article "Vowel amplitude and phonemic stress in American English,"[2] to a continued preoccupation with the phonetic realization of suprasegmental features, and to the quest for phonetic reality of which the present essay constitutes a part.

CONSTRAINTS UPON PRODUCTION

It seems reasonable to assume that no phonetic feature can have linguistic function unless it is subject to voluntary control. Likewise, for any phonetic feature to function significantly within a sound system, it must be audible. To quote from a classic treatise, "We speak in order to be heard in order to be understood."[3] Phonetic reality is thus bounded by our control over speech production on the one hand, and by our perceptual mechanism on the other. One way to get closer to phonetic reality would be to explore these two boundaries.

[1] Ilse Lehiste, *Suprasegmentals*. To be published by M.I.T. Press.

[2] Ilse Lehiste and G. E. Peterson, "Vowel amplitude and phonemic stress in American English," *Journal of the Acoustical Society of America* 31 (1959), pp. 428-435.

[3] R. Jakobson, C. Gunnar M. Fant, and Morris Halle, *Preliminaries to Speech Analysis: The distinctive features and their correlates*, Technical Report No. 13 (May 1952), Acoustics Laboratory, M.I.T., Cambridge, Massachusetts.

In the present essay, I should like to consider the production and perception of suprasegmentals—quantity, pitch and stress.

When we claim that duration and tempo may have linguistic function, we must assume that we have control over the rate of articulation. If tone and intonation function significantly in a language, the speakers of that language must have control over the rate of vibration of the vocal folds. Considering the suprasegmental feature of stress, we assume that the speaker has control over whatever physiological process is involved in its generation. These assumptions are frequently not made explicit, but they are present, underlyingly, in any claim that features of tone, stress and quantity may have linguistic function.

In trying to assess to what an extent these assumptions are based on phonetic reality, it is necessary to ascertain to what an extent the speaker is in fact able to control the respiratory musculature, the muscles of phonation, and the muscles involved in articulation. Let us begin with the physiological mechanism involved in the suprasegmental feature of quantity. In order for the feature of quantity to function significantly in language, it must be true that articulatory movements, the duration of articulatory gestures, and their ordering in sequences are not completely determined by physiological constraints such as the mechanical time constants of the motor structures.

The mechanical time constants themselves can be inferred from the upper limits of movement of which the articulatory organs are capable. Some basic information about the maximum rate of articulation was provided by Hudgins and Stetson.[4] The average rates of articulation which they established were 8.2 per second for the tip of the tongue, 7.1 for the back of the tongue, and 6.7 both for the lips and for the velum. One might assume that these rates are completely determined by the size, mass, and shape of the articulators: the tip of the tongue being the smallest, its inertia is less than that of the other articulators. However, there is a much more basic reason for the magnitudes of these average rates; it can be shown that inertia, size and shape are not sufficient to explain the observed facts.

I performed a brief experiment to test the notion that the rate of articulation is determined by the mechanical time constants of the articulators. I compared the rate of tongue-tip closures in the production of a trilled long [r:] and in sequences of articulations of [tə]—syllables [tətətətətətətə]. I selected these two, since the production of the consonant gesture is superficially very similar in the articulation of single-tap [r] and [t], and [ə] is acoustically practically identical with

⁴ C. V. Hudgins and R. H. Stetson, "Relative speed of articulatory movements," *Archives néerlandaises de phonétique expérimentale* 13 (1937), pp. 85-94.

the vocoidal part of the trilled [r]—the vocalic sound produced between the individual closures. I averaged 8 [tə]-syllables per second. This is very close to Stetson's results, who had reported averages of 8.2 syllables per second in productions of [tat tat tat tat]. In the production of the trilled [r], however, I produced an average of 28 taps per second.

Now we have the same articulatory organ in both cases, engaged in the same movement. The mechanical time constants should be the same. But there is a basic difference in the two articulations: with [tə]-syllables, each movement is under voluntary control, whereas in the production of [r:], we are dealing with an aerodynamic process, in which muscle tension and rate of airflow are balanced against each other to produce a vibratory movement of the tip of the tongue. We seem to be getting closer to what really determines the rate of articulation: it is the speed with which voluntary movements can be performed, which in turn depends on the speed with which neural commands can be translated into articulatory movements.

The latency period of a simple motor reaction to a sound signal is of the order of 110-150 milliseconds; the time delay in responding to a proprioceptive signal is about 100 msec.[5] And consonant articulations in rapid trains of CVCVCV syllables follow each other at intervals which seem to be very close to time periods determined by the response capability of the neural pathways.[6]

The production of sequences of articulatory gestures introduces a further problem. Muscles have to be activated in a different order from the actual, final output of speech sounds, since there are differences in the length of the neural pathways leading to the different muscles, and there are differences in the rate of response and of movement of which the muscles are capable. The ordering in time of the signals sent to individual muscles cannot, therefore, be the same as the ordering of articulatory movements in actual performance.

This can only be explained if we assume that whole trains of articulatory movements are programmed at a higher level and triggered off as a whole.[7] One reason why such preprogrammed trains

[5] V. A. Kozhevnikov and L. A. Chistovich, *Speech: Articulation and Perception*, Moscow-Leningrad, 1965. Translated by J. P. R. S., Washington, D. C., No. JPRS 30.543.
[6] It is interesting that voluntary finger movements have an upper limit of the same magnitude—about 8 times a second, although a finger can be moved faster by electrical stimulation. Cf. Kenneth J. W. Craik, "Theory of the human operator in control systems," *British Journal of Psychology* 38 (1947), pp. 56-61 and 38 (1948), pp. 142-148.
[7] Cf. Craik, op. cit., and K. S. Lashley, "The problem of serial order in behavior," reprinted in S. Saporta (ed.), *Psycholinguistics: A Book of Readings* (New York: Holt, Rinehart and Winston, 1961), pp. 180-198.

of events have to be assumed is the sheer number of the individual muscular adjustments which have to be made during speech: Lenneberg has shown[8] that the rate at which individual muscular events occur throughout the speech apparatus is of an order of magnitude of several hundred events every second. The activation of so many muscles in such a short time cannot depend on volition alone; there must be preprogrammed trains of events that run off automatically in much the same way as a pianist performs a complicated cadenza.

The existence of such patterns is further supported by anticipatory lapses in ordering: the well-known phenomena of metathesis and distant metathesis (spoonerisms). Since such lapses involve the interchange of elements in sequences that have yet to be realized, their occurrence clearly implies the existence of a program for the realization of the sequence.

The time patterns of these articulatory sequences are correlated with linguistic units of what has been called the phonological hierarchy. They include a basic unit of the size of a syllable, and a larger unit of about six or seven syllables, which corresponds in size to the tone-group of Halliday[9] and the phonemic clause of Trager and Smith.[10] And it appears, as Lenneberg has suggested, that the rhythmic structure of speech is ultimately related to the relatively constant rhythmic patterns of the electrical activity of the brain, one of which has a frequency of approximately 6 cycles per second. It is surely no accident that this frequency is very close to the frequency with which syllables are produced in speech.

But let us return to the question of voluntary control, and consider the problem of the independent control of pitch and stress. It has been assumed for some time—explicitly or implicitly—that stress and pitch are independent of each other. Now there are two ways of controlling the rate of vibration of the vocal folds: a) by a controlled adjustment of subglottal pressure, and b) by a controlled adjustment of the tension of the vocal folds. There is good experimental evidence that independent control is indeed possible.[11]

However, at the level of the acoustic signal, there is no way to separate the increase in fundamental frequency due to increased

----

[8] Eric H. Lenneberg, *Biological Foundations of Language* (New York: John Wiley & Sons, Inc., 1967).

[9] M. A. K. Halliday. "The Tones of English," *Archivum Linguisticum* 15 (1963), pp. 1-28.

[10] G. L. Trager and H. L. Smith, *Outline of English Structure*, Studies in Linguistics No. 3 (Norman, Oklahoma), 1951.

[11] Jw. van den Berg, "Subglottal pressures and vibration of the vocal folds," *Folia Phoniatrica* 9 (1957), pp. 65-71; P. Ladefoged, *Three Areas of Experimental Phonetics* (London: Oxford University Press, 1967).

tension from the increase due to higher subglottal pressure. It is tempting to assume that the controlled tension of the vocal folds is associated with tonal features, and subglottal pressure increases are associated with stress features; but even if this were so for the speaker, there is no evidence that the *hearer* can separate the two kinds of increases in fundamental frequency—the increase due to greater tension of the vocal folds, and the increase due to higher subglottal pressure.

It is, of course, possible to counterbalance the two physiological mechanisms. Speakers of English habitually use higher pitch on a stressed syllable; but speakers of Russian frequently use stressed low-pitched syllables under analogous conditions. It is also possible to keep the fundamental frequency constant (by a compensatory adjustment of the vocal folds) and increase subglottal pressure. The result is a sound wave of greater amplitude. This means that each individual pulse produced by the vocal folds contains a greater amount of acoustic energy. Increase in the amplitude of a sound wave normally results in an impression of greater loudness, since a greater amount of energy reaches the ear in a given unit of time. However, from what is known about the integrating time-constant of the ear, it seems that the same effect should be achieved by a greater number of pulses reaching the ear per unit time. Higher frequency thus should result not only in an impression of higher pitch, but also in an impression of greater loudness. At the frequencies of the human vocal range, the ear is also increasingly sensitive to higher frequency. An increase of perceived loudness thus can be caused by both greater amplitude of the individual pulses (produced by increased subglottal pressure) and by a greater number of these pulses reaching the ear per unit time (as a secondary result of higher subglottal pressure, or as a primary result of increased tension of the vocal folds). It is not surprising that the listener may attribute both types of increases to the same underlying cause and call it by a common name such as stress.

As I already mentioned, there is no evidence that a listener can distinguish between increases in fundamental frequency that are caused by the two possible physiological mechanisms. However, it is probable that the *speaker* can distinguish between them, since the two mechanisms involve different—and widely separated—organs. The speaker 'knows' which syllable he has stressed; the listener uses his knowledge of the language in addition to the phonetic cues present in the sound wave to determine which syllable was stressed. This analysis-by-synthesis approach to stress was anticipated by Daniel Jones, who also discussed the problems involved in identifying the location of stress in unknown languages, and the pitfalls of interpreting prominence achieved by other means as being due to stress.[12]

While it is certainly possible that the production of stress and pitch may be independently controlled, it seems much less likely that they are always independently perceived. Another bit of negative evidence might be considered here: the fact that there is no phonetic evidence for differences in degree of expiratory stress. And there is probably a very good reason why fine gradations in stress cannot be expressed in phonetic terms. It appears to me that word-level stress is in a very real sense an abstract quality: a potential for being stressed.[13] Word-level stress is the capacity of a syllable within a word to receive sentence stress when the word is realized as a part of the sentence. The degrees of stress of other syllables within the word are usually predictable by rules and are therefore non-contrastive.

The only way to handle stress within phonology seems to be this way of viewing stress as an abstract quality, since up to now nobody has succeeded in establishing unambiguous phonetic correlates of stress. As was mentioned earlier, fundamental frequency does not provide an unambiguous cue, since we can obviously have stressed low-pitched syllables. Greater respiratory effort, resulting in higher subglottal pressure, likewise cannot be used to identify stressed syllables, since experiments have shown that not all syllables which are perceived as stressed are associated with peaks of subglottal pressure. Every utterance, if it is long enough, has one or more peaks, but not every stressed syllable has a peak. It appears that what is realized phonetically is sentence-level stress rather than word-level stress. In other words, our knowledge of the structure of the language informs us which syllables have the potential of being stressed: we 'hear' the underlying phonological form. Here we have arrived at a point where it is necessary to distinguish psychological reality from phonetic reality; I shall return to this after a more detailed consideration of perception.

CONSTRAINTS UPON PERCEPTION

In this quest for phonetic reality, I have tried to show to what an extent phonetic reality may be found in a study of speech production. But, if I may return to my initial quotation, "We speak in order to be heard in order to be understood." If a phonetic feature is to be considered significant, it is obviously also necessary that it be audible. No phonetic phenomenon can have linguistic significance if it falls below

---

[12] Daniel Jones, *An Outline of English Phonetics* (New York: Dutton), 6th edition, 1940.

[13] Uriel Weinreich, "Stress and word structure in Yiddish," *The Field of Yiddish Language, Folklore and Literature,* edited by Uriel Weinreich (New York: Linguistic Circle of New York, 1954), pp. 1-27.

the perceptual threshold. It is frequently true that physical measurements can be made with a precision that is greater than the discriminatory capacity of the ear. The phonetic reality of speech events is bounded by constraints on perception as well as by constraints upon production.

The just noticeable differences or differential thresholds (= difference limens) have been established for the various acoustic parameters of the speech signal. As a first approximation, the jnd of duration is between one and four centiseconds in the range of the durations of speech sounds—from about 3 to 30 csec. The jnd for fundamental frequency is of the order of $\pm 0.5\% - 1\%$ for a vowel having a fundamental frequency in the neighborhood of 120 Hz. The jnd for intensity is approximately 1 dB for a synthetic vowel; but in a separate study of the difference limens for changes in the amplitude of the second formant, the jnd for intensity was found to be 3 dB.[14] It is frequently assumed that the same relationships hold for actual speech, but this is not always the case. Let us look again at the problems connected with establishing the phonetic reality of stress.

It seems likely that in terms of production, stress is the result of increased activity of expiratory muscles, causing higher subglottal pressure and a higher rate of airflow. All other factors being kept constant, higher subglottal pressure should result both in a higher fundamental frequency (unless checked by a compensatory adjustment of vocal fold tension) and in a higher amplitude of the sound wave. Now it has been known for some time that given the same input energy, the output energy—the intensity of the sound wave—is not constant for different speech sounds. There is a correlation between tongue height (or degree of jaw opening), degree of lip rounding, and output intensity, so that the more open vowels have greater output intensity than the higher and more rounded vowels. In the study referred to at the beginning of this essay, I established the so-called intrinsic intensities of English syllable nuclei. The average difference between /i/ and /a/ turned out to be about 5 decibels. This difference is above threshold and should be audible. The same study showed, however, that this was not so: although a difference in intensity was present, listeners heard vowels produced with subjectively equal effort as being equally loud. I assumed then, and still consider it to be plausible, that listeners associate a certain intrinsic relative amplitude (or perhaps average power) with each vowel spectrum, and apply a corresponding 'correction factor' to the incoming signal.

[14] J. L. Flanagan, "Estimates of the maximum precision necessary in quantizing certain 'dimensions' of vowel sounds," *Journal of the Acoustical Society of America* 29 (1957), pp. 533-534.

Although the listeners were told to mark which syllable was louder, they were obviously responding to subjective effort; they were making a linguistic judgment in terms of stress rather than loudness. Psychophysical experiments with pure tones and white noise show a very different pattern of dependence of perceived loudness upon intensity and frequency. The perception of loudness and the perception of stress seem to be separate things. Interpretation of an incoming signal in terms of linguistic stress presupposes a speech setting, and, if the notion of 'correction factors' has some validity, also a certain amount of learning. Daniel Jones is the only older phonetician who has explicitly stated that stress perception also involves knowledge of the language in which the utterance is spoken. Jones seems to have anticipated the motor theory of speech perception when he suggested that a person familiar with a language would not perceive the sounds objectively from the physical stimulus, but perceives them in a subjective way: the sounds he hears call up to his mind the manner of making them, and by means of immediate 'inner speech' he knows where the stress is.

Another problem in the interpretation of intensity data is the interaction between formant frequency and fundamental frequency. The relative independence of the glottal and subglottal effects makes possible the mathematical description of speech sounds by specifying the source function and the filter function, which together determine the system function.[15] Such a specification indicates that the glottal output serves to excite a resonating system whose characteristics determine the various spectra associated with vowels. The spacing of the harmonics generated at the glottis is independent of the center frequencies of the resonances of the vocal tract. If the articulatory configuration of the vocal tract remains fixed and the fundamental frequency of the voice is changed, extensive changes in over-all level will occur; the amplitude will increase, if a harmonic coincides with the frequency of one of the lower formants, especially the first formant— since most of the energy of the vowel is contained in the first formant.

This 'optimal vocal frequency' was studied with synthetic vowels by House,[16] who found that the overall intensity of synthetic vowels could fluctuate by as much as 5-6 dB depending on whether harmonic frequency coincided with the first formant. Peterson-McKinney[17] and

---

[15] Gunnar Fant, *Acoustic Theory of Speech Production* ('s-Gravenhage: Mouton and Co., 1960).

[16] A. S. House, "A note on optimal vocal frequency," *Journal of Speech and Hearing Research* 2 (1959), pp. 55-60.

[17] G. E. Peterson and N. P. McKinney, "The measurement of speech power," *Phonetica* 7 (1961), pp. 65-84.

Ladefoged-McKinney[18] observed similar fluctuations in real speech, when test words were produced with long falling pitch. They observed one to four prominent peaks—of several decibels—in the output intensity; however, there was only one peak of subglottal pressure and apparently only one peak of loudness. Again, these fluctuations are physically larger than the differential threshold of the ear for differences in intensity; they should be audible, but are not reacted to when the stimulus is interpreted as speech.

There is a further factor which makes the interpretation of intensity curves in terms of stress extremely difficult, and this is the difference in intensity between a vowel target and the transitions to and from adjacent consonants. The intensity of the vocalic portion of a syllable nucleus depends on its formant structure; however, the formant structure does not remain constant throughout the vowel, since the initial and terminal frequencies of the formants are determined by the preceding and following consonants. For example, in sequences involving a high vowel flanked by dental/alveolar consonants, the intensity of the syllable nucleus is greater during the transitions than during the target portion of the vowel.

This means that it is impossible to establish any phonetic correlates for differences in *kind of stress* that have been claimed to exist: crescendo stress, diminuendo stress, rising-falling stress, two-peaked stress within one syllable, etc. Whatever the psychological reality of these claimed distinctions, their phonetic reality is yet to be established.

PHONETIC REALITY AND PSYCHOLOGICAL REALITY

This leads us back to the possible difference between the phonetic reality and the psychological reality of linguistic phenomena. I have already suggested that stress at word level need not necessarily be phonetically realized; it is a property of a word, the *stressability* of one of its syllables, which is realized when the word is assigned a certain degree of stress within the sentence. The potential for stress is part of the underlying phonological shape of the word. There is no question in my mind but that underlying phonological shapes have a kind of psychological reality. Let me present another example in support of this reality taken from historical linguistics.[19]

[18] P. Ladefoged and Norris P. McKinney, "Loudness, sound pressure, and subglottal pressure in speech," *Journal of the Acoustical Society of America* 35 (1963), pp. 454-460.

[19] Paul Kiparsky, "Phonological change." Unpublished dissertation, Massachusetts Institute of Technology, 1965; Carl Darling Buck, *Comparative Grammar of Greek and Latin* (Chicago, The University of Chicago Press, 1933).

Already in Proto-Indo-European, there was a rule of regressive voicing assimilation, according to which the first, voiced member of a consonant cluster (consisting of plosives and/or fricatives) became voiceless, if the second member of the cluster was voiceless. Now in Latin, which represents a stage historically far removed from Proto-Indo-European, another rule operated which is know by the name of Lachmann's Law: a short vowel was lengthened before a cluster whose first member was voiced. As a result of this rule, a long vowel appeared in *āctum*, while a short vowel appeared in *factum*. *Actum* is, of course, derived from the verbal stem *ago*, and *factum* from *facio*—both verbs having a short vowel in the stem. It is crucial to remember that after the operation of the IE regressive assimilation, there were no clusters of this type in Latin whose first member could have been voiced and second voiceless; in all such clusters, the first member was devoiced already in Proto-Indo-European. How could the speakers of Latin know which vowel to lengthen? How could they know which consonants had been voiced in Indo-European?

The paradox can be explained only if we assume that in the underlying phonological form, the stem-final consonant of *ago* was still voiced, although its phonetic realization was always voiceless in clusters of this type. Lachmann's Law operated on the underlying phonological shape, which must have possessed psychological reality for the speakers of Latin.

There are numerous other examples that would illustrate the psychological reality of underlying phonological forms, but let this one suffice.

I have proposed for some time that one of the main functions of suprasegmentals is to establish patterns whose domains are higher-level phonological units, such as syllables, words, and phonological phrases. These patterns clearly have a certain kind of psychological reality— they constitute a Gestalt, if you will. In spoken language, the underlying phonological shapes are given phonetic form. It is this phonetic form which is accessible to direct observation, and which possesses phonetic reality. The underlying forms can only be inferred from the linguistic behavior of speakers and listeners; their reality is psychological, but the patterns are no less real than their actualizations.

Let me now return to my original quotation: "We speak in order to be heard in order to be understood." We cannot escape the constraints of our humanness: we cannot understand signals which are below the perceptual threshold, and we cannot expect features to have a linguistic function over which we do not have articulatory control. Phonetic reality operates within limits determined by our neural and muscular makeup.

Linguistics is an empirical science. As such, it describes observed linguistic facts, seeks to explain them, and attempts to set up predictions. The validity of the predictions and explanations depends in a very real way upon the correctness of observations. A comparison of predictions with actual realizations provides the ultimate test of the correctness of the predictions. Without such verification, predictions are largely meaningless. And this is the point at which phonetics plays a crucial role: it provides us with a possibility to subject linguistic theories to experimental verification. It is this much larger context in which the quest for phonetic reality finds its ultimate justification.

HOW DOES RHYTHMIC PROSE WORK?

ARCHIBALD A. HILL
University of Texas

Disputes over the nature of English metre are notorious; so much so, in fact, that in more pessimistic moods, older scholars have been known to tell their younger colleagues to leave the subject alone for fear of hopeless embroilments. The nature of rhythm in English literary prose is less controversial, perhaps, but only because it is less often written about. The basic disagreements are found there also, so that it is quite as possible to display them, and perhaps to resolve some of them in a discussion of prose as it is in an examination of verse. We can proceed with quotation of a famous example of prose that all critics have called rhythmic:

> Laodemeia died; Helen died; Leda, the beloved of Jupiter, went before. It is better to repose in the earth betimes than to sit up late; better, than to cling pertinaciously to what we feel crumbling under us, and to protract an inevitable fall. We may enjoy the present while we are insensible of infirmity and decay, but the present, like a note in music, is nothing but as it appertains to what is past and what is to come. There are no fields of amaranth on this side of the grave: there are no voices, O Rhodopè, that are not soon mute, however tuneful: there is no name, with whatever emphasis of passionate love repeated, of which the echo is not faint at last.

The passage is from Walter Savage Landor's *Aesop and Rhodopè,* and can be taken as a sort of *locus classicus* for discussion of rhythm in English prose. It has been noticed as an example of rhythmic quality by Saintsbury, by Sir Walter Alexander Raleigh, Sir Herbert Read, and Paull Franklin Baum, yet just about the only clear convergence among these critics is that the passage is indeed rhythmical. In part, however, I think it is possible to reconcile some of the several statements, and it is also possible to reject some as erroneous. The final result should be to show not only something of the sources of success in this particular passage, but also to throw at least a little light on the nature of rhythmic prose in general.

I can begin with Sir Walter Alexander Raleigh, whose statement is one of the briefest, and also one of those most easily refuted. He speaks of the last part of the passage as being blank verse.[1] Just what

---

[1] Quoted in the introductory essay in *Landor, Poetry and Prose . . . with an Introduction and Notes* by E. K. Chambers, Oxford (Clarendon Press, 1946), p. xxxiv.

blank verse is, is another problem, but here the statement must mean that the last lines are iambic pentameter without rhyme. Without rhyme they certainly are, but I would not read the material from *there are no voices* on as essentially iambic. My transcription of this material would be as follows—

there are no voices | O Rhodopè | that are not soon mute |

however tuneful | there is no name | with whatever

emphasis of passionate love | repeated | of which the echo

is not faint at last.

The transcription I have just given takes account of two kinds of things only; the stresses, arranged in a Tragerian scheme of four contrasts, and the terminal junctures, also arranged in a scheme of four. There are two reasons why I do not think that these lines can be called blank verse. First, there is no regularity of phrasing, corresponding to the ten syllable unit of a verse line. The first phrase has five syllables; the next, four; the next, five; the next, five; the next, four; the next, fifteen; and the last, ten. Second, it is true that there are alternating stronger and weaker syllables, but these are not arranged more regularly than the successive syllables of any English utterance. I would subscribe, certainly, to the Jespersen formulation that the several grades of English stress are reduced to two, a strong and a weak, for the purposes of scansion, with the strongest and the weakest stresses fixed, but the middle grades variable in accord with whether they are surrounded by stresses stronger or weaker than themselves. Even making full allowance for this type of relativism in the succession of stresses, it is not possible to see here a succession of weak-strong feet. On this scheme the first phrase would be weak-weak-strong-strong-weak, and the next would be strong-strong-weak-strong, with the possibility of regarding the first part of the second phrase as more or less unmetrical on the ground that there are two syllables with the same grade of linguistic stress, not clearly definable as weak or strong.

We can agree with Sir Walter only that the lines are poetic. Yet their poetic quality is certainly not to be sought in the mere succession of syllables. Here is an utterance which is strictly iambic, and in which there are exactly twenty syllables, yet I doubt if any one in his senses would say that what is presented is two lines of blank verse:

∪ ∧ ∪ ∧ \ ∧ ∪ ∧ ∪ ∧ ∪ / ∪
Alicia Smith went out and bought a loaf of bread | that

∧ ∪ ∧ ∪ ∧ ∪ /
wasn't fresh or good at all #

The critic who has been most dogmatic on this passage is Saintsbury. He scans the passage altogether in terms of the feet of classic poetry. I quote only the first few lines. The marks are to indicate long and short syllables, and the bars, the boundaries of feet.

∪ ∪ ∪ — ∪ — — ∪ — — ∪ ∪ ∪ — ∪ ∪ — ∪ ∪
Laodameia | died; | Helen | died; | Leda | the beloved | of Jupiter |

∪ ∪ — ∪ ∪ — ∪ ∪ ∪ — ∪ ∪ — ∪ —
went before. | It is better | to repose | in the earth | betimes |

∪ ∪ — ∪ —
than to sit up late;[2]

Of these markings he says that "the scansion should speak for itself to all who are able to hear it." The only other statement specifically bearing on this passage is "Elsewhere Landor, with his usual precision (oh, call it not pedantry!), prefers the form 'Helena' as more classical. But here the three final *a*'s of the names would be importunate, and he admits the English shortening." Importunate is a slightly curious term to apply to rhythmical arrangement; presumably it means monotonous. Another possible reason for not using the form 'Helena' might be that Landor wished to use the same long-short or strong-weak pattern that he employs in 'Leda.' Since Saintsbury puts his objection firmly on subjective reaction, however, there is no disputing him.

It is, as a first step, quite easy to point out that Saintsbury has not found any noticeable patterning in the passage quoted. The first foot is of five syllables; the second of one; the next of two; the next of one; the next of two; the next of four, and so on. I think it is quite possible to hear Saintsbury's scansion, but if it speaks for itself, it does not explain to me why this passage is markedly rhythmic. Elsewhere in the volume, he develops his basic ideas more fully. Thus he says "The Rhythm of Prose, like the Metre of Verse, can, in English as well as in the classical languages, be best expressed by applying the foot-system, or system of mathematical combination of 'long' and 'short' syllables."[3] There are at least two things that can be objected to in this statement. First, Saintsbury's table of feet gives feet of one, two, and as many as five syllables, with as many as fifteen different

[2] George Saintsbury, *A History of English Prose Rhythm,* 1912 (Reprinted Indiana University Press, 1965), p. 340.
[3] Saintsbury, p. 478.

four-syllable feet, and the five-syllable feet left uncounted because too numerous. There is further, no principle governing the division of sequences into feet, so that the reader is left to guess why 'Helen died' is given as two feet rather than one. In Saintsbury's scheme, 'Helen died' could have been a single foot, which would then have been a long-short-long, or cretic. I can only guess the principles which led him to call it a single foot, but it would seem to be true that his maximum length for feet is five syllables. The first phrase, 'Laodameia died,' would exceed this maximum, if treated as a single foot. Therefore he breaks it into two, setting off the verb as a single, monosyllabic foot. Having separated the verb in the first phrase, he does so in the second also, preserving consistency. But a second principle which also must be at work is reliance on normal English phrasing. Thus the maximal English phrase, 'the beloved of Jupiter,' is divided before the preposition, as it would be in normal speech, rather than with a division before 'Jupiter.' Yet though it is possible to discover why Saintsbury divides into feet as he does, a foot-segmentation based on normal speech, no matter how reasonable, destroys much of his argument that rhythm is best described by measuring the feet. In foot-measured verse, the feet, whether iambs, trochees, dactyls or whatever, are decided on beforehand by the poet, and it is his task in composition to make the phrasing of the text correspond, or at least not contradict them. If the phrasing consists of irregular numbers of syllables as in normal speech, it seems impossible to conclude that fixed feet are relevant to the rhythm at all.

The second part of Saintsbury's theory of rhythm is that the feet are successions of long and short syllables. He thus defines quantity in English:

'Quantity' as used in this book, means the property of syllabic length or shortness, and this property is acquired in English—as in classical languages, though to different extents and in different manners,—by three conditions:

1. 'Vowel-value' itself, which is not, however, by any means so sovereign as in Greek and Latin.

2. 'Position' which, again, is very much less uniformly powerful than in the ancient languages, and, unless assisted by something else, may, as in the leading case of 'car*pente*r,' be quite inefficient.

3. 'Stress' of one kind or another, either that of the ordinarily pronounced 'accent'; or something resembling the *arsis* and *thesis* of the ancients; or, further, special emphasis of the poet, *metri* or *sensus gratia*.[4]

It must of course be remembered that these statements were made

---

[4] Saintsbury, pp. ix-x.

in the days before formulation of modern linguistic theory, and that therefore they require a certain amount of translation into the currently more familiar terminology. For 'vowel-value' Saintsbury can be presumed to mean the contrast between the vowels of *bit* and *beat,* whether the contrast is thought of as one in short and long vowel, simple vowel and vowel nucleus, or lax vowel and tense vowel. Whatever the terminology, it is generally agreed that the vowel of *beat* is longer than that of *bit.* An example where in Saintsbury's terms, vowel-quality is not sovereign, would be the second syllable of *concrete,* noun, if the word is pronounced with the major stress on the first syllable.

'Position' of course, means position of the vowel before two or more consonants in the same syllable. His example of failure of position to establish length is satisfactory except for the fact that a reader may be permitted to wonder if the syllable division might not be before rather than after the /t/. An example which would not be subject to that difficulty might be the second syllable of 'longest,' clearly shorter than the first syllable, yet clearly ending in two consonants.

His discussion of stress is least clear of the three properties he discusses, and I confess that I do not know what he means by *arsis* and *thesis* as applied to English. In general, however, it would seem that stress of 'one kind or another,' refers to the several grades of English stress as now often (though not universally) formulated. That is, his special emphasis would seem to mean the sentence stress which comes just once in a phrase and which indicates the center of information as in a pair of sentences like 'John went HOME,' and 'John WENT home.' In addition it should be pointed out that Saintsbury can give no example of a fully stressed syllable which is also short. It is also worth noting that other investigators of metrics and rhythm have never had any difficulty in translating Saintbury's markings from long-short to strong-weak.

It is perhaps worth while to summarize the relations of quantity and stress as they occur in Modern American English. First, the syllables which receive secondary or primary stress are never short, though some are longer than others. Under stress, then, there is usually no contrast at all in length, though in my own idiolect and that of some other speakers, there is an isolated contrast between long and short /a/, as in *balm* (long) and *bomb* (short). Generally speaking the longest syllables contain syllabic nuclei rather than simple vowels and end in voiced consonants, particularly nasal clusters. Also it should be said that in much American and British speech a syllable ending in a voiced consonant or cluster is still further prolonged if it falls under sentence stress and before a terminal juncture. Syllables with tertiary or weak stress are always short, so that there is no possibility of contrast in length. Though it is a hackneyed example, Latin *mensa* (nominative), and *mensā* (ablative) form a semantically relevant difference which is independent of stress.

It would seem therefore that there are two reasons against Saintsbury's conclusion that differences in English quantity are the organizing principle of English metre and rhythm. The most compelling is that he can find no examples of quantity independent of stress. Therefore one can conclude that stress alone gives an adequate explanation of metrical variation. To rely on the extra hypothesis of mixed stress and quantity is both to be less than economical and less than clear. In fact, I would advance it as an axiom that the basic organization of metre and rhythm in any language must make use of items which make a relevant difference in the structure of the language, and only of these items. Further, the items so made use of must appear at the level of words and phrases, not merely at the level of sentences. That is, English sentences are often distinguished by pitch, but English words never are. It follows that English verse can not make use of patterns of pitch difference as a basic organizing principle, but that Chinese verse, in a language where pitch does indeed distinguish words, can use pitch as the organizing principle of some of its verse types.

Since quantity is either quite isolated in English (as in my *balm-bomb*) or appears only as a characteristic of final stressed, voiced monosyllables, it also follows that it can not be made the organizing principle of verse or rhythm as in the classic tongues. An example, however, of very skilful secondary use of quantity is to be found in W. S. Gilbert's line

> As you walk down Picadilly with a poppy or a lily
> In your mediaeval *hand*.

The structure of English makes it at least possible to put a great extension of quantity on the last syllable, which then makes a noticeable (and pleasant) contrast with the series of much shorter syllables which precede. Yet I am sure that this kind of variation in quantity, even though it may on occasion explain a literary effect, is quite different from the kind of quantitative variation which Saintsbury was talking about. The uncertainty in deciding quantity, which springs from the fact that Saintsbury sets up three variables (quality, position, stress) is something that gives him a considerable leeway in interpretation. Thus he marks *went* in 'went before' as long, which it is by position, though since it has a secondary stress, it might have been

marked short, making the foot in which it occurs an anapaest rather
than a cretic. Saintsbury seems to have been aware of this element of
uncertainty, and been willing to exploit it, since he says "the quanti-
fication of the following pages expresses it is believed, the 'length' and
'shortness' of syllables as they would be spoken by the best tongues and
heard by the best ears in the passages given." Since there is no way of
defining 'the best tongues' except to say that they are those that agree
with Saintsbury, the statement is obviously meant to dispose of possible
disagreement. Finally, it is once again possible to show that the arrangement of feet in the Landor passage, whether they are thought of
as longs and shorts, or as strongs and weaks, does not produce the
effect of rhythm. I give a sentence similar to that from Landor, composed for the occasion—

$$\breve{}\ \breve{}\ \breve{}\ \overline{}\ \breve{}\quad \overline{}\qquad \overline{}\ \breve{}\quad \overline{}\qquad \overline{}\ \breve{}$$
The first of April | came | money | went | Jimmy

$$\breve{}\ \breve{}\ \overline{}\quad \breve{}\quad \breve{}\!-\!\breve{}\breve{}\quad \quad \breve{}\ \overline{}$$
who believed in | ability | went berserk.

The sentence just given agrees closely with the scansion that Saintsbury gives for the first of the Landor passage, except for the secondarily
stressed *first,* which he might have marked as long, though as I have
tried to show, marking as a short is also a possibility. If then, rhythm is
not based on quantity, sequences of feet do not constitute prose patterns, and finally, if a pattern of scansion identical with that of the
passage discussed fails to produce the effect of rhythm, there is very
little left of the Saintsbury treatment.

Sir Herbert Read approaches the problem in another way. He says
of the Landor passage "The rhythm of this passage is controlled by
the subtle distinction in value made between the colon and semi-colon.
The semi-colon seems to mark a carrying over of an even beat; the
colon, the recovery of an initial emphasis."[5] The comment is curious
since at first it seems nearly incomprehensible. There is no pattern of
phrase- or sentence-end intonation which corresponds to the semi-colon
in the way that a period often indicates a different terminal intonation
pattern from that indicatd by a comma. Nor is any terminal intonation
pattern a matter of beat or emphasis—these are phenomena that be-
long with stress, not intonation. Yet it seems clear that Sir Herbert is
talking sensibly enough, and is merely handicapped by lack of terminology. What he apparently means is variation in juncture patterns.
One such pattern consists in mere elongation without modification in
the pitch levels of the preceding syllables. This is a pattern which

---

[5] Sir Herbert Edward Read, *English Prose Style* (New, revised edition.
London, G. Bell & Sons, 1952), p. 47.

falls at the end of phrases and clauses, rather than complete sentences. This pattern could then be said to "carry over an even [pitch]." This pattern is written / | / and is called 'single-bar.' It usually follows a syllable which at least ends on the next to the lowest pitch, written /2/. It can be very roughly correlated with the comma.

A second terminal pitch and juncture pattern is that of a fall in the level of a syllable or syllables from pitch three, the next to highest, to pitch one, the lowest. This fall is then followed in turn by a still further half-level fall, which constitutes the terminal juncture. The pattern is written /31#/, i.e. three-one double-cross. The pattern marks at least relative completeness of an utterance, and corresponds roughly with a period.

These two patterns are all that Sir Herbert takes account of, though there are at least two more. One is a variant of the comma pattern described above, and consists in a half-level upturn after a syllable which ends on pitch two. The pattern is written /2 |||/, or two double-bar. Since there is an upward pitch break, it could not be said to "carry over an even [pitch]." But, though Sir Herbert says nothing about it, in my reading of the Landor passage double-bars occur after both *Leda* and *Jupiter*.

Another variety of terminal pitch and juncture pattern which Sir Herbert does not mention is a double-bar falling after a syllable with pitch three. This is used for echo questions as in "John went home?" It obviously does not occur in the Landor passage given.

We can agree, then, with Sir Herbert that there are variations in the terminals which end the separate phrases, but it is still true that his statement is confused and confusing. For one thing, he is wrong about which punctuation marks correspond to the terminals he attempts to describe. Landor's periods, colons, and semi-colons all correspond to double-cross terminals—the correspondence is not limited to colons as Sir Herbert says. Also it is the commas in the passage, not the semi-colons which correspond to single- or double-bar. It is also true that Sir Herbert speaks somewhat confusingly both here and elsewhere of the role the punctuation marks perform, since his language implies that the writer is free to choose whatever punctuation he wishes, producing a harmony by judicious mingling of varieties. It is impossible to say whether this is what he really means, or whether once again his lack of terminology has produced a superficial confusion. At any rate, it is clear that it is the basic pattern of lexical and grammatical content which produces the intonation pattern, and it is not possible for the writer to punctuate as he chooses, imposing an intonation foreign to the subject matter. A sufficient example of how the grammatical

and lexical content resist arbitrary punctuation-change is this nonsensical bit of student composition:

"I do not like fish. However, it is cooked."

When Sir Herbert's statements have been sufficiently edited, I think
it is possible to find an element of sound analysis in them. If we con-
centrate on the first sentence alone, it is true that we have two double-
cross terminals after the two occurrences of *died*, then after the next
proper name where we might again expect *died* and a third double-
cross, we get instead a single- or double-bar, followed by a phrase which
runs on to *Jupiter*, and is ended by a second single- or double-bar.
The whole is then concluded with a three syllable phrase with once
more a double-cross. I do not believe that this arrangement of terminals is alone enough to account for the impression of rhythm, but it
certainly is a contributing factor, and to this extent Sir Herbert is
right.

The only critic who has paid attention to the content of the Landor
passage is Paull Franklin Baum. He says:

> In a favorite form of this parallelism the final member is ex-
> panded . . . as in 'Where is the wise? Where is the scribe? Where
> is the disputer of this world? (I Cor. 1:20) or Landor's 'Laodameia
> died; Helen died; Leda, the beloved of Jupiter, went before.'

He continues:

> The next sentence turns on 'better . . . than,' the latter part of
> the comparison being protracted by additional modifiers. The
> third has a simple balance ('enjoy the present . . . insensible of
> decay') varied by the extra phrase 'of infirmity'; then 'the present'
> is repeated precisely 'like a note in music.' The final sentence
> comprises the threefold anaphora, with considerable expansion
> like the gradation of the first sentence. From such sentences . . .
> one can see what Landor meant when he wrote: 'Good prose to
> say nothing of the original thought it conveys, may be infinitely
> varied in modulation. It is only an extension of metre, and am-
> plification of harmonies, of which even the best and most varied
> poetry admits but few.'[6]

The two terms needing explication here are gradation and ana-
phora. The first is borrowed from Saintsbury, and means the kind of
parallelism with final expansion quoted from *Corinthians*, and the
first Landor sentence. The second is classical, and means the kind

[6] Paull Franklin Baum, "The Other Harmony of Prose," quoted in
Modern Essays on Writing and Style, ed. Paul C. Wermuth (New York, 1964),
pp. 74, 77.

of parallelism with deletion of identical material which is found in the last sentence, with identical or near identical material enclosed in brackets:

> There are no fields of amaranth on this side of the grave [which are not soon faded]: there are no voices [on this side of the grave], O Rhodopè, that are not soon mute; there is no name [on this side of the grave] with whatever emphasis of passionate love repeated, of which the echo is not faint at last.

It seems to me that Baum's comment, like that of Sir Herbert, is genuinely insightful, but also incomplete. He is right, certainly, in that a large part of the sense of patterning which the passage gives is due to the various kinds of parallelism which it employs. I think I would add to it only that another important part of the content is the highly compressed analogy in the last lines, that is,

> repetition of a name, finally dying away
> echo of a name, finally dying away

Perhaps also the allusiveness of names like Laodameia, Helen, and Leda, and even amaranth (though we may not know how this imaginary unfading flower looks) contribute to a more generalized impression of rhetorical quality. Yet, as I have said, I think Sir Herbert is right too. That is, I think that it is in general the organization of content which produces rhythm, and the intonation pattern in which it is realized. Further, in the statement I have just given, I think there is a possibility of reconciling not only Baum and Read but also the views of transformational students of syntax and those of more conservative students of phonology. The one group tends to view rhythm in prose as largely a matter of grammatical organization; the other, as a pattern of intonation contours. As so often happens, both are right.

I think we can now leave the Landor passage, but there is certainly more to say about rhythmic prose elsewhere. One of the types of rhythm which is possible in English, since we have a significant word-stress, is a pattern of strong-weak alternation, with the units set off by pauses. Such rhythms reduce prose to percussive patterns like drum-beats or thumps on a table. English, like many languages, has percussive patterns which we all know, and to which we fit various sets of words. A typical one is

DA da-da-DA-da da-DA

To this we fit either 'Shave and a haircut, six bits,' or 'Down by the gasworks, dead drunk.' Another such pattern is

DA-da-da da-DA-da da-da-DA DA DA

To this rhythm we can fit either 'All I want for Christmas is a new front tooth,' or 'The man who came to see me had a long, white beard.' It is of course true that these rhythms make use of patterns involving time, so that they might seem to contradict the statement made earlier that since English does not have significant time differences as word-distinguishers, English can not make use of patterns of longs and shorts. The contradiction is only apparent, however, since the element of time in these percussive patterns is in the arrangement of syllables in relation to pauses, with differences in the length of syllables as usual automatically produced by the stresses. Another point about such patterns is that the intonation patterns contribute to the rhythmic effect also. Thus in the one just quoted, the intonation pattern is

The man who came to see me || had a long | white | beard #

The pitch on the last syllable, and the terminal after it, work together to give the impression of the final completion of a unified, rhythmic pattern.

It is worth mentioning also that languages like some of those of Central America, where pitch is significant on the word level, have very similar rhythms, based on patterns of pitch. In fact this sort of tune-pattern is sometimes sufficiently extended, as in Masateco, so that it is possible to carry on a conversation by whistling, quite without words.

What seems to happen in English prose is that not infrequently the first phrase or sentence of a passage in which the writer is striving for a rhythmic effect, is one in which one of the recognizable percussive rhythms is employed. Thus one of the justly celebrated rhythmic sentences is that which concludes Sir Walter Raleigh's *History of the World* of 1614:

O eloquent, just, and mighty Death!

This is

da DA-da-da DA da-DA-da DA

I would refrain from calling it iambic in spite of its regular alternation, because of the spacing which makes the first four syllables a unit, the fifth a single unit, the next three a unit, and the final again a single unit. Here also the intonation contributes, since we have three double-bar terminals, and then a final double-cross. After having, so to speak set the tone in this opening, Raleigh goes on with parallels arranged in sets of three, with expansion in the last member after the fashion noticed by Baum, and clearly marked by the terminals:

whom none could advise | thou hast persuaded #
what none hath dared || thou hast done #
and whom all the world hath flattered || thou only hast cast
out of the world | and despised #

Then follows a sentence with a quadruple complement, once again giving the pattern of three double-bars and a final double-cross:

thou hast drawn together all the far-stretched greatness ||
all the pride || and ambition || of man #

The final clause breaks the pattern, but still gives at least one double-bar, before finishing the whole with a double-cross:

and covered it all over with these two narrow words ||
Hic jacet #

Perhaps a reasonable way of concluding this discussion, and of showing the range of variation in English rhythmic prose is to take up a bit of a very different kind of composition. The quotation is from Kipling's *Sing Song of Old Man Kangaroo,* the opening sentence:

Not always was the Kangaroo as now we do behold him, but a different animal with four short legs.

The first phrase ends with *him,* and contains fifteen syllables. The second, eighth, and fourteenth syllables are metrical strongs, and this symmetrical arrangement is enough to establish the phrase as rhythmical. Notice that a long string of fifteen syllables can hardly be scanned as a succession of feet. It is the total phrase that is the unit. Having established a rhythmical pattern, Kipling goes on to a different type of construction, a multiple complement not unlike that in the Raleigh sentence:

. . . with four | short | legs. #

The sentence indicates the rightness of the statement of Landor, quoted by Baum, that rhythmic prose is "an extension of metre, and amplification of harmonies, of which even the best and most varied poetry admits but few." Rhythmic prose, since it must be prose, can not admit the regular patterning in successive phrases which characterizes verse. Consequently each phrase, or phrase group, establishes its own pattern, and no single pattern is carried throughout. The prose patterns pass from percussive sequences to grammatical parallelisms, to symmetrically arranged pitch contours, and depend always and to a large measure on successful organization of content.

SOUND, SYNTAX, AND SENSE—AND MEANING

JOHN B. NEWMAN

Queens College of the City University of New York

A speaker may be said to "have access to a language" if (a) he has the ability to produce sentences he has himself never previously uttered nor ever heard anyone else utter, (b) he can understand what he is saying as he is doing this sort of thing, and (c) he can make himself understood by doing this to others who have similar "access" to the same language. At the same time, he must be able to understand sentences of this sort produced by others. As for the use of repetitions and reiterations—that is, sentences or parts of sentences that were previously produced or were heard (or seen) previously produced by others—a speaker may be considered to have "language access" if he has the ability to understand the relationship of such replications to the situation, or to particular aspects of the situation, in which such utterances are used. As intricate a complex of abilities as this obviously implies a vast number of factors. In this discussion we shall limit our consideration to those factors that pertain to what is commonly referred to as "the 'meaning' of what is said."

Perhaps the greatest problem encountered in considering the meaning of human utterances is engendered by the meaning of meaning itself. Still, it would be possible to discuss meaning without becoming entwined, like the Trojan Laocoön, in the serpentine coils of the meaning of "meaning" (and, inevitably, the meaning of "the meaning of 'meaning' "). We could do so simply because, as readers (and speakers) who have "language access," we somehow "know" what meaning is! The reason is not at all mysterious or elusive. It is simply a function of our "access" to language. We "know" what "meaning" is because we *have* what "meaning" is when we have "language access."

Before dismissing this observation as circular, if not ranting, gibberish, we should be fully cognizant of the problem faced by anyone trying to analyze the meaning *in* language by means *of* language. Using language to analyze the meaning of language is similar to what would have taken place if Noah had attempted to rebuild his ark, plank by plank, at the height of the flood while trying to keep himself and his whole ménage (and menagerie) afloat all the while he was doing so. Furthermore, the comprehension of the meaning of an utterance in a language that is ordinarily used cannot be explained by translation;

for there is no more familiar idiom into which it could be transposed.[1] We must, therefore, use our understanding of ordinary talk to understand our understanding of ordinary talk *while we go on talking*.

One point that might be helpful, however, is that the English word "meaning" implies two poles. One pole refers to *that which something signifies*; the other to *the value or significance of what is signified*. "Thus if we ask what is the meaning of life, we may be asking a question about the signification of the term 'life,' or asking a question about the value or significance of living—or both."[2] *Signification*, then, should be distinguished from *significance* in any consideration of the meaning of "meaning."

Suppose, however, we were to be asked a question that unequivocally concerns the signification of the term involved, a question such as "What does 'light' mean?" An answer is not easy to come by. Even modern physicists have a difficult time of it, and the reason is not the paucity of their knowledge of the phenomenon. With eyes to see, we all *know* what light is; but we would indeed be hard put to *tell* someone what it is, even if the person is possessed of eyes at least as well-sighted as our own. "Meaning" thus implies two other poles. In this paper we shall call these poles *sense* and *substance*: with *sense* referring to that which we can explain to someone in words; and *substance* referring to that which we *know* (as we *know* what "light" is).

But where does the dictionary stand in this respect? What function does it serve as regards "meaning"? What do we find when we look up a word in the dictionary? We find a *definiens*, or a statement in words, which purports to clarify the "meaning" of the *definiendum*, or the word in question. Words about words are used to explain other words. Look up, for instance, the treatment of the word "light" in any dictionary and you will probably find that it is surprisingly well done. But we can come to such a conclusion only because we previously *knew* what light was before we looked up the dictionary's explanation of it. In sum, we *knew* the *substance* of the word "light" before we got the *sense* of the term from the dictionary. The dictionary merely presented a way of telling us what was previously known. Try looking up a totally unknown term. (Word-puzzle fans are used to this.) At most, you will get a *sense* of the term. If you are lucky, you might come to know how you might use the word in a sentence purely as a result of looking it up in the dictionary. (More to the point, you

---

[1] Although I have embellished it here with Pentateuchal reference, the image of rebuilding a boat while staying afloat in it is Otto Neurath's, and is cited in Willard Van Orman Quine, *Word and Object* (Cambridge, Mass., 1960), p. 3.

[2] Charles Morris, *Signification and Significance* (Cambridge, Mass., 1964), p. vii.

may be able to fit the proper letters into the proper boxes of the puzzle, regardless of whether the puzzle is a cross-word—or the encoding or decoding of a thought in speech or writing.) It is doubtful, however, that you will come to *know* what a word refers to extensionally —that you will come to *know* its *substance*—as a result of consulting the dictionary. In those cases where you experience the feeling of "So *that* is what an *x* is!"—you probably *knew* what *x* was previously, you probably already *knew* its *substance*. The dictionary merely informed you of "its 'name,'" or "the word for it."

To illustrate the extent of the function that the dictionary serves as a source of the "meaning" of a word, let us see what happens in the case of the word "fanon," a word that we will assume is not generally known. Look it up in the dictionary, and you will discover that "fanon" means "maniple." This might be a revealing (even if a not particularly interesting) fact if only we know what "maniple" meant. Well, we have probably learned from previous similar experiences that it is necessary to "look further," perhaps in a "better" dictionary.

Without passing judgment on any one of them, let me report that I have on my desk before me three dictionaries. Regardless of their individual or collective merits, they can at least serve to make the point. I have no doubt that other lexicographical publications might (or might not) be said to be more thorough (?), more authoritative (?), perhaps clearer (?) than the ones I shall cite. Still, I shall cite: (1) *Webster's New Collegiate Dictionary*, based on *Webster's New International Dictionary, Second Edition*, published by the G. & C. Merriam Company of Springfield, Massachusetts, dated 1951; (2) *Funk & Wagnalls' Standard College Dictionary, Text Edition*, published by Harcourt, Brace & World of New York, dated 1963; and (3) *The Universal Dictionary of the English Language*, edited by Henry Cecil Wyld, "with Preface to the American Edition" by Allen Walker Read, published by the Standard American Corporation of Chicago, Illinois, dated 1939. The Merriam publication reports "fanon" as follows: "a. a maniple. b. a short cape or deep collar worn by the pope at solemn pontifical Mass." The Harcourt publication reports: "1. A maniple worn by a celebrant at Mass. 2. A cape worn only by the Pope, as he presides at solemn pontifical Mass." The Standard American Corporation publication reports: "An ornamental scarf worn over the left arm by the Pope when celebrating Mass."

Do you know what a fanon is? Would you recognize one if you saw it? Is it a cape, a collar, or a scarf worn over the arm?

Let's check "maniple" while we're about it. The Merriam publication reports as the ecclesiastical use of the term: "A narrow band of the same material and color as the chasuble carried suspended from the left arm by the celebrant and ministers at Mass." The Harcourt publication reports: "A band worn on the left arm as a eucharistic vestment, usually by Roman Catholic clergymen." The SAC publication reports: "Sort of scarf or stole worn on left arm by celebrant at the Eucharist."

Do you know what a maniple is? Would you recognize one if you saw it? Is it a band suspended from the arm, a band worn on the arm, a scarf, or a stole? Does this knowledge add to your understanding of what a fanon is?

Someone once told me that he had recently purchased a new room air conditioner of some number of thousands of "B.T.U.'s." "What's a 'B.T.U.'?" I asked. "A 'British thermal unit,'" I was told. Of course! Apparently I was supposed to know what a "B.T.U." was upon being told that it was an abbreviation for "British thermal unit." Do you know what a "British thermal unit" is? Would you know what it is—much less how it pertained to the cooling of the air in a room in your home—if you were told that a "British thermal unit" is "the quantity of heat required to raise the temperature of one pound of water one degree of Fahrenheit at or near its point of maximum density"? That is what my Merriam dictionary tells me a "British thermal unit" is. The explanation in my Harcourt dictionary is somewhat simpler: it ends with the word "Fahrenheit" and omits the words "at or near its point of maximum density." Otherwise, the explanation is the same as the Merriam's. My SAC dictionary, dated 1939, does not even have an entry for "British thermal unit." Though "British thermal unit" is a "technical term" (and so, presumably, beyond the ken of ordinary mortals), we nonetheless go on using "British thermal units" and "B.T.U.'s" in generating grammatical sentences, regardless of the help the dictionary may (or may not) afford us as regards their meaning. We cannot help thinking of the aptness of George Miller's observation that "the fact that we have no idea what we are talking about does not stop us from talking."[3]

It would seem, then, that what a dictionary gives as the definiens of a term is an explanation of the use of the definiendum in the language. The user of the language may then be able to apply the term in question to make *sense* in encoding or decoding a grammatical sentence. It is doubtful, however, that one could get the *substance* of a term from a dictionary. No one ever gained access to a language by means of a dictionary. Ask anyone who has ever toured in a foreign land. The unfolding of intimate experience that subsumes the *substance* of a term can scarcely be supplied by words alone. Listen to the way a student responded to a lecture by Ludwig Wittgenstein:

[3] *Language and Communication* (New York, 1951), p. 171.

I thought, at the time, I'd undergone a conversion, but what I'd received, I realize now, was a philosophy shown, not a philosophy argued. Wittgenstein had uttered what he felt could be uttered (and it was very important), but what he displayed could only be felt and seen. . . . It now seems inevitable that [his] *Tractatus* [*Logico-Philosophicus*] should have stressed, so much, the difference between what can be *said* (and anything that can be said can be said clearly), and what can only be shown.[4]

The intimacy of the experience of confrontation, of being *shown*—regardless of the particular sensory modality involved—is the basis of language *substance*. It is the stuff of which "deep" language structure is made. A series of "upward" transformations will result in a "surface" language structure which can then be produced as speech. Speech must make *sense* in order to be comprehended and decoded. But the comprehension of speech implies another, converse, series of transformations, which will make a produced sentence understood as *substance*. Words arranged in sentences, even grammatical sentences, cannot themselves have the "deep" *substance* that can alone have meaning in the truest sense of that perpetually protean term. Words arranged in sentences are all that is available in language, but they are not themselves meaningful in *substance*.

But no one ever speaks in such a "substantive" fashion—for any length of time. As T. S. Eliot once said, "I gotta use words when I talk to you." But all too frequently that is exactly what we do. We "use words" when we talk; and we even "use words" when we try to communicate. One need not be a psychologist to realize that an important phase of language behavior is play, whether it take the form of an interpersonal game or a manifestation of oral autoeroticism. And so, the use of words *per se* (*i.e.*, their choice) is frequently a form of play, or what might be called "linguistic creativity." Though it is most apparent in verse and poetry, and in what is called rhetorical "style," as well as in punning and other forms of humor, wit and word-play, linguistic creativity, or language play, is an inevitable part of all verbal expression because it is inherent in the structure of language itself.

Language has three dimensions. They are (1) the diacritical, which pertains to the rules for the production of the isolates or discrete units of the language (*e.g.*, the sounds in spoken language, the letters in written language, the movements in gesture language, etc.); (2) the syntactic, which pertains to the rules for the arrangement of the sets of the language (*e.g.*, the words or lexical units); and (3) the semantic

[4] William H. Gass in *The New Republic* of June 22, 1968, p. 30.

which pertains to the rules that define (a) the *sense* of the patterns[5] (*e.g.*, the sentences) generated in accordance with the syntactic rules and (b) the *substance* of the information being communicated, regardless of the form it may take in utterance. Linguistic creativity, or language play, is a consequence of the unitary character of each of these dimensions of language. Though they are coterminally related in that their interaction results in meaningful sentences, neither is a function of the other, and, to certain extents, neither is dependent upon the other. Small wonder, then, that there is an infinity of sentences available to those with access to language! We can say just about anything we want to. In fact, we can say virtually anything at all. We can pack a lot of meaning into a few words. We can utter a lot of words that mean nothing at all. We can express thoughts whose phonetic representations refer to nothing at all, and we can say things that refer to anything we may have in mind in sounds that are neither well-ordered nor sensible. We can say things whose sounds have no *substance*, though the words uttered are well-ordered and so make a certain amount of *sense*. Indeed, our voices may be puny, to paraphrase William Faulkner, but our ability to talk is inexhaustible. Let us now look at some of the types of sentences we can produce to see if we can gain some insight into the meaning they may or may not contain or convey.

As for such expressions as are produced without sounds, we can cite any number of instances. The report of Wittgenstein's student cited above is only one. Any example of what is generally known as "non-verbal communication" could serve for the virtually infinite number of others.[6]

As examples of utterances whose sounds refer to nothing at all, we have at least an equally vast number from which to choose. There are, first of all, such paravocal emissions as sighs, coughs, hums, sniffs, snorts, sneezes, breath-intakes, hisses, throat-clearings, and belches which all of us produce throughout a day. These noises have no meaning, at least not in the sense that they refer to anything. They are merely acoustic indications of our physical, psychological, or psychophysical state at a given moment in a particular set of circumstances. It should be understood, however, that sighs, coughs, and other such noises can be used to refer to something other than themselves or the inner state of their emitter. In certain societies, for in-

---

[5] For a full description of the function of isolates, sets and patterns in the structure of languages, see Edward T. Hall, *The Silent Language* (New York, 1959), pp. 119-164 *et in passim*.

[6] For a brief, but comprehensive, introduction to this whole vast area of study, the reader is referred to Albert Mehrabian, "Communication Without Words," *Psychology Today*, 2 (September, 1968), pp. 53-55.

stance, a belch is used as a means of indicating the satisfaction given by the food that was just eaten; and in certain instances in our own society, a throat-clearing can signify a reminder, a reprimand, and perhaps a dozen other things as well. But, for the most part, paravocal emissions of this sort serve merely as symptoms of the emitter's inner state at the moment of their occurrence.

The tones, tempos, rhythms, and qualities of voice that inevitably accompany all of our verbal utterances are further examples of sounds which represent nothing other than themselves or the inner state of their emitter. Though these so-called suprasegmental aspects of speech contribute to the total meaning of the utterance as a whole, none of these aspects are representational in themselves. Usually, they are mere indications or outward manifestations of our inner states, but they can, of course, be controlled. They can be suppressed or purposefully used, but such sounds serve no semantic function other than to indicate the inner state of their source.

But what of otherwise meaningless concatenations of sounds that somehow resemble a reference to something other than themselves or the physical state of their source? In the story, "Ladle Rat Rotten Hut," its author tells us that "hairs annulled furry starry, toiling udder warts, warts welcher alter girdle deferent firmer once inner regional virgin."[7] Though nonsensical in appearance in print, this seeming gibberish becomes recognizable (*i.e.*, "accessible," and hence meaningful) as each phrase is read aloud with the proper inflection. For those who do not "get it" (*i.e.*, do not have access to this specimen of "Anguish Languish"), this cryptograph may be deciphered as the story, "Little Red Riding Hood." The cipher goes on to say that "here's an old fairy story, told in other words, words which are altogether different from the ones in the original version."

Were the entire scheme of this game of "Anguish Languish" not based on a phonological similarity to a grammatical text, it would, beyond the shadow of a doubt, be nothing but sheer noise. Yet despite the level of phonetic, lexical, syntactic, and semantic "noise in the channel," a speaker with access to English could decode and comprehend a "furry starry" such as "Ladle Rat Rotten Hut" on the basis of its sound alone. It could, of course, be argued that a previous knowledge of the original is necessary for the comprehension of a parody. But there are other such compositions which parody nothing

---

[7] This entire story, attributed to Professor Howard Chace, then of Miami University, Oxford, Ohio, and author of other examples of "Anguish Languish," may be found in *Word Study* (A Publication of G. & C. Merriam Company, Springfield, Mass.), Vol. XXXVIII, No. 5, p. 4 (May, 1953). The discussion which appeared in several of the following issues is equally interesting and delightful.

but themselves.[8] So if it is possible for such concatenations of disparate orthographical items, otherwise without trace of any linguistic context save a sort of phonic resemblance to spoken English, to convey even an echo of reference to something other than the sounds themselves or the state of their source, then any doubt of the conveyance of meaning by means of sound alone should be dispelled. Were this not so, the entire concept of phonetic symbolism[9] and onomatopoeia would have no basis whatsoever; and punning would not be possible at all.

More interesting in a formal sense (and hence, presumably, more productive) is the question of the semantic interpretation of sentences that are deviant according to the "scale of grammaticalness"[10] that every speaker with access to the language has "built into him," as it were. This notion can perhaps best be explained briefly with the following anecdote. I once asked a resident native of a small New England village I was visiting if he could speak for either of the two dentists in town. Yes, he allowed as how he could speak for one of them "because of the great job he once did in pulling out several teeth from one of my sisters' heads. . . . Uh . . . Well, I can't say 'one of my sisters' *head*' can I? . . . Uh . . . Dammit! You know what I mean." Well, I did. But I laughed just the same. And after a bit, he did too. Perhaps there were no hurt feelings because both of us had access to the same scale of grammaticalness. As speaker and hearer, we both recognized the attempt to formulate what was meant as being grammatically deviant because it made no *sense*. Still, we both *knew* what had been intended to be said because the sentence, no matter its grammatical deviance, had *substance* to which both of us had access.

We shall make no attempt to explain grammatical deviance here. Anyone interested in pursuing that question may well begin with

---

[8] Although his scholarship encompassed all of the linguistic sciences, the late Professor Lee S. Hultzén was especially devoted to all of *ars phonetica*, including this game of phonic equivalence. He once showed me a letter he had written to a George W. (it is a bit long to present here in its entirety) which was addressed to "Dirge Orgy" and was signed "Yearn Aussie ate eddied mirror, Elles Ache," the initialed signature to be pronounced, according to a footnote, as it was in the "16th cent or earlier."

[9] For a fuller discussion of this subject, including its pros and cons, see, among others, Otto Jespersen, *Language: Its Nature, Development and Origin* (New York, 1949), pp. 396-411; Edward Sapir, "A Study in Phonetic Symbolism," *Journal of Experimental Psychology*, 12 (1929), pp. 225-239; Stanley S. Newman, "Further Experiments in Phonetic Symbolism," *American Journal of Psychology*, 45 (1933), pp. 53-75; and John B. Carroll, *The Study of Language* (Cambridge, Mass., 1959), p. 238n.

[10] The phrase is Noam Chomsky's. I got it from his *Aspects of the Theory of Syntax* (Cambridge, Mass., 1965), though it may occur elsewhere in his writings as well.

Noam Chomsky's *Aspects of the Theory of Syntax,* and go on from there (if there is any further to go). What we are interested in here is the degree to which a sentential construction may be grammatically deviant, and still make *sense.* If some light can be shed on that, we may then consider the extent to which such constructions may or may not have *substance*—that is, have a meaning which can be made *known* to more than one person. With such "knowledge," a reader or listener can prove the degree of his "access" to the language by supplying that part of the context which may be missing from the text,[11] and so demonstrate his understanding of its "meaning."

Let us begin by considering a series of ten words selected at random from a dictionary. "Without any constraints due to adjacent words," a string of ten words, such as:

(i) byway consequence handsomely financier bent flux cavalry swiftness weather-beaten extent[12]

has what has been called "a zero order of approximation to English."[13] In other words, the string makes no *sense* at all. Even the separate words in the string cannot really be said to have any meaning, for they do not indicate or convey anything, individually or in conjunction with any of the other words in the string.[14] At best, they are simply orthographic representations. They appear to resemble words by their shape rather than by any syntactic or semantic function they perform in the string. In short, they are not true lexical items in which some kind of meaning may inhere or to which some kind of meaning may be attached syntactically as a consequence of their conjunction.

In order to obtain what could be considered a "first order approximation," words would have to be selected on the basis of the frequency of their occurrence in English speech rather than merely on the basis of their listing in the lexicon of the language. In order to accomplish this:

a scrambling of the words in the higher orders was used. By drawing words at random from the contextually determined lists,

[11] Cf. the definition of meaning attributed to I. A. Richards by Geoffrey Wagner, *On the Wisdom of Words* (Princeton, New Jersey, 1968), pp. 248, 255.

[12] George A. Miller & Jennifer A. Selfridge, "Verbal Context and the Recall of Meaningful Material," in Sol Saporta & Jarvis R. Bastian (edd.), *Psycholinguistics: A Book of Readings* (New York, 1961), p. 205.

[13] *Ibid.,* p. 202.

[14] Cf. George A. Miller's statement that "Words standing alone have no meaning . . . or, more precisely, have no single meaning. The dictionary definitions are derived from the contexts in which the word occurs." See his *Language and Communication, op. cit.,* p. 112.

we obtained as good an approximation to the relative frequencies of individual words in English as these higher order lists provided. The alternative method of selecting words at random from a newspaper might have given a sample quite different in difficulty (familiarity).[15]

An example of "a first order approximation to English" in a ten word string that was so derived is:

(ii) abilities with that beside I for waltz you the sewing[16]

If we were to go on to construct a series of such ten word strings in which each word was determined by the juxtaposition of one, two, or more words in the string, we could derive a series of orders of approximation to English up to what should amount to a well-formed or "grammatical" ten word sentence. Thus, if each word in a string were determined in the context of only one preceding word, then each successive pair of words could go together in a sentence. We would then have "a second order approximation" in a string of ten words, such as:

(iii) was he went to the newspaper is in deep and[17]

To construct higher orders of approximation:

> [one] person would see a sequence of words and would use the sequence in a sentence. Then the word he used directly after the sequence would be added, the first word of the sequence would be dropped, and the new (but overlapping) sequence would be presented to the next person.[18]

Generated in this fashion, examples of the fourth and fifth orders of approximation would be, respectively:

(iv) saw the football game would end on January
(v) they saw the play Saturday and sat down beside him[19]

Anyone capable of reading this discussion obviously has access to the language, and so he will appreciate the semantic ebb and flow in (iv) and (v). In both of these strings, something "meaningful" seems to be in the process of being formulated for several words running; but then the *sense* seems to "drop off," as it were. One has the feeling that another "sensible fragment" could then begin, were the

[15] Miller & Selfridge, *op. cit.*, p. 202.
[16] *Ibid.*, p. 205.
[17] *Ibid.*
[18] *Ibid.*, p. 202.
[19] *Ibid.*, p. 206.

string longer by a number of words. The method by which these strings were constructed would indeed justify that feeling.

But consider the following:

(vi) to both married aunts of mine are to John's parents

As in the case of (iv) and (v), something "meaningful" seems to be in the process of being formulated for several words running; but then the *sense* seems to "drop off." One has the feeling that another "sensible fragment" could then begin, were the string longer by a number of words. In other words, (vi) appears to be an order approximation similar to (iv) and (v) that was probably constructed in the same way. The fact is that it was not. Actually, (vi) was constructed by rearranging the words in an otherwise syntactically well-formed ten word sentence so as to make the scrambled form appear to be an order approximation string.

The reason why this was done was not because of some devious desire on my part to deceive anyone by changing the meaning of the original sentence. There is no question of the fact that word order is fundamental and basic to the semantics of English and to the meaning of any sentence in it. The reason why the sentence from which (vi) was derived was scrambled was to take us out of—to transport us beyond—the volatile nature of the language to which all of us, as its speakers and readers, have access. It has been said that language is like carbon monoxide gas—colorless and odorless, but highly dangerous. It is only in unusual circumstances that we become at all aware of the capriciousness of language, as when a riddle is explained to us.[20] In order to understand everyday language more accurately, it becomes necessary for us to "climb out through [it], on top of it, and over it," as Ludwig Wittgenstein put it.[21] By rearranging the words in an otherwise syntactically well-formed ten word sentence so as to make the scrambled form resemble an order approximation string, we force ourselves to become aware of the sorts of meaning-types inherent in the course (and discourse) of ordinary language—most specifically the difference between *sense* and *substance*.

The original sentence from which (vi) was constructed reads as follows:

(vii) both of John's parents are married to aunts of mine[22]

---

[20] A student once tried to nettle me by asking, "If I took two apples away from three, how many apples would I have?" I was, of course, wrong when I said one, for if he took two apples, he would, naturally, have two.

[21] *Tractatus Logico-Philosophicus*, trans. C. K. Ogden (New York, 1922), p. 189.

[22] Chomsky, *op. cit.*, p. 77.

The ten words in (vi) thus make sense together in (vii). All ten words "fall into their proper places," as it were, each in the context of the others, constituting what anyone with access to the language would recognize as a "grammatical" sentence.

But what does the sentence *tell* us? Or, in the clumsy terminology of ordinary language, what does the sentence mean? We know that both of John's parents could, in easily understood circumstances, be married to different spouses—but only one of them could be married (legally, at any rate) to my aunt! Sentence (vii) thus has no *substance,* for we *know* that what it says cannot be so. As a ten word string the construction may make *sense,* but as a sentence its incongruity or deviance lies in its lack of *substance.*[23]

This example is not unique. We chose it simply because it consisted of ten words. Chomsky lists four others,[24] but the number of further examples that are continually available are at least as numerous as there are speakers of the language. Everyone at some time in his daily verbal behavior is party to this sort of utterance. It is not necessarily indicative of a lapse of mind or the loss of ability to use the language effectively. It is simply in the nature of discourse consisting of utterances that must be generated according to the rules of the language being used. Anyone who has ever worked on the composition of a statement for publication is aware of this.

Consider, for a moment, a sentence such as:

(viii) a unicorn may be captured by making it run its horn into a tree, behind which the huntsman has dodged

Why, it may be counterargued, can't we understand such a sentence? Well, of course, we can "understand" it! It is grammatical, and it makes *sense.* We can "envision" what the sentence is saying. We all know (?) what a unicorn is. (If we don't know what a unicorn is, we can always, as Lewis Carroll said of a griffin, "look at the picture.") We can see (?) how a beast with a single sharp-pointed horn protruding from its forehead could run it into a tree while charging a dodging huntsman. And so on. In the same way, using the same "logic," it can be argued that we can "understand" (perhaps better, we can rationalize) a sentence such as "both of John's parents are married to aunts of mine."

It is interesting, incidentally, to notice who argues that sentences such as (vii) and (viii) "make sense." (It should, of course, be noted again that we do not deny that such sentences make *sense.* We merely

[23] As Chomsky puts it, the "incongruity" of the sentence is "purely semantic (or 'pragmatic')." *Ibid.,* p. 76.
[24] *Ibid.,* p. 77.

stress the fact that they have no *substance.*) Are such challengers rationalists? What rationalist would argue for the "substance" of unicorns? Are they sceptics? What sceptic would argue for the reality of unicorns? Are they realists? nominalists? What are they? One could not even call them sophists, for that would desecrate the etymon of that name! One must conclude that such challengers are simply nuisances!

But coming back to sentence (vii), notice what happens if it is itself embedded in such frames as:

(ix) it is nonsense to speak of both of John's parents being married to aunts of mine

(x) aunts of mine cannot be married to both of John's parents

(xi) both of John's parents cannot be married to aunts of mine[25]

Oddly enough, we can accept these enlarged sentences not only as making *sense* but also as having *substance.* It is interesting to consider the reason why. In his discussion of sentences of this type, Chomsky says that although they violate strict syntactic subcategorization rules, the reason why they are not unnatural, or semantically incongruent, is because of "the semantic properties of certain lexical items and certain constructions."[26] For want of further explanation, it would seem that, despite the semantic incongruity of sentence (vii), it is the incorporation of lexical items and constructions associated with or signifying negation that makes sentences of this type semantically congruent. From a strictly semantic point of view, this can be explained on the basis of metalanguage.

Ordinary language is ordinarily used for purposes of interaction, and is merely a means of accomplishing that purpose. The user of ordinary language is seldom aware of what he is saying or the way he is saying it. (Else why do we react the way we do when what we have said is played back to us mechanically, or "thrown back at us" conversationally?) If it is our desire to analyze what we are saying or writing, we must "climb out through ordinary language, on top of it, and over it" in order to understand it.

This can be done by inventing a language that will permit us to talk *about* ordinary language *and about nothing else;* for if this invention would permit us to talk about anything else, it would be nothing more than ordinary language in the first place. Thus, *stone,* referring to a physical object (which can be kicked),[27] would be a word in ordinary

---

[25] These frames are patterned after ones in Chomsky, *op. cit.,* p. 157, 158.
[26] *Ibid.,* p. 158.
[27] Willard Van Orman Quine, in remarking on Dr. Johnson's demonstration of the reality of a stone by kicking it, said that "To begin with, at least, we have little better to go on than Johnsonian usage. The familiar

language; whereas "stone," referring to the word *s-t-o-n-e* in ordinary language, would be a word in metalanguage. The metalanguage word "stone" is as distinctly different from the ordinary language word *stone* as semanticists are so very careful to distinguish the ordinary language surrogate from the physical object for which it stands. As a result, the metalanguage word "stone" becomes a linguistic object to be examined, analyzed, and evaluated *independent of the ordinary language word* stone *and its referent.* The linguistic objectivity referred to by the word "stone" in metalanguage is distinctly different from, *and is not to be confused with,* the physical objectivity referred to by the word *stone* in ordinary language. The two are not the same. They are not identical. They do not have the same referent. In short, *they are not the same word!* The fact that both are commonly thought of as the same "word," that they are spelled the same way and pronounced the same way (and consequently erroneously explicated lexicographically in the same way) gives rise to their being used in the same way syntactically. On the basis of their identical orthography and orthoepy, they *appear to be* identical; and so they are used as though they "make the 'same' *sense.*" The most that can be said about them is that they are heteronyms, and so they are at least as different, one from the other, as one stone is from another!

Thus, if I were to say:

(xii) the stone has diabetes

I would be using ordinary language to refer to physical realities which pertain to the physical objects that are being talked about. Though the sentence would be syntactically congruent (*i.e.,* it makes *sense*), it would be semantically incongruent (*i.e.,* it has no *substance*). When, however, sentence (xii) is itself embedded in such frames as:

(xiii) it is nonsense to speak of a stone having diabetes
(xiv) a stone can't have diabetes[28]

no consequent unnaturalness or semantic incongruity is evident. The reason is that sentences (xiii) and (xiv) *are not sentences in ordinary language.* These sentences *appear* to be talking about stones and their

material objects may not be all that is real, but they are admirable examples." See his *Word and Object, op. cit.,* p. 3. Perhaps a major part of Alexander Bryan Johnson's theory of language is based on a similar premise. See, for instance, *A Treatise on Language,* ed. David Rynin (Berkeley, California, 1959) and *The Meaning of Words* (Milwaukee, Wisconsin, 1948).

[28] These examples, as well as the two following, were suggested by the ones to be found in James D. McCawley, "The Role of Semantics in a Grammar," in *Universals in Linguistic Theory,* ed. Emmon Bach & Robert T. Harms (New York, 1968), p. 128.

physical properties, but actually they are not. For they are talking about sentence (xii)! They are commenting on it, examining, analyzing, and evaluating it; and so sentences (xiii) and (xiv) must be considered to be sentences in metalanguage. As such, they do not refer to the physical facts pertaining to *the excess sugar in the blood of stones* but rather to the linguistic facts pertaining to a sentence regarding "the excess sugar in the blood of stones." Sentence (xii) is phrased in ordinary language. As such, it may make *sense,* but it has no *substance*: because we *know* (as we *know* what light is) that its referents, the physical realities it is talking about, are simply not so, nor can they be. Any negation of sentence (xii), however, not only makes *sense,* but also has *substance*: because it must be couched in metalanguage. As statements in metalanguage, sentences (xiii) and (xiv) refer to the linguistic reality of sentence (xii)—regardless of what it says.[29]

Suppose now, instead of negating sentence (xii), we were to ascribe it as a statement made by someone, as, for instance:

(xv) John said that the stone had diabetes
(xvi) I cannot conceive of anyone saying that a stone has diabetes

Here, again, as in the case of sentences (xiii) and (xiv), no consequent unnaturalness or semantic incongruity is evident. Though a case could be made arguing that any such ascription must also be in metalanguage, we would be inclined to go along with B. F. Skinner, who distinguishes "autoclitic expressions" from metalanguage. The term *autoclitic,* according to Skinner, is "intended to suggest [verbal] behavior which is based upon or depends upon other verbal behavior."[30] Autoclitics may be positive (as in sentence (xv)) or negative (as in sentence (xvi)). Though they may appear to be the same as metalanguage expressions, autoclitics are distinctive in at least one respect. The speaker who utters an autoclitic may be said to be two steps *away from* the subject being discussed because of his attribution of the statement to someone at some time. Metalanguage, on the other hand, by talking about ordinary language *and about nothing else,* may be said to be two steps *above* the subject being discussed.

As speakers and readers having access to the language, we are usually in no doubt as to whether a term belongs to ordinary parlance or technical terminology. "If it is a vernacular term," according to Gilbert Ryle, "then nearly everybody will know its stock use."[31] But

[29] Cf. B. F. Skinner's observation that "once verbal behavior has occurred and become one of the objects of the physical world, it can be described like any other object." See his *Verbal Behavior* (New York, 1957), p. 319.
[30] *Ibid.,* p. 315.
[31] "Ordinary Language," *The Philosophical Review,* 62 (1953), p. 168.

this seems hardly to be so in the case of the term "meaning." Although there is no question that the term belongs to ordinary parlance, nearly everyone does *not* know its stock use. In fact, hardly anyone does. Ogden and Richards found that "no less than sixteen groups of definitions [actually, they list twenty-three!] may be profitably distinguished in a field where the most rigid accuracy is desirable."[32] And Leo Abraham culled from the literature more than fifty uses of the term.[33] But it is not even a matter of number (which implies a "correct" or specific tally). The reason for this semantic frustration lies in the multiordinality of the term "meaning" itself. According to Alfred Korzybski:

> The main characteristic of [multiordinal terms] consists of the fact that on different levels of orders of abstractions they may have different meanings, with the result that they have no general meaning; for their meanings are determined solely by the given context, which establishes the different orders of abstractions.[34]

If such are the circumstances surrounding the term "meaning" in ordinary parlance, who could be blamed for not knowing its "stock use," whatever that might be or ever have been?

Is "meaning," then, a technical term? Hardly. The fact that a technical (semantic) interpretation may be made of its use in the language no more changes its status as a term in ordinary parlance than would a lexicological account of its etymology change its current dictionary definition, such as it is or may be.

In the flood of daily communication, we manage somehow to remain afloat, for the most part, with ordinary words in ordinary parlance. In extraordinary cases, we do the best we can. "In doing physics, for example, where our language is tightened up in order precisely to describe complicated and unusual cases concisely, we prepare linguistically for the worst."[35] But even here our ark is frequently swamped, as is evident, for instance, in the dilemma of the corpuscular/undulatory conception(s) of light.[36] In the ordinary use of ordinary language we rarely bother to prepare linguistically for the worst (if, indeed, we bother to prepare for anything at all!). And even if we are prepared, we would find that we could not manage it anyway. And so words fail us. Technical as it may be, semantic

---

[32] *The Meaning of Meaning*, 6th ed. (New York, 1943), pp. 186-187.
[33] "What is the Theory of Meaning About?" *The Monist*, 46 (1936), pp. 228-256.
[34] *Science and Sanity*, 3rd ed. rev. (Lakeville, Connecticut, 1948), p. 14.
[35] J. L. Austin, "The Meaning of a Word," in *Philosophical Papers*, ed. J. O. Urmson & G. J. Warnock (Oxford, 1961), p. 36.
[36] See *The Limits of Language*, ed. Walker Gibson (New York, 1962), pp. 15-28.

analysis remains, therefore, continually justified, if not essential, in order to permit us to know what is going on in the language in which we are presumably communicating—even if we may not know what we are talking about.

Ordinary parlance permeates our entire existence as *human* beings. As Dwight Bolinger describes it:

> The running account that a child is able to give of a series of actions that he performs or sees performed betokens an organized activity that is not enclosed within itself but relates at all times to something else. It would seem absurd to us to be told that every time we stood up, sat down, reached for a chocolate, turned on a light, pushed a baby carriage, or started the car we should, at the same time, be twitching in a particular way the big toe of our left foot. But just such an incessant accompaniment of everything else by our speech organs does not surprise us at all. Other activities are self-contained. That of language penetrates them and almost never stops. It must be developed not separately, like walking, but as part of whatever we do. So it must be on hand from the start.[37]

Were this penetration of all our activities always and necessarily in reference to them, we might have here a possible basis for the explanation of meaning. But the incessant twitching in a particular way of our speech organs is one thing, while the meaning of what we are saying is quite another. The former purports to describe the signal, while the latter refers to the message. The signal, however, is as discrete and separable from the message as are the interests of the repairman and the drama critic, both of whom could be looking at the same television screen at the same moment. An adult's ordinary parlance. just as a child's, is preponderantly phatic,[38] if not actually "egocentric."[39] The "incessant accompaniment of everything else by our speech organs" may not, then, have anything at all to do with anything else that is going on at the time—or ever.

Although our ability to participate in the dialect of our speech community may not develop separately in us, that does mean that that dialect itself is not therefore self-contained. We must penetrate our dialects, and we must never stop doing so, in order to maintain our language access. For it is that access which reveals meaning to us. Just as we heard the sounds of our dialects, just as we encode and decode its sentences, so are we able to make *sense* of them, or com-

[37] Dwight Bolinger, *Aspects of Language* (New York, 1968), p. 2.

[38] See Bronislaw Malinowski, "The Problem of Meaning in Primitive Languages," in Ogden & Richards, *op. cit.*, pp. 313-316.

[39] See, for instance, Jean Piaget, *The Language and Thought of the Child*, trans. Marjorie Gabain (New York, 1955), p. 32 *et in passim*.

prehend them. Whether we understand them, whether the *sense* has *substance*, depends on whether we "know" (or *can* "know") that what is communicated is so, or at least possibly so. But neither sound, nor syntax, nor *sense*, nor any combination of the three, is essential to the communication of *substance*. Balzac must have had that in mind when he said that men are so made that they can resist sound argument, and yet yield to a glance.

If it is true that meaning can be determined by the ability of the language user to supply that part of the context which is missing from the text, then there should be no reason why, at this point, I could not say, in J. L. Austin's words:

"Here I leave and commend the subject to you."[40]

---

[40] "A Plea for Excuses," *op. cit.*, p. 152.

FIVE POEMS

KENNETH L. PIKE

Center for Advanced Study in the Behavioral Sciences, Inc.

Lonely

Whose Priority?

Communication

Placard at Wake Island

Not Many Noble

Lonely

Drifting clouds in pale dull sky
  Frame the streaming sound of cars
Rushing past from where to there
  Without me.

Apartment-high I sit and sigh alone.
  No wife with cup and cheer
To talk about the weather. I'll
  Write a letter.

Words bring us closer. Thoughts and hearts
  are found in phrases bound by love.
Pain, grief, or hope can only ache their
  Worse when wordless.

Articulate the loss, and distance
  By itself grows shorter, home nearer.
I call her "Joy in Flowing Song." Dear—
  Let's talk!

(P.S. I wish we could also walk together.)

Whose Priority?

Here.
There.
Here!
Where?
There!

It's clear,
there look!!

The corner of
the eye lies.

Shift
the focus
and blur
sets in
again.

How aim?

My by-product
is your priority.

Mark 7:27-28

Communication

The thrust of
metaphor
cannot be parried
before it meets the mark,
before defence is set.

Usually
His parables forced
surrender—or
murder.

Steel upon steel,
this time
reply in kind.

The Syrophoenician woman
knew she didn't
own the right.
She saw the
Power—
and reached the switch
with parable.

Live
communication is
parabolic art—and arc.

Mark 7:28

Placard at Wake Island

"The U.S. day begins at Wake"—
Start the clock;
run the full race
to end—and early sleep.

String from
Pole to Pole
marks life in two.
"Hello Wednesday!"
"Goodbye Tuesday."

Someone must begin,
lest all die.
Spin the world's dial:
come the sun.
Warm hands by day,
rest by night—
or care for airstrip
so others may embark.

Our day is done.
Who carries on
in wind and tropic rain
on journey round the clock?

Not Many Noble

Again, sheer Goodness.
They saw it, shimmering,
wistfully saw it,
sidled up to it,
felt the contrast,
sensed its Alien Source—
and approved.

But would they buy?
Could they buy?—
They, the almost-good,
      the almost-wise,
      the almost-rich,
      the almost-strong?

The cost to them:
loss, of hope in goodness,
      of pride in wisdom,
      of trust in gold,
      of lust for power.

To Him, the cost:
      a Cross.

Mark 10:17-22

Ergo sum

Allomorph in infinite free variation,
uncomplementarily distributed
by the nonstructure of the universe
as we do not know it;
yet, maintaining a chronetic similarity,
somehow a class of one multiple distinctiveness—
phonemic, as it were, until the ultimate
double-cross juncture.

Cj STEVENS
Herbert H. Lehman College
of the
City University of New York

INTERCONSONANTAL DIFFERENCES

John W. Black
Ohio State University

Two purposes underlay the study that is reported here. The first was to establish groupings of consonants in keeping with factors isolated by the statistical procedure of factor analysis. The groupings might or might not correspond with the adjectival categories plosive, fricative, lateral, glide, etc., or with systems of distinctive features. The second purpose was to estimate the relative psychological distances among the initial consonants of English.

PROCEDURES

Stimuli and responses. Twenty-four consonants that are used in the initial positions of English syllables were selected for study. These were paired with five vowels in consonant-vowel syllables and spoken in the following order, as disyllables with equal stress.

```
Speaker 1: /pi-pi, pi-bi, pi-mi ·····························pi-ji/
Speaker 2: /be-pe, be-be, be-me ·····························be-je/
Speaker 3: /ma-pa, ma-ba, ma-ma ·····························ma-ja/
Speaker 4: /no-po, no-bo, no-mo ·····························no-jo/
Speaker 5: /tu-pu, tu-bu, tu-mu ·····························tu-ju/
                 · · ·
Speaker 24: /jo-po, jo-bo, jo-mo ····························jo-jo/
```

The successive initial consonants beyond the /t/ of Speaker 5 were: [d, θ, ð, f, v, k, g, s, z, ʃ, ʒ, tʃ, dʒ, w, ʍ, r, l, h, j]. As implied in the outline of the preceding paragraph, there were 24 speakers. Each read his pairs of syllables at six-second intervals, paced by a sweep-hand timer. The reading was done in a sound isolated room (IAC-403) and the recording was made with a chest-type microphone feeding a Wollensak T-1500 recorder. The speakers were undergraduate students, both males and females, who had studied no phonetics. A number of equally stressed disyllables were spoken as practice under close supervision. The entire recording session was monitored for satisfactoriness. A few readers were asked to re-record. Equal levels from speaker to speaker were achieved at the recorder and in re-recording.

Twenty-four undergraduate students listened individually to the twenty-four recordings and assigned values to the individual items in the manner of magnitude estimation. The task required one hour. The instructions were:

> You will hear many pairs of syllables. The first list will be for practice. Please assign a value to the sameness (difference) in the sound of the two syllables that are spoken in rapid succession. If they seem to be identical, assign a small value; if they are greatly different in sound, assign a larger value. A separation or difference that is double another will be assigned a rating twice as large as the smaller one. You may use any scale you wish, that is numbers of any size and any range. Now listen to a list for practice. . . . Are there questions?

The foregoing procedure yielded from each listener an outcome that can be visualized as 24 rows (one row per speaker—and ipso facto per initial syllable of each pair of syllables) and 24 columns (one column per initial consonant of the second syllable of the pair). Each row was a series of values that represented the acoustic proximity of the consonants of the first and second members of the 24 pairs. In order to equate the work of the different judges, each entry was converted to a proportion of the sum of the values of the row. The matching rows from the 24 judges were then pooled. This yielded a composite set of 24 x 24 values with the rows and columns as above. These are presented in Table 1. Each row should summate to 100 per cent or *units of proportionality*. Illustrative of the table, while /p/ (row one) differs from /j/ by 2.12 units, it differs from /dʒ, z, w/ by more than twice this amount.

PART I—CONSONANTAL GROUPINGS

Two statistical procedures were followed. First, the data of the rows of Table 1 were correlated. Second, the data of the columns of Table 1 were subjected to a factor analysis (rotated factors) in which twelve factors were isolated.

RESULTS

The intercorrelations of Table 2 provide a direct assessment of the similarity of rows of pairs of consonants and are helpful in anticipating the results of the factor analysis. Any coefficient that exceeds 0.40 is significant at the 5 per cent level of confidence. For example, the rows of values of Table 1 generated by the reference sounds /p/ and /b/ were statistically significantly correlated. The ones generated by /p/- and /d/-comparisons were not significantly correlated.

The significant values of Table 2 have been extracted and the corresponding phonemes entered in Table 3. In instances in which there

TABLE 1

THE RELATIVE DISTANCE (IN PER CENT) BETWEEN THE COMPARISON SOUND AT THE LEFT AND EACH PHONEME OF THE ROW

	p	b	m	n	t	d	θ	ð	f	v	k	g	s	z	ʃ	ʒ	tʃ	dʒ	w	ʍ	r	l	h	j
p		3.02	4.08	3.90	4.15	3.82	4.06	4.20	4.18	3.47	4.50	4.72	4.99	5.16	4.99	5.30	4.92	5.06	5.12	4.82	4.74	4.26	4.13	2.12
b	3.05		3.67	3.91	3.11	3.50	3.21	3.64	3.91	3.50	4.62	3.54	4.90	4.72	5.08	4.66	5.08	4.59	4.81	4.81	4.64	4.96	4.44	4.40
m	4.33	3.67		2.74	4.80	4.88	4.61	4.10	4.76	4.99	5.39	5.62	5.09	4.37	5.03	5.67	5.40	5.19	3.35	3.25	3.60	3.47	3.19	3.24
n	3.75	3.91	2.74		4.46	5.47	4.40	3.38	3.58	3.46	4.93	4.79	5.00	4.49	5.53	5.02	5.74	4.99	4.27	4.22	3.79	3.82	3.63	3.56
t	3.62	3.11	4.80	4.46		5.98	5.47	4.40	3.45	3.40	4.69	4.35	4.96	4.61	5.53	5.02	4.08	3.35	6.76	4.91	5.38	4.61	4.59	5.39
d	3.96	3.94	4.88	3.04			3.04	3.46	3.45	3.40	4.69	4.35	4.96	4.61	4.77	4.22	4.08	3.35	5.27	5.21	4.87	4.31	3.67	2.69
θ	3.67	3.97	4.59	4.61	4.66	2.83		2.75	1.72	2.60	4.84	4.67	2.63	3.77	4.70	4.54	5.09	5.12	5.13	5.05	5.51	5.40	4.45	5.06
ð	3.51	4.09	4.24	4.61	4.04	2.50	2.85		2.67	2.24	4.85	4.67	4.63	4.31	4.80	4.31	5.33	4.80	4.86	4.83	4.67	4.96	4.09	5.17
f	4.18	3.81	4.82	5.08	4.58	2.50	2.85	2.64		2.64	4.56	5.47	4.95	4.64	5.18	4.81	5.08	5.04	4.32	4.04	4.03	4.96	4.61	5.16
v	4.09	3.99	4.21	4.94	4.84	4.36	3.84	3.42	3.84		5.38	4.82	5.16	4.82	4.67	4.18	4.92	4.44	2.42	2.11	3.78	4.63	4.41	5.10
k	4.11	4.26	4.58	4.54	4.35	4.02	4.07	4.07	4.57	3.59		4.02	4.50	4.59	5.08	4.77	4.16	4.05	4.79	4.33	4.51	4.64	4.59	3.86
g	3.66	4.09	3.98	4.60	3.58	3.87	3.69	3.54	4.25	3.74	3.56		4.65	4.33	5.12	4.91	3.86	3.61	4.88	4.83	4.51	4.94	5.03	5.00
s	4.14	4.64	4.57	5.13	4.66	3.36	4.09	4.25	4.19	4.28	4.19	4.59		2.51	3.14	3.46	3.65	3.99	4.90	4.92	4.86	5.58	5.13	5.56
z	3.49	4.09	4.18	5.07	4.35	4.20	4.17	3.81	4.25	4.28	5.18	5.11	2.96		3.00	3.44	3.93	3.11	4.51	4.55	4.38	5.29	4.68	4.92
ʃ	4.35	4.43	4.74	4.82	4.99	3.86	3.79	3.81	3.81	3.58	4.78	4.94	3.45	3.04		2.39	3.93	2.88	5.06	4.98	5.57	5.58	4.68	5.07
ʒ	4.23	3.86	4.65	4.88	4.65	4.07	3.60	3.76	3.76	3.26	5.03	4.99	4.83	3.96	3.15		2.99	3.07	5.06	4.66	4.99	5.23	5.12	4.90
tʃ	4.32	4.66	4.43	4.35	4.38	3.94	3.75	4.02	4.02	4.22	4.80	4.63	3.40	3.73	3.13	2.82		4.52	4.84	4.64	4.66	5.33	4.65	5.14
dʒ	4.44	4.89	5.06	5.28	4.66	4.22	3.74	3.55	3.55	4.03	5.43	5.21	5.23	4.11	3.44	2.35	2.52		4.49	4.64	4.79	5.18	4.93	3.73
w	3.99	4.14	4.34	5.14	4.46	3.96	3.87	3.25	3.25	3.06	5.05	4.80	5.21	4.43	4.91	4.33	5.16	4.54		3.14	2.85	4.49	3.09	4.80
ʍ	4.12	4.53	4.62	4.99	4.82	4.07	3.97	3.54	3.54	3.70	5.05	5.54	5.14	4.13	5.10	4.88	5.07	4.63	1.92		3.11	4.03	2.73	4.66
r	4.23	4.01	4.57	4.49	4.51	3.84	4.35	4.25	3.96	4.00	4.98	4.73	4.56	4.18	4.74	4.54	4.88	4.36	3.32	3.62		4.28	4.21	3.72
l	4.19	3.99	4.06	5.22	4.56	3.98	4.75	3.96	3.96	3.54	5.34	4.36	4.24	3.72	4.93	4.73	5.07	4.78	4.03	3.87	2.99		3.88	4.15
h	3.50	4.29	4.42	5.02	4.55	3.77	3.76	3.57	3.57	4.12	4.75	4.85	4.71	4.59	4.64	4.29	4.72	4.73	3.77	3.61	3.99	4.57		4.02
j	4.37	4.52	4.34	5.15	4.94	4.38	4.21	4.10	4.10	4.08	5.17	5.36	4.44	4.23	4.42	3.07	4.40	3.95	3.66	3.97	3.88	4.07	4.05	

TABLE 2

CORRELATIONS AMONG ROWS OF TABLE 1, THAT IS, CORRELATIONS AMONG THE SEPARATION DISTANCES OF PAIRS OF PHONEMES

	p	b	m	n	t	d	θ	ʒ	f	v	k	g	s	z	ʃ	ʒ	tʃ	dʒ	ʍ	r	l	h	j
p	.600	.075	.134	.188	.274	.072	.088	−.014	.123	.099	.194	−.113	−.261	−.287	−.384	−.307	−.327	−.291	−.231	−.207	−.000	.090	.203
b		.053	.194	.265	.616	.074	.123	.021	.250	.095	.482	.294	−.412	−.391	−.318	−.302	−.262	−.356	−.336	−.167	.023	−.094	.057
m			.833	−.102	−.166	−.341	−.020	−.306	−.231	−.172	−.128	−.255	.106	−.151	−.047	−.233	−.087	−.227	−.304	−.013	−.055	.172	.267
n				.535	−.094	−.100	.156	.172	−.007	−.230	−.128	−.103	−.255	.106	−.151	−.047	−.233	−.065	−.013	−.116	−.136	−.136	.263
t					−.094	−.100	.535	.107	−.036	−.079	.155	.071	−.119	−.148	−.127	−.073	−.293	.081	−.013	−.113	−.171	−.032	−.125
d						.616	.172	.168	−.071	−.015	.169	−.255	.106	−.178	−.198	−.145	−.145	.107	−.262	−.224	−.197	−.123	.109
θ							.156	.596	.819	−.000	.073	.023	−.079	.019	.124	−.169	−.073	.152	−.404	−.204	−.227	−.055	−.357
ʒ								.596	.651	.403	.073	−.017	.106	−.178	−.177	−.198	−.206	.010	−.386	−.119	−.277	−.013	−.319
f									.819	.651	.503	−.255	.019	−.178	−.127	.010	.091	.107	−.331	−.204	−.119	−.180	−.389
v										.403	.503	.633	.106	−.178	−.198	.010	.091	.152	−.262	−.224	−.197	−.227	−.382
k											.491	−.065	.071	−.148	−.177	.010	−.073	.107	−.331	−.204	−.277	−.277	−.048
g												.491	.106	−.178	−.198	−.145	−.145	.152	−.386	−.119	−.119	−.365	−.188
s													.732	.544	.283	.010	.091	.131	−.266	−.298	−.449	−.307	−.368
z														.732	.544	.415	.311	.309	−.057	−.116	−.316	−.431	−.339
ʃ															.673	.544	.340	.650	−.184	−.369	−.532	−.429	−.290
ʒ																.797	.415	.701	−.288	−.335	−.516	−.484	−.180
tʃ																	.753	.724	−.143	−.454	−.545	−.507	−.197
dʒ																		.650	−.297	−.313	−.433	−.198	−.198
ʍ																			.640	−.370	−.252	.494	.127
w																				.884	−.251	.589	.059
r																					.758	.435	.216
l																					.706	.603	.492
h																						.483	.281

were not two significant positive values and no significant negative co-efficients the highest available values were used and the corresponding phonemic symbols in Table 3 marked with an asterisk. In keeping with this rule, both /b/ and /d/ are shown in Table 3 to be positively correlated with /p/. Although the correlation was not statistically significant it was the second highest of the values of the /p/-row.

One feature of Table 3 is that each significant correlation of Table 2 is represented twice. For example, since /b/ is positively related to /p/, it is inevitable that this relationship will appear again in Row 2, i.e. the /b/-row.

TABLE 3

PAIRS OF PHONEMES REPRESENTED BY SIGNIFICANT CORRELATION COEFFICIENTS IN TABLE 2. HIGH NONSIGNIFICANT VALUES HAVE BEEN ADDED TO MAKE AT LEAST A PAIR OF POSITIVE CORRELATIONS PLUS AT LEAST ONE NEGATIVE CORRELATION. THESE EXCEPTIONS ARE MARKED WITH ASTERISKS. ENTRIES ARE LISTED IN ORDER OF THE MAGNITUDE OF THE CORRELATION, HIGH VALUES FIRST

Reference Phoneme	Positive Correlations	Negative Correlations
p	b, d*	ʒ*
b	d, p, g	z
m	n, l	tʃ, ʒ, dʒ, ʃ
n	m, l	tʃ, ʒ, ʃ
t	d, b*	w
d	b, t, g	w
θ	f, ð, v	w*
ð	f, θ, v	r*
f	θ, ð, v	j*
v	f, ð	j*
k	g, d	w*
g	k, b, d	ʍ
s	z, ʃ	l
z	s, ʃ, ʒ	b
ʃ	ʒ, tʃ, z, dʒ, s	l, h, m, b
ʒ	ʃ, tʃ, dʒ, z	m, l, n, h
tʃ	ʒ, ʃ, dʒ	l, m, h, n, r, ʍ
dʒ	ʒ, ʃ, tʃ	h, m, l
w	ʍ, r, h	t, d
ʍ	w, r, h, l	tʃ
r	w, ʍ, l, h	tʃ
l	r, m, j, h, ʍ, n	tʃ, ʃ, ʒ, s
h	ʍ, w, l, r	dʒ, tʃ, ʃ, ʒ
j	l, h*	f*, v*

Factor analysis. The foregoing correlations suggest that some con-sonants evoke like estimates of aural similarity when they are com-pared with the remaining consonants. In these instances, relatively large values would fall in some columns; likewise, relatively small values would fall in the same columns. Three specific observations about the rows and the columns of Table 1 are pertinent. First, the constant reference phoneme is heard as the first of a pair of syllables in the stimuli that generated the values of the rows; it is heard second as the data are viewed in relation to the reference consonant heading a column. This is remindful of the order effect in the procedures of paired comparisons. The values—percentages of rows—tend to become percentages of columns. The discrepancy is measurable. While the rows uniformly represent 100 per cent, the summated values of the columns range from 83 to 112 "per cent." Second, the stimuli that generate a row of data in Table 1 were spoken by a single speaker. Thus a comparison between two rows is confounded with a comparison between two speakers. The columns, however, represent responses to stimuli spoken by 24 voices. Third, a row refers to responses to a single vowel; the values of the columns relate to syllables that contain five different vowels. These later considerations particularly led to a more detailed examination of the data as arranged in *columns* rather than in *rows*.

The columns of Table 1 were subjected to a factorial analysis with a Varimax rotating program through 12 factors. This accounted for at least 88 per cent of the variance associated with the columns of Table 1. The results, factor-by-factor and the over-all commonality, are shown in Table 4. If the factor loadings of Table 4 are viewed as correlation coefficients, values of .40 are significant at the 5 per cent level. The significant cells are extracted from Table 4 and presented in Table 5 in phonetic symbols. High values of like sign are designated *in positive agreement*; of different sign, *in opposition*. In instances in which the cut-off of .40 would give a single consonant to a factor or no sound "in opposition" the consonants with the highest ranking significant and non-significant values in Table 4 have been added to Table 5 and marked with an asterisk. Thus there are a minimum of two *positive* and one *negative* consonants in Table 5.*

A discussion of the individual factors follows. Factor I is bipolar and puts in contrast two groups of consonants /m, n, l/ and /ʒ, tʃ, dʒ/. This is the only factor to which /m, n/ contribute importantly, suggesting the designation *nasality*. However, the bi-directional strength emphasizes the opposition between much and little *sonority*, or a *smooth-rough* dichotomy.

---

*Plus and minus values in Table 4 have been either retained or reversed throughout a column to facilitate reading. Therefore, positive and negative signs in Table 4 do not necessarily agree with "positive agreement" and "opposition" in Table 5.

TABLE 4

A FACTOR ANALYSIS OF THE COLUMNS OF TABLE 1 THROUGH 12 FACTORS (VARIMAX ROTATING PROGRAM; IBM 7094 COMPUTER)

	I	II	III	IV	V	VI	VII	VIII	IX	X	XI	XII	h²
/p/	.13	.15	.04	—.06	.08	—.08	.93	.09	—.07	.09	—.02	.00	.95
/b/	.15	.15	.05	—.27	—.06	—.05	.63	—.04	—.47	—.19	.05	.33	.89
/m/	.91	—.09	—.24	—.09	—.08	.03	—.01	.00	.07	.11	—.11	—.10	.96
/n/	.91	.07	—.18	—.13	—.11	.10	.03	.02	.06	—.07	.04	.04	.92
/t/	—.04	.25	—.00	—.15	.06	—.91	.07	—.09	—.20	—.02	.02	.01	.97
/d/	—.09	.23	.00	—.23	.05	—.30	.16	.07	—.82	.04	—.06	.21	.96
/θ/	—.09	.21	.89	.22	.08	—.13	—.00	.00	—.13	.08	.02	.07	.95
/ð/	.12	.32	.69	—.21	—.03	.03	—.03	—.21	—.08	.02	.51	—.02	.94
/f/	—.11	.05	.94	—.05	—.07	.03	—.01	—.12	.07	.00	—.01	—.13	.94
/v/	—.06	—.10	.64	—.36	—.06	.11	.20	—.40	.07	—.36	.14	.04	.92
/k/	—.06	.16	—.04	—.01	.94	—.06	.03	.01	—.01	—.07	—.01	.18	.96
/g/	.02	.22	—.13	—.08	.35	—.01	.13	—.20	—.24	—.08	.03	.81	.96
/s/	—.14	.25	.14	.86	.12	.09	—.06	—.12	.10	—.05	.19	.01	.93
/z/	—.13	.06	—.18	.87	—.18	.08	—.15	—.12	.13	—.11	—.14	—.06	.94
/ʃ/	—.51	.36	—.29	.45	.22	.10	—.16	.20	.29	—.12	.05	—.15	.92
/ʒ/	—.63	.38	—.22	.93	—.29	.18	—.27	—.10	.26	—.20	.02	.13	.92
/tʃ/	—.59	.51	—.37	.13	.01	.01	—.34	—.16	—.06	—.06	.06	—.09	.93
/dʒ/	—.57	.27	—.36	.01	—.05	—.18	—.23	—.08	.41	—.28	—.21	.21	.96
/w/	.03	—.83	—.10	—.12	—.11	.38	—.13	—.07	.14	.12	.03	.21	.97
/ʍ/	.08	—.86	—.10	—.14	—.04	.01	—.12	—.12	.15	.25	.02	.24	.95
/r/	.18	—.86	—.14	—.04	—.09	.10	—.13	.20	.00	.01	.05	.08	.88
/l/	.51	—.46	—.18	—.23	—.15	—.13	—.06	.41	.01	.14	.32	.11	.90
/h/	.21	—.41	.01	—.21	—.11	.04	.07	.10	—.00	.82	.01	—.09	.96
/j/	.16	—.01	—.30	—.29	.06	.15	.12	.81	—.07	.09	.06	—.18	.94

TABLE 5

ENTRIES FROM TABLE 4 THAT EXCEED .40 PLUS SUFFICIENT HIGH-RANKING ENTRIES—DESIGNATED BY ASTERISKS—TO PROVIDE AT LEAST TWO ENTRIES "IN POSITIVE AGREEMENT" AND ONE "IN OPPOSITION"

I	II	III	IV	V	VI	VII	VIII	IX	X	XI	XII
				In Positive Agreement							
m	ʍ	f	ʒ	k	t	p	j	d	h	ð	g
n	r	θ	z	g*	d*	b	l	b	ʍ*	dʒ*	b*
l	w	ð	s								
	l	v	ʃ								
	h										
				In Opposition							
ʒ	tʃ	tʃ*	v*	ʒ*	w*	tʃ*	v	dʒ	v*	l*	j*
tʃ		dʒ*									
dʒ											

Factor II shows heavy loadings on /ʍ, r, w, l, h/. These include three of the conventional glides, all except /j/, and include also /r, l/. Already, we have a second use of /l/. In this group, as in Factor I, /l/ is in opposition to the affrication of /tʃ/. While the essential feature of /l/ in Factor I may have related to nasal resonance, sonority, vowelness, or smoothness, here it apparently contributes to the glide-consonantal character of English.

Factors III and IV together suggest three degrees of friction, light (/f, θ, ð, v/); medium (/ʒ, z, s, ʃ/); and heavy (/tʃ, dʒ/). A second and equally applicable distinction between the positive elements of the two factors would be *less intense* and *more intense* fricative consonants. All of the "positive" consonants of Factor IV are listed by Fletcher (1953) as having more intensity than the weaker ones of Factor III. Third, the two groups can be distinguished by Wickelgren's distinctive feature of place, or fourth, by Singh and Black's categories of duration. Importantly, there are two categories, or, in the present instance, two factors represented by these consonants. It is also noteworthy that the opposition to the light friction group is a greater degree of the same characteristic, friction, and that /v/ of the light friction group contrasts with /ʒ, z, s, ʃ/ or the medium friction group of Factor IV. The feature that distinguishes the two factors, amount of friction, seems also to account for the bipolar aspects of each of the factors.

Factors V, VI, VII are voiced and voiceless counterparts of consonants usually termed plosives. In conjunction with Factors IX and XII, these factors suggest that conventional descriptions may place too much emphasis on plosiveness as a feature. If plosiveness were a first-order feature of consonants it would be expected to show up in this analysis as a unique factor, contrasting to nonplosiveness. Rather there are five plosive factors, three parallel ones separated by place of articulation and two that show a "sameness" among voiced plosive consonants and differences between places of articulation. The contrast between /d/ and /dʒ/ has relevance to an occasional practice of including /d/ and /ʒ/ separately in tallies of phonemes instead of /dʒ/ (Voelker). Here, quite apart from its phonemic character, the distinguishing characteristic of /dʒ/ appears to be its fricativeness.

Factors VIII and X suggest a singular and differentiating duality among some of the glides, the ones of Factor X /h, ʍ/ possibly having an aspirate or whisper quality that is not present in /j, l/. Both of these groups tend to contrast with /v/.

Factor XI principally identifies the uniqueness in /ð/. The character of this trait is somewhat present also in /dʒ/ and tends to be absent in /l/.

Discussion

Several aspects of the portion of the study summarized here bear noting. First, the judgments were made by individuals who had not studied phonetics. A pilot procedure with some of the material indicated that persons who are familiar with phonetic categories—plosive, fricative, and the like—tend to read these values into their judgments and thus simply preserve the status quo. Nor did it appear possible to avoid an influence of prior phonetic experience. The novices, however, had no prior clue to bias their judgments. Moreover, they did their judging reliably. A split half correlation of the twenty-four judges, corrected for length, yielded a correlation coefficient of, $r = .90$.

Second, the foregoing correlation coefficient, as well as pertaining to the reliability of the phonetically naive judges, relates to the applicability of the method of magnitude estimation. It yielded consistent results. Although the method permits the use of any numerical scale, fractions were rare, as were numbers in excess of 100. Possibly prior experience with rating scales tended to limit the subjects' range of measures.

Third, the nature of the factors themselves bears scrutiny. The several factors may be more than are feasible in categorizing consonants. Yet it is reassuring to have confirmation that consonants fall into groups in keeping with the way they sound.

There are some surprises, for example the glide aspect of /l/ and /r/, the possible nasal component of /l/, the separating of /j/ from /w, ʍ, h/, and the dividing of sounds that contain friction. Moreover, two principles emerged: voicing and the lack of voicing do not in themselves either constitute a factor or cause a pair of voiced-voiceless cognates to fall into different groupings. Contrariwise, the place of articulation apparently puts a stamp of aural uniqueness on the phonemes. Factors III and IV can be differentiated by amounts of sound pressure or equally well by place. The former falls into Wickelgren's place categories 0-1, and the latter in his categories 2-3. Also, the plosiveness of some consonants may be a secondary attribute to the place of their articulation.

Part II—Visual Stimulation

Some of the procedures of Part I were replicated in a pseudo listening procedure. The second "listening task" occurred about two weeks after the first. It was a group exercise that involved the same twenty-four students who had made the earlier judgments. This time they sat in a language laboratory and heard 90 dB (re .0002 microbar) of white noise while making the judgments required by the following directions.

> Earlier you evaluated the similarity-dissimilarity of the initial sounds of pairs of recorded syllables. Please make this judgment again from your own conceptualization of how the syllables sound. Again use any scale of values you wish to indicate the sameness-disparity distance between two consonants. Two consonants that "sound alike" will receive a small rating. Ones that are twice as far apart will be given double this value. Your first answer sheet provides spaces for your comparisons of the first sound of *pat* and the first sounds of *pat, bat, mat . . . year*—not the word, not the whole syllable, only the first sound. You may pronounce these sounds if you wish. In fact, we expect you to say them, but you will not be able to hear yourself because of the noise in your headset. There are 24 answer sheets. Please work through them in order.

The purpose of the headset and noise was to minimize the "listener's" hearing of his own vocalization. The outcome of this procedure was treated as the earlier one and the resulting values are enumerated in Table 6. For example, in row one /p/ is seen to differ minimally from /b/ (2.19 units) and maximally from /ʃ/ (5.32 units).

Results

The statistical procedure for Part II involved comparing the ratings that were made of the aural stimuli and the ones that were made from viewing the pairs of consonants as initial sounds (letters) of common words. This was done by correlating values of each of the

TABLE 6

THE RELATIVE DISTANCE (IN PER CENT) BETWEEN THE STANDARD PHONEME FOR A ROW, AT THE LEFT, AND EACH PHONEME AT THE HEAD OF A COLUMN. VISUAL STIMULI ONLY; JUDGMENTS MADE IN NOISE

	p	b	m	n	t	d	θ	ð	f	v	k	g	s	z	ʃ	ʒ	tʃ	dʒ	w	ʍ	r	l	h	j
p	2.19	3.41	3.79	3.67	3.52	4.09	4.30	4.34	3.86	4.54	4.39	4.95	5.03	5.32	4.75	4.73	4.28	4.79	4.64	4.92	4.57	4.54	4.61	
b	2.45	3.16	3.75	3.70	3.17	4.06	4.06	4.34	3.52	4.27	4.37	4.99	5.16	5.14	5.06	4.79	4.46	4.42	4.62	4.73	4.90	4.03	5.31	
m	3.95	3.47	2.14	3.88	4.13	3.90	4.41	4.64	4.80	4.26	4.69	4.73	4.69	4.66	4.75	4.85	4.97	4.25	4.00	4.40	4.59	4.22	4.50	4.29
n	4.22	4.02	2.48	3.44	4.26	4.41	4.16	4.42	4.27	4.26	4.83	4.73	4.98	5.00	4.81	4.81	4.76	4.47	4.46	4.40	4.34	4.06	4.25	4.48
t	3.34	3.45	4.13	4.20	2.51	2.86	3.09	3.28	3.73	4.23	3.89	4.00	4.13	4.66	4.88	5.03	4.75	4.42	4.62	4.97	5.04	4.95	5.16	5.06
d	3.38	3.33	3.90	4.07	2.51	3.97	4.00	3.61	4.23	3.89	4.08	3.84	4.65	4.92	4.70	4.16	3.89	4.74	4.87	4.65	4.89	4.92	4.88	4.99
θ	4.19	3.89	4.64	4.67	3.69	4.00	1.44	3.31	3.61	3.14	4.77	4.00	4.73	4.32	4.53	4.16	4.39	4.44	4.54	4.89	4.97	4.71	4.42	5.07
ð	4.48	4.09	4.80	4.42	3.94	4.22	1.44	3.56	3.56	2.33	4.52	4.45	4.84	4.76	4.97	4.19	4.53	4.44	4.54	4.74	4.89	4.71	4.42	5.00
f	3.98	4.17	4.42	4.33	4.33	4.56	3.26	3.37	3.37	4.45	4.16	4.45	4.14	4.42	4.51	4.54	4.98	4.53	4.41	4.53	5.05	5.26	4.47	4.68
v	3.41	3.60	4.51	4.56	4.78	4.55	3.73	3.35	2.34	3.97	4.84	4.90	5.06	4.82	5.18	4.57	4.73	4.40	3.58	4.05	4.64	4.99	4.23	4.28
k	3.75	3.75	4.55	4.49	3.59	3.85	4.19	4.06	3.97	4.36	2.89	2.89	4.87	4.73	4.59	4.19	4.17	4.61	4.80	4.71	4.96	4.85	4.18	4.71
g	3.40	4.40	4.66	4.40	3.64	3.60	4.60	4.37	4.62	4.36	2.34	4.40	4.61	4.94	5.20	3.38	3.96	3.96	4.62	4.97	4.69	4.68	4.72	4.58
s	4.66	4.97	4.84	4.66	4.69	5.11	4.62	4.28	3.63	3.85	4.65	4.40	4.61	1.94	2.48	3.18	3.77	4.26	4.79	4.77	5.35	5.45	4.68	4.64
z	4.52	4.75	4.96	4.72	4.72	4.47	4.51	4.28	4.49	3.99	4.47	5.33	2.39	3.05	3.25	3.16	3.85	3.61	4.70	4.64	4.73	5.16	4.06	4.77
ʃ	4.98	4.76	5.05	4.79	4.59	4.46	4.34	4.46	4.03	4.29	5.33	3.30	3.11	3.93	2.78	2.79	3.12	2.85	4.14	4.62	5.07	5.10	4.92	4.63
ʒ	4.51	4.67	5.28	5.07	4.59	5.07	4.56	4.33	4.56	4.39	4.56	3.60	3.11	3.93	2.78	2.78	2.12	2.07	4.50	4.55	5.10	5.64	4.06	5.01
tʃ	4.83	5.04	5.31	4.93	4.59	4.97	4.29	4.35	4.33	4.56	4.64	4.47	4.20	3.57	2.42	2.16	2.12	2.16	4.21	4.76	5.19	5.34	4.57	4.59
dʒ	4.56	4.73	5.10	5.45	4.38	4.44	4.81	4.42	4.80	4.37	4.73	4.80	4.44	3.59	1.74	2.16	2.13	2.16	4.52	4.44	4.73	5.25	4.90	4.47
w	4.82	4.76	4.72	4.59	5.10	4.81	4.75	4.57	3.99	4.25	4.57	4.25	4.81	4.67	4.94	2.16	4.45	4.09	1.34	1.56	3.40	4.47	3.29	3.50
ʍ	4.66	4.66	4.59	4.46	4.91	4.82	4.57	4.44	4.25	4.36	4.75	4.99	4.95	5.04	4.65	1.74	4.99	4.28	1.34	4.04	3.22	4.04	3.08	3.60
r	4.65	4.66	4.29	4.74	4.60	4.63	4.53	4.69	4.25	4.43	4.46	4.51	4.76	4.59	4.57	4.37	4.56	4.29	3.11	3.27	3.84	3.75	3.73	3.62
l	4.35	4.31	4.21	4.53	4.53	4.44	4.47	4.30	4.43	4.16	4.65	4.60	4.75	4.72	3.92	4.23	4.32	4.44	4.18	4.12	3.84	3.78	3.29	3.09
h	4.66	4.67	4.87	4.83	4.75	4.11	4.30	4.16	4.93	4.60	4.46	4.78	4.74	3.92	4.23	4.07	4.01	3.48	3.38	4.46	3.93	3.06		
j	4.68	4.70	4.82	4.93	4.55	4.35	4.23	4.22	4.66	4.43	4.74	4.81	4.52	3.95	4.05	4.04	3.79	3.58	4.03	3.93	3.06			

24 pairs of matching columns of Tables 1 and 6. The coefficients of correlation are shown in Table 7. Nineteen of the 24 values were statistically significant and the median coefficient was, $r = .64$.

TABLE 7

CORRELATION COEFFICIENTS BETWEEN MATCHED COLUMNS OF TABLE 1 (AUDITORY STIMULI) AND TABLE 6 (VISUAL STIMULI). N = 24. ANY VALUE EXCEEDING .40, SIGNIFICANT AT THE 5 PER CENT LEVEL

p	.51
b	.69
m	.81
n	.88
t	.40
d	.64
θ	.64
ð	.68
f	.48
v	.65
k	.67
g	.32
s	.61
z	.86
ʃ	.91
ʒ	.79
tʃ	.84
dʒ	.48
w	.83
ʍ	.74
r	.78
l	.84
h	.56
j	.16

DISCUSSION

Special consideration should be given to the similarity of the judgmental responses to aural stimuli and to letters. There was insufficient time for the listeners to repeat the pairs of aural syllables over and over. Yet saying them aloud in the presence of a masking noise was the rule rather than the exception in the circumstance in which they rated the sameness of the sound of consonants while viewing appropriate letters. The extent of the correlation between the judgments evoked by aural and visual stimuli is important. The judges were allotting psychological space similarly in the two tasks. This is in keeping with a conjecture that some motor—perhaps neural— activity intervened or mediated in the aural experience akin to the observed activity in the second. Alternatively or additionally the judgments made in the presence of masking noise may have been influenced by "auditory imagery."

PART III

Although a factor analysis established the clusters of consonants, there remained the objectives of establishing the relative distances between pairs of consonants. Of course, direct quantitative evidence of interphonemic distances is available from Table 1. These are tallied in Table 8 in a manner to show their distributions. The extreme interphonemic distances were 1.72 and 6.76 units of proportionality. There were 20 comparisons of 2.75 or less and an equal number of 5.45 or more. The data of Tables 1 and 8 include two values of each comparison. For example /p, b/ is shown in row one of Table 1 as 3.02 and /b, p/ in row two as 3.05. This particular discrepancy, 0.03, is unusually small. The median discrepancy for the similar comparisons of the entire table is 0.60. Table 9 presents a single pooled value for the pairs representing similar comparisons in Table 1. Tables 10 and 11 present similar data in different forms. In Table 10 the separations between phonemes are ordered from the smallest to the largest. For example in row one, /ʃ/ is the pivotal sound. The phonemes /ʒ, tʃ, dʒ . . . l/ are arranged in keeping with successively larger differences. left to right, between each of them and /ʃ/. Similarly, /w/ was judged to be most like /r, v, h/. Ties in rows are indicated by asterisks. The rows are ordered, one to the next, to accommodate the factors established in Table 5 except that each pivotal sound is included but one time. The utility of the table lies in the quick reference it provides for near and distant consonants.

The arrangement of the data of Table 11, a matrix of ranks with a minor adjustment, accommodates a statistical treatment. The adjustment was to add 1 to each cell in the table. The adjusted matrix was treated to an analysis of variance by ranks (Xr^2). The obtained value for $Xr^2 = 64.05$, is highly significant. This indicates that the ranks were not randomly distributed among the columns but that certain columns tended to contain low ranks and others high ones. The mean ranks of the different consonants are also shown in Table 11. They range from 5.2 to 17.5 units of proportionality. Thus /v, f, ð/ either tend to be relatively similar to other consonants or, alternatively, markedly similar to several. Contrariwise, /l, t, k/ are distinctly apart from most of the consonants.

Another guideline to evaluating the distance between phonemes is to compare the average within-factor interconsonantal distance to the average between-factor distance. The mean differences among the con-

TABLE 8

THE NUMBER OF PHONEMES THAT ARE SEPARATED FROM THE COMPARISON PHONEME (LEFT OF THE ROW) BY
THE AMOUNT INDICATED IN THE HEADING OF THE COLUMN

	<2.50	2.50 2.60	2.70 2.80	2.90 3.00	3.10 3.20	3.30 3.40	3.50 3.60	3.70 3.80	3.90 4.00	4.10 4.20	4.30 4.40	4.50 4.60	4.70 4.80	4.90 5.00	5.10 5.20	5.30 5.40	5.50 5.60	5.70 >5.80
p	2.12			1		1			1 1 2	3 2		1	2 1	3 1	2	1		
b				2	1		2 1		2		1	2 1	3 1	3 2	2 2			
m			1		1 2	1 1	1			1	2 1	1	1 2	1 2	1	1 1	2	
n	1.97					1 1	2 1	3 1		2	2	1	2 2			1 1	1 1	1 5.98
t			1		1		2 4	1	1 1		1 2	1 3	1	2		2		6.76
d		1		1	1		1	1 2 1	3 1	1 1	1		1 1 2		3		2	
θ	1.72	2 1						1 1	1		1 1	2 3	1 1	3 2			2	
ð	2.24	1	1				1		1		1 1	2 3	1 1	3 2	1 1			
f		1 1	1						1 3	1 1		4	5 1	1	2	1 1		
v	2.42			1		1		1	2 1	1	2 2	1 2	2 3	2	1			
k							1 1	2 1	1 1	1 2		3	2	2	1			
g					4 3		2	5	3 1		6 1	2		1				
s		1		1	1 1	1 1	1	2	1 1		1	2 2	2 2	1				
z			1 1		2			1 1	2		2 2	2	2	2		2		
ʃ	2.39		2	1		1 1	1 2		1 1	3 3	3	2 1	1 1	2 1		2		
ʒ			1 1	1 1		1				1 1		2 1	4 3			2		
tʃ		1	1		1	1 1	1 2		1		3	1 2	3 2	1				
dʒ	2.35	1			1	1 1	2	1 1	1	3 1	1 4	2 2		1	1			
w			1	2 1 1				1	1 1	1	2	2	1 2	1 1	1 3	1		
ʍ	1.92	1		1			1	1 1	1	1 2	3 1	2	1 1	2 1				
r				1			1	2	1 2 3		1 4	1	1 1	1 2		1 1		
l			1		1		1	1 1	3	1 4	2 1	4	2 1	1				
h						1	1 2	4 2	2 1	1	1	3	1 1	1 1				
j		1				2 1 3		1 1 1 2		1	3 2	4 1	1					
						1	1	1 1 3	3 3	1			1	2	1			

TABLE 9

MEAN INTERPHONEMIC DISTANCES (COMPUTED FROM TABLE 1)

	p	b	m	n	t	d	θ	ð	f	v	k	g	ŋ	s	z	ʃ	ʒ	tʃ	dʒ	w	ʍ	r	l	h	j
p		3.04	4.21	3.83	3.89	3.87	3.86	4.18	3.78	4.31	4.19	4.57	4.33	4.67	4.77	4.62	4.75	4.56	4.47	4.49	4.23	3.82	3.25		
b			4.24	3.85	4.09	4.09	4.09	3.87	3.75	4.60	4.17	4.21	4.52	4.51	4.18	4.24	4.36	4.55	4.37	4.21	4.33	4.48	4.37		
m				2.36	4.09	4.61	4.35	4.03	3.86	4.20	4.52	4.43	4.27	3.00	3.99	4.24	4.55	4.31	4.52	4.67	4.09	4.09	3.81	3.79	
n					4.96	4.69	4.71	4.01	3.67	3.98															
t						3.51	4.03	4.35	4.01	3.98															
d							4.01	3.67	4.12	2.11	2.76														
θ								2.79	3.48	3.04															
ð									2.11	2.76															
f										3.03															
v																									

TABLE 10

RANK ORDER OF PROXIMITY—LEFT TO RIGHT (NEAR TO FAR). TIES ARE INDICATED BY ASTERISKS THAT MARK THE ADJACENT ENTRIES OF A ROW. THE SOUNDS ARE GROUPED ACCORDING TO FACTORS EXCEPT THAT EACH CONSTITUENT SOUND IS LISTED ONLY ONE TIME, THIS BEING WITH THE FACTOR WITH WHICH IT IS FIRST IDENTIFIED

TABLE 11

RANK ORDERS OF THE DIFFERENCES BETWEEN THE COMPARISON PHONEMES AT THE LEFT OF ROWS AND THE CONSONANTS INDICATED IN THE COLUMN HEADINGS

	v	f	ʒ	θ	o	p	b	n	z	h	r	d	ʍ	m	ʒ	dʒ	w	j	tʃ	s	ʃ	g	l	t	k
v		3	5	3	11	8	7	6	10.5	12	4	18	2	10		13	1	21	19	22	15	16.5	14	20	23
f	2		3	2	3	7	4	15	12	11	5	16	6	13	14	18	8	21	19.5	16	22	23	17	19.5	9
θ	1	2	4		6	4	7.5	8	10	7.5	13.5	13	17	13		15.5	19	21	23	12	25	13.5	20	11	18
ð	2	10	11		9	5	2	5	22	8	23	7	17	12	20	20	21	18	19	3	18.5	14	22	11	16
o	3	7.5	5		13	1	8	7.5	16	11	15	2	16	6		20	21	11	17	18.5	22.5	14	12	9	13
p	3	11	8		10	7	6	9	14	16	14	20	18.5	14	12	12	18.5	10	22.5	20	21	15	21	17	13
b	2	2	4		5	4	10.5	17	15	18	15	13	11	12	17	17	12	4	21	18	2	21	10	23	16
n	9	11	13		4	10	16	8	8	9	7	13	3	14	20	20	16	19	9	1	16	20	23	20	22
h	5	6	6		3	9	2	13.5	18	2	15	16	19	14	14	14	5.5	8	22	18	21	12	14	23	21
z	5	4	8		12	9	12	11.5	10.5	2	7	13.5	4	10.5	15	15	20.5	3	11	22	20	23	12	15	23
r	5	13	5		9	9	14	15	8	22	18.5	11.5	20.5	14	9	9	5	16	19	18	17	18.5	13	10	16
d	16	4	6		7	9	16	10	8	17	14	13	12	18	2	2	13	17	21	15	3	17.5	6	18	22
ʍ	4	5	10		6	10	9	12	13	3	1	14	5	12	16	16	11	5	2	21	19	23	23	16	20.5
m	7	9	5		3	8	19	12	11	6	3	20	15	19	4	4	2	17.5	16	23	17	14	19	22	23
ʒ	8	7	7		3	9	17.5	12	4	16	17.5	11	19	17	13	13	21	22	6	18	2	13	15	21	20
dʒ	8	5	18		8	10	14	10	1	20.5	16	15	17	11	3	3	18	22	8	3	23	15	17	21	22
w	7	14			7	16	11	11	12	22	22	18	17	12.5	5	5	19	20.5	8	5	20	15	23	10	20
j	6	7	6.5		3.5	3	3	16	3	5	13	16	19	17	2	2	18	12	10	16	18	12.5	23	20.5	11
tʃ	3	6.5				8.5	3		15.5	14	21	1	12		5	5	10	12	22	14	23	3.5	20	14	13
s	3.5				7		3	16	18.5	18.5	15	8.5	19	12.5	2	2	23	22		20			15.5	15	23
ʃ	2				3.5		11					1	12	17	10	5	22	2		14		15	20	22	1
g	4																					12.5		13	23
l	1																					3.5			17
Mean	5.2	6.7	6.8	7.4	7.8	9.0	10.3	11.1	11.6	11.8	11.9	12.0	12.1	12.2	12.5	13.3	13.3	14.7	15.5	15.9	16.2	16.5	16.6	17.5	

sonants of each factor as well as between factors are shown in Table 12. For example, the mean between the pairs of positively loaded consonants of Factor I is 3.34. It is separated from Factor VIII by only 0.55 units of proportionality.

The foregoing values, if reliable, provide a means for comparing the present classification of consonants with ones established in keeping with distinctive features. Most of these relate closely to the system proposed by Jakobson, Fant, and Halle (1952). The values of interconsonantal distance as determined here were applied to the consonants of five categories of their system:

> compact-diffuse
> grave-acute
> tense-lax
> continuant-interrupted
> strident-mellow

If these features or any pair of them relate to aural interconsonantal differences, the intra-group mean values should be less than the intergroup values. Moreover, the median minimal difference separating contrasting factors might serve here to measure whether the features are importantly separated. The mean values, determined as in the measures of Table 12, are summarized in Table 13. Categories *2, 4,* and *5* show greater similarities within each group than between groups.

Miller and Nicely downgraded the perception of 16 consonants in two manners, first by attenuating the level of presentation of syllables to listeners and second, by high- and low-pass filtering. The substitutions that were made for 16 consonants were published. A separate matrix was published for each of six levels of presentation and for each of the conditions of filtering. The 16 stimulus consonants designated the rows and the 16 response consonants, the columns. The first row in each instance was the stimulus /p/. For present purposes, the six rows of responses to /p/ were pooled; etc. This gave the frequencies with which 16 consonants were substituted for /p/ under conditions of distortion by level of presentation. These frequencies were correlated with the 16 related values of aural proximity. This process was repeated for each of 16 consonants and for the results of the different types of distortion used by Miller and Nicely. Interest focused on whether or not small separation distances between consonants were associated with high rates of consonantal confusion.

Wickelgren studied the consonantal errors made in a task involving short-term memory. His object was to study the errors made in recalling syllabic tests and to find whether the error responses tended to preserve the distinctive features of the stimulus list. His procedure

TABLE 12

THE MEAN INTERCONSONANTAL DIFFERENCE BETWEEN THE POSITIVELY LOADED CONSONANTS OF A FACTOR AND BETWEEN THE POSITIVELY LOADED CONSONANTS OF DIFFERENT FACTORS

	Intra-factor Distances	Inter-factor Distances										
		II	III	IV	V	VI	VII	VIII	IX	X	XI	XII
I	3.34	3.99	4.35	4.86	4.77	4.69	4.14	3.89	4.40	4.04	4.79	4.41
II	3.58	—	4.17	4.81	4.85	4.87	4.39	4.06	4.55	3.76	4.70	4.66
III	2.87		—	4.20	4.44	4.06	3.91	4.59	3.94	4.07	4.02	4.16
IV	3.27			—	4.80	4.90	4.57	4.75	4.77	4.81	4.03	4.69
V	3.79				—	4.36	4.13	4.84	4.11	4.92	4.35	3.93
VI	3.51					—	3.74	4.61	3.56	4.72	4.23	3.89
VII	3.04						—	4.11	3.34	4.33	4.45	3.60
VIII	4.11							—	4.30	4.14	4.72	4.69
IX	3.09								—	4.54	4.39	3.52
X	3.17									—	4.56	4.79
XI	4.11										—	4.39
XII	3.57											—

TABLE 13

MEAN INTERCONSONANTAL DISTANCES OF THE CONSONANTS WITHIN AND BETWEEN THE DICHOTOMOUS GROUPS OF CONSONANTS AS CLASSIFIED BY JAKOBSON, FANT, AND HALLE

Category	N	Mean	Category	Mean	N	Contrasting Categories	Difference	N
1. Tense	36	4.23	Lax	4.23	72	T-L	4.23	72
2. Compact	15	3.97	Diffuse	4.03	66	C-D	4.47	72
3. Grave	10	3.94	Acute	4.14	21	G-A	3.99	35
4. Continuant	28	3.71	Interrupted	4.19	28	C-I	4.34	64
5. Strident	6	3.72	Mellow	3.99	6	S-M	4.38	16

yielded an error matrix representing a closed set of 23 consonants, all of the ones of the present report except /ʍ/. Thus, the frequencies with which the 22 available consonants were substituted for each of the stimulus consonants were available. Here again, high rates of consonant confusion might be expected to relate to minimal interconsonantal distance.

Four sets of correlations are shown in Table 14: interconsonantal acoustic distance *vs.* Wickelgren's substitution errors due to forgetting; acoustic distance *vs.* Miller and Nicely's errors caused by low level; acoustic distance *vs.* their errors caused by frequency distortion; and acoustic distance *vs.* the combination of low level and frequency distortion. Twenty-two of the 23 correlations between Wickelgren's substitution scores and the present acoustic distances were significant. Likewise, essentially all of the correlations with the substitutions made by Miller and Nicely's subjects were statistically significant.

TABLE 14

CORRELATION BETWEEN INTERCONSONANTAL ACOUSTIC DISTANCES AND CONSONANTAL CONFUSIONS

	1. Wickelgren*	2. M-N Level Distortion**	3. M-N Frequency Distortion**	4. M-N Combined Distortion**
p	—.75	—.82	—.74	—.72
b	—.73	—.25	—.77	—.76
m	—.69	—.86	—.87	—.87
t	—.64	—.75	—.72	—.72
d	—.71	—.70	—.73	—.72
n	—.66	—.71	—.73	—.71
tʃ	—.71	—	—	—
dʒ	—.30	—	—	—
k	—.97	—.86	—.91	—.89
g	—.62	—.72	—.78	—.78
f	—.46	—.75	—.73	—.70
v	—.71	—.87	—.89	—.89
θ	—.53	—.84	—.82	—.81
ð	—.69	—.77	—.77	—.77
s	—.54	—.74	—.79	—.79
z	—.63	—.56	—.76	—.76
ʃ	—.62	—.75	—.76	—.74
ʒ	—.63	—.77	—.83	—.82
w	—.53			
r	—.72			
l	—.58			
j	—.73			
h	—.83			

*Any value of .40 significant at the 5 per cent level.
**Any value of .51 significant at the 1 per cent level.

Greenberg and Jenkins employed various scaling methods including magnitude estimation in scaling the psychological distances between the six conventional plosives of English /p, t, k, b, d, g/. These six consonants yielded 15 distances /p-t, p-k . . . d-g/ ($\frac{6 \times 5}{2}$). These 15 distances, obtained by the method of magnitude estimation, correlate with the present ones, $r = .73$.

DISCUSSION

The purposes of the study reported here were to establish and test a concept of interconsonantal distances. The pooling of the pairs of equivalent measures of Table 1 provides a scale with units of proportionality. This scale assigns relatively small mean values to the intra-phonemic distances of the consonants of a *factor*, and relatively large ones to the mean distances between the consonants of different factors. Thus, interphonemic distances went into the isolating of the factors. These were shown in Table 5. However, it would be expected that any grouping of consonants on the basis of a common property would likewise yield small intra-class distances of separation and larger inter-class distances. This principle operates in the instances of compact *vs.* diffuse consonants, continuant *vs.* interrupted ones, and strident *vs.* mellow ones; not in the instances of tense *vs.* lax, nor grave *vs.* acute.

Intuitively, it would seem that consonants that sound alike, that is occupy much the same space, would be likely to be confused, and that ones that are remote from each other would seldom be confused. This confusion might be enhanced by increasing the difficulty of the listening circumstance or the nature of the verbal task. Three sets of confusion data were compared to the interphonemic distances. Almost without exception the anticipated relationships were demonstrated. It is noteworthy for investigators in this field that the measures of phonemic disparity were related in the same degree to consonantal substitutions that accompanied an attenuated signal and one that was distorted in spectrum. Also, in a comparison of one sub-set of phonemic distances with values that were derived separately by a similar procedure the similarity between the results was evident.

The intra-group differences of the *tense* and *lax* consonants was as great as the inter-group difference. Thus, the present procedures do not confirm the validity of this dichotomy. The differences between *compact* and *diffuse* consonants exceeded the intra-group means by .47 unit. This is as much as separates some **factors**. The present results are in keeping with the validity of the dichotomy. Continuant consonants are more homogeneous than interrupted ones, and the inter-group distance exceeded the mean intra-group distances.

The foregoing procedure can be viewed as a test of a system of distinctive features or as a test of interconsonantal distances. Other comparisons with interconsonantal distances are available through data provided by Miller and Nicely (1955), Wickelgren (1966), and Greenberg and Jenkins (1964).

REFERENCES

Fletcher, Harvey. *Speech and Hearing in Communication.* New York, 1953.

Greenberg, J. H., and J. J. Jenkins. "Studies in the Psychological Correlates of the Sound System of American English," *Word,* 1964, pp. 157-177.

Harris, J. D. "The Loudness Discrimination Area," *J. Speech and Hearing Dis. Monogr.,* Supp. 11, 1963, pp. 18-23.

Jakobson, R., C. G. M. Fant, and M. Halle. *Preliminaries to Speech Analysis.* Massachusetts Institute of Technology, 1952.

Lane, H. "The Motor Theory of Speech Perception," *Psychol. Review,* 72, 1965, pp. 275-309.

Liberman, A. M., P. Delattre, and F. S. Cooper. "The Role of Selected Stimulus Variables in the Perception of Unvoiced Stop Consonants," *Amer. J. of Psychol.,* 65, 1952, pp. 497-516.

McGee, Victor E. "Determining Perceptual Spaces for the Quality of Filtered Speech," *J. Speech and Hearing Res.,* 8, 1965, pp. 23-38.

Miller, G. A., and P. E. Nicely. "An Analysis of Perceptual Confusions among Some English Consonants," *J. Acoust. Soc. Amer.,* 27, 1955, pp. 338-352.

Peters, R. W. "Dimension of Quality of the Vowel [æ]," *J. Speech and Hearing Res.,* 6, 1963, pp. 239-248.

Singh, S., and J. W. Black. "Study of Twenty-Six Intervocalic Consonants as Spoken and Recognized by Four Language Groups," *J. Acoust. Soc. Amer.,* 39, 1966, pp. 372-387.

Stevens, S. S. "On the Psychophysical Law," *Psychol. Review,* 64, 1957, pp. 153-181.

Voelker, C. H. "A Comparative Study of Investigations of Phonetic Dispersion in Connected American English," *Archives Néerlandaises de Phonétique Expérimentale,* 13, 1937, pp. 138-152.

Wickelgren, Wayne A. "Distinctive Features and Errors in Short-Term Memory for English Consonants," *J. Acoust. Soc. Amer.,* 39, 1966, pp. 388-398.

This research was supported by a contract between the Office of Naval Research (Nonr 495(18)) and The Ohio State University Research Foundation, and conducted in 1966. Parts I and II were reported to a Psycholinguistic Seminar in Rome, May 19; and another in Milan, May 26, 1967. Part III was reported at the Tenth International Congress of Linguists, Bucharest, August 28-September 2, 1967.

A COMPARATIVE STUDY OF JAPANESE AND ENGLISH CONSONANT PHONEMES

SHIGERU TAKEBAYASHI

Tokyo University of Foreign Studies

1.1 This paper compares Japanese and English consonant phonemes which are roughly matched in both languages. It also aims at describing the phonemic and phonetic status of the unmatched consonants of one language from the viewpoint of the other. The dialect of Japanese treated in this paper is the so-called "Standard Japanese" spoken by the educated people born and bred in Tokyo. The phonetic descriptions of this Standard Japanese are based on S. Hattori's *Onseigaku* (Phonetics) (Iwanamishoten, Tokyo, 1951) and *Gengogaku no Hōhō* (Methods in Linguistics) (Iwanamishoten, Tokyo, 1960), H. Kindaichi's *Nihongo On-in no Kenyū* (Studies in Japanese Phonology) (Tōkyōdōshuppan, Tokyo, 1967) and on my own observations. The type of English dealt with here is what is often referred to as "General American," and is fully described in such phonetics books as J. S. Kenyon: *American Pronunciation* (George Wahr, Ann Arbor, Mich., 10th ed., 1951), C. M. Wise: *Applied Phonetics* (Englewood Cliffs, N. J., 1957), C. K. Thomas: *The Phonetics of American English* (2d ed., New York, 1958) and A. J. Bronstein: *The Pronunciation of American English* (New York, 1960) and is recorded in Kenyon and Knott's *A Pronouncing Dictionary of American English* (2d ed., Springfield, Mass., 1949).

1.2 The Japanese language has five vowel phonemes /i, e, a, o, u/ and the phoneme /:/, which is the lengthening element of the preceding vowel and constitutes a syllable by itself. Thus /kado/(corner) is disyllabic while /ka:do/(card) is trisyllabic. There is a contrast between /sato:ya/(sugar dealer) and /satooya/(foster parent).[1]

General American has eight vowels: /i, e, æ, a, ɔ, o, u, ə/ plus accompanying vowel glides which may be used to describe this type of American English. The exact analysis of the vowels does not concern us here.

The systems of the Japanese and the English consonant phonemes may be diagrammed as follows:[2]

---

[1] Cf. Kindaichi: *op. cit.*, pp. 133-153.
[2] In this diagrammatization I am indebted to W. G. Moulton: *The Sounds of English and German* (The University of Chicago Press, Chicago and London, 1962), p. 27.

	JAPANESE						ENGLISH			

JAPANESE						ENGLISH			
p b	t d	c	k g			p b	t d	c ʃ	k g
	s z		h		f v	θ ð	s z	ʒ	h
m	n	ŋ		m	n			ŋ	
	r				l	r			
y	w			y		w			
ṇ		q							

The Japanese phonemes that are enclosed by solid lines are those which lack counterparts in English and the English phonemes enclosed by dotted lines are those which are not matched in Japanese. The Japanese phonemes /ṇ/ and /q/ are syllabic, but they are conveniently included in our comparison because most of their allophones are phonetically consonantal. Both Japanese and English /y/ and /w/ are phonetically vocalic or "vocoid" according to Pike's terminology,[3] but they too are included in this paper because they are nonsyllabic and hence phonemically consonantal.

1.3 The structure of a Japanese syllable is fairly simple. It is typically /CV/, i.e., it is usually composed of one consonant phoneme and one vowel phoneme. /C/ can be zero, i.e., there are syllables of /V/ only: /e/(picture), /ue/(upper part), /aoi/(blue). /C/ also allows the semivowel phoneme /y/ to intervene between it and the following vowel: /kyu:ri/(cucumber), /byo:ki/(illness), /hyaku/(hundred). In such cases the syllable structure is /CyV/ (see further 6.1). The phonemes /:/, /ṇ/ and /q/ are unique in that they occur only after /(C)V/. Thus we have /(C)V/ in /o:ki:/(big), /(C)Vṇ/ in /oṇdaṇ/ (warmth) and /(C)Vq/ in /iqpai/(full) and /maqtaku/(quite).

On the other hand there are rather complicated consonant clusters in English syllables: /CV-/(*team*), /CCV-/(*snow*), /CCCV-/(*strong*) and /-VC/(*it*), /-VCC/(*box*), /-VCCC/(*tempt*), /-VCCCC/(*texts*). Therefore English consonant phonemes may appear in preconsonantal, postconsonantal and interconsonantal positions in addition to prevocalic, postvocalic and intervocalic positions. In Japanese, it should be noted that syllable divisions are fairly clear-cut and that, consequently, consonant phonemes appear only in prevocalic positions due to the syllable structure /CV/ noted above.

Japanese consonant phonemes (except /ṇ/ and /q/ never appear finally. Thus Japanese tend to replace English final consonant /-C/ by their /-Cu/. In Japanese /u/ (phonetically an advanced variety of un-

---

[3] Cf. K. L. Pike: *Phonetics* (The University of Michigan Press, Ann Arbor, 1958), p. 78.

rounded back vowel [ɯ]) is the most neutral and weak vowel like English or French [ə]. English *rope* is turned in Japanese into /ro:pu/, *cheese* into /ci:zu/, *time* into /taimu/. But as we shall see in 2.5, there are no combinations /tu, du/ in the language and English final /t, d/ are usually replaced by Japanese /to, do/. Thus *boat* is converted into /bo:to/, *record* into /reko:do/.

2.1 English stop consonants are often unexploded as the /k/ in *act*, /g/ in *begged* or /p/ in *attempt*, while Japanese stops, which have only prevocalic allophones as stated above, are *always* exploded. In Japanese, when a stop is pronounced with a considerably long retention (as in English /kk/ in *bookcase* or /tt/ in *hot-tempered*) that part of retention is perceived to be not a stop phoneme but the phoneme /q/ which will be treated in 8.1 and 8.2. The Japanese also perceive English stops which are pronounced rather long after checked vowels to be /q/ plus stop phonemes, while comparatively short stops after free vowels are recognized as simple stop phonemes. Thus *kick, head, cup* are for the Japanese /kiqku, heqdo, kaqpu/, while *talk, road, keep* are /to:ku, ro:do, ki:pu/. It is interesting to note that /p, b, t, d, k, g/ are more adequately referred to as stops rather than as plosives in English but vice versa in Japanese.

2.2 Japanese voiceless stop consonants are not so fortis as English. English /p, t, k/ are aspirated before stressed vowels unless preceded by /s/, but Japanese /p, t, k/ are usually unaspirated or weakly aspirated. As regards aspiration, Japanese /p, t, k/ are related not to the English /p, t, k/ in *peace, talk, cool* but to those in *speak, stay, school* or in *upper, better* (when pronounced voiceless), *locker*.

Likewise, English voiced stops are not so lenis as Japanese. This is most noticeable in /b/. Japanese /b/ tends to become fricative in intervocalic positions as is the case with Spanish /b/, especially in easy or careless conversation. Thus /b/'s in /abunai/(dangerous), /kubomi/(hollow place), etc. are often [β] in my speech.

Intervocalic /g/ is usually or regularly replaced by [ŋ] in Standard Japanese (see 4.2). However, some speakers use fricative [ɣ] for intervocalic /g/ (see also 4.2).

2.3 Word-initial allophones of English voiced consonant phonemes are often partially devoiced as the /b/ in *back*, /d/ in *day*, and /g/ in *get*. Japanese initial voiced consonants are fully voiced as in many Romance languages. This case holds true not only in voiced stops but also in voiced fricatives, nasals and liquids. So the comparison will not be made any further.

2.4 English /t, d/ are alveolar consonants unless they stand before /θ/. In Japanese most speakers use dental /t, d/, but some employ dento-alveolar or even alveolar /t, d/.

The so-called "voiced t" of American English presents a special difficulty to Japanese hearers. This will be treated in 5.2.

2.5 In Japanese the combinations /ti, di/ and /tu, du/ do not usually occur. Some Japanese therefore find it difficult to pronounce English *teach, tin, deal, Dick, tool, took, doom.* They replace English /ti, di/ by Japanese /te, de/ or /ci, zi/ (which will be discussed in 3.3 and 3.4) and /tu, du/ by /cu, zu/. But many people, especially younger ones, have little difficulty in pronouncing /ti, di/ and /tu, du/, owing to the rapid spread of English teaching after the war. Among these speakers new phonemic combinations /ti, di/ are beginning to be established. They use the combinations in the following loan words from English and other European languages:

/ti/: /tiː/(tea), /tiːmu/(team) (Many, however, still use the conventional form /ciːmu/ instead), /tiːn̥eizyaː/(teen-ager).

/di/: /diːdiːtiː/(DDT), /dinaː/(dinner), /diːzeru/(diesel engine) (But here some use the conventional /ziːzeru/).

2.6 Both English and Japanese /k, g/ have prevelar, postvelar and mediovelar allophones according to the tongue-positions of the following vowels. In English prevelar allophones appear before front vowels as in *keep, get, cat,* postvelar allophones before back vowels as in *court, cold, goose* and mediovelar allophones before central vowels as in *cut, cart, girl.* In Japanese, too, prevelar /k, g/ occur before front vowels as in /kinu/(silk), /gen̥zai/(present), postvelar /k, g/ before back vowels as in /kuru/(come),[4] /gomi/(rubbish) and mediovelar /k, g/ before central vowels as in /kasa/(umbrella), /gaqko/(school).

English prevelar allophones of /k, g/ which appear before /æ/ as in *cat, gang* present a peculiar problem to Japanese learners of English. The Japanese language possesses only one low vowel phoneme, namely /a/, and most Japanese usually substitute this /a/ for /æ, a, ə/ in learning English. They find it hard to distinguish *back* from *buck, ran* from *run, hut* from *hot* or *hat.* They, however, can distinguish *cat* from *cut, began* from *begun.* The situation is as follows:

The Japanese perceive all these vowels as their /a/; thus /Kaqto/

[4] Japanese /u/ is actually a fairly advanced variety of the unrounded back vowel [ɯ] (see 6.3). Thus to put it more exactly, Japanese /k, g/ before /u/ are just intermediate between postvelar and mediovelar.

for *cat* and *cut* and American *cot,* and /bigan/ for *began* and *begun.* Now in Japanese, as stated above, mediovelar, not prevelar /k, g/, stand before /a/. Therefore it is very easy for the Japanese to recognize /k, g/ in *cut, cot* and *begun* where mediovelar allophones appear, but not so in *cat* and *began* where prevelar, not mediovelar allophones as they expect, appear. Here it should be remembered that Japanese syllable structure permits /CyV/ besides the normal /CV/ (see 1.3). This semivowel phoneme /y/ as well as the high front vowel /i/ requires that the allophones of the preceding consonants be palatalized or, in case of /k, g/, advanced (i.e., prevelar) (see further 6.2). In English, palatalized allophones do not appear before /æ/ but prevelar allophones of /k, g/ do. This prevelarity makes the Japanese hearers perceive the sounds to be the pre-/y/ allophones of their /k, g/-phonemes. Thus the Japanese recognize *cat* as /kyaqto/ in their own way, distinguishing it from *cut, cot* (both /kaqto/).[5] Likewise *began* (/bigyaṇ/) is distinct from *begun* (/bigaṇ/). Thus after /k, g/ distinction between /æ/ and /ə, a/ in English is converted into that between /y/ and /∅/(zero) in Japanese.

3.1 English fricative consonant phonemes /f, v/ do not find their counterparts in Japanese. Naturally the Japanese replace these two sounds by some phonetically related sounds in their language. Here it is very interesting to observe the Japanese response to these two sounds. They take English /v/ as their /b/, but not /f/ as their /p/. As noted in 2.2 Japanese /b/ tends to be fricative especially in an intervocalic position. There is a considerable phonetic similarity between this fricative [β] and English [v]. The Japanese find it hard to distinguish *very* from *berry* or *bury, rove* from *robe,* or even *lover* from *rubber.* (As for the confusion of /l/ with /r/, see 5.1).

The case is quite different for /f/. The nearest Japanese sound to English [f] is [ɸ], which, though it may seem quite arbitrary to the Americans, is an allophone of /h/ before the vowel /u/ (phonetically [ɯ]). Accordingly, when the Japanese hear English /fu, fuw/ they take them as /hu, hu:/; thus, *foot* as /huqto/, *full* as /huru/, *who* as /hu:/, *fool* as /hu:ru/. Consequently this causes confusion of /fu, fuw/ with /hu, huw/ among Japanese hearers of English. Many Japanese respond alike both to English /fu, fuw/ and /hu, huw/.

The Japanese have traditionally regarded /C/ not an independent phonological unit. The psychologically smallest unit of the language for them is /CV/, hence their use of *kana* syllabaries instead of alphabets. Japanese [ɸ] is thus not an independent element. Instead,

---

[5] The Japanese usually cannot distinguish /ə/ in *cut* from /a/ in *cot.*

[ɸɯ](phonemically /hu/) is an established one. For this reason when the Japanese hear English /f/, they perceive it [ɸ] and immediately relate it to their /hu/([ɸɯ]). Thus when /f/ precedes consonants or stands finally it is perceived by Japanese to be /hu/: *fry* and *fly* both become /hurai/, *golf*, /goruhu/, *safe*, /se:hu/, etc.

When /f/ precedes a vowel other than /u/ it is often perceived by the Japanese to be /hu/ plus another vowel phoneme. Thus *feet* is often taken as /hui:to/ (four syllables!), *finger* /huiŋga:/, *fan* /huaṇ/, etc. But it is not rare for Japanese who are more or less familiar with English to replace /f/ by [ɸ]. Thus *film* is converted to [ɸirɯmɯ], *fair* to [ɸea], *face* to [ɸe:sɯ], *fan* to [ɸaỹ], *form* to [ɸo:mɯ], etc. It is very interesting to note that new combinations like [ɸi, ɸe, ɸa, ɸo] have thus emerged in addition to the established [ɸɯ](/hu/). This [ɸ] before vowels other than /u/ should phonemically be analyzed as /hw/: the words above being /hwirumu, hwea, hwe:su, hwaṇ, hwo:mu/. There is a contrast like this: /huaṇ/ (three syllables (anxiety) — /hwaṇ/ (two syllables) (fan) — /haṇ/ two syllables) (seal). In present-day Standard Japanese we have no combination of [ɸV] other than [ɸɯ], but formerly [ɸ] did stand before every vowel.[6] Such combinations seem to have revived at least in some speakers of Standard Japanese due to contact with English and other European languages.

If English loan words that begin with /f/ and a vowel are much more Japanized or spoken by those who know little English, /hu/ or /hw/ is often completely reduced to simple /h/. Thus *foul* (in sports) is turned into /ha:ru/, *fork* into /ho:ku/ (identical with that resulting from *hawk*), *folk dance* into /ho:kudaṇsu/.

3.2 English /θ/ and /ð/, too, have no counterparts in Japanese. Most Japanese usually take them as /s/ and /z/, and they find it rather difficult to distinguish *thigh* from *sigh*, *thick* from *sick*, *path* from *pass*, or *thee* from *z*, *breathe* from *breeze*, *clothing* from *closing*.

3.3 The correlations of Japanese /s, z, c/ and English /s, z, ʃ, ʒ, c, j/ are very complicated.

It will be convenient at first to list the allophones of the three Japanese phonemes:

---

[6] For example, a Japanese-Portuguese dictionary entitled *Vocabvlario da Lingoa de Iapam*, published at Nagasaki in 1603, includes such words as *fana* (flower), *fito* (man), *feri* (border), *fotondo* (almost). These *f*'s seem to have represented [ɸ].

1. /s/: [s] before /e, a, o, u/ — /semento/[semento](cement), /sakura/[sakɯɾa] (cherry), /sode/ [sode] (sleeve), /susumu/[sɯsɯmɯ] (advance).

[ɕ] or [sʲ]⁷ before /i/ — /sizumu/[ɕi(d)zɯmɯ, sʲ—] (sink).

2. /z/: [dz] initially before /a, e, o, u/ and after /n/ — /zero/ [dzeɾo] (zero), /zaqsi/[dzaɕɕi, dzasʲsʲi] (magazine), /zo:/[dzo:] (elephant), /zurui/[dzɯɾɯi] (cunning).

[dz] or [dʲzʲ] initially before /i/ — /zisin/[dʑiɕiɣ̃, dʲzʲ—] (earthquake).

[z] or [dz] intervocalically before /e, a, o, u/ — /kaze/[ka(d)ze] (wind), /mazaru/[ma(d)zaɾɯ](mix), /ko:zo:/[ko:(d)zo:] (structure), /mizu/[mi(d)zɯ](water).

[ʑ], [zʲ] or [dʑ] or [dʲzʲ] intervocalically before i — /kozin/ [ko(d)ʑiɣ̃, ko(dʲ)zʲiɣ̃](individual).

3. /c/: [ts] before /u/ — /cubaki/[tsɯbaki](cammelia). /c/([ts]) rarely appears before /a/ — /otoqcan/[otottsaɣ̃](daddy).

[tɕ] or [tʲsʲ] before /i/ — /cikai/[tɕikai, tʲsʲikai](near).

It is to be noted that in Standard Japanese opposition between the voiceless fricative [s] and the voiceless affricate [ts] is phonemic — [sɯki](/suki/(plow)) contrasts with [tsɯki](/cuki/)), while the voiced fricative [z] and the voiced affricate [dz] are merely positional variants or are in free variation with each other. As stated above many speakers (including myself) use [dz] initially or after /n/ and [z] in intervocalic positions, where [dz] also appears especially in slow or careful speech. Likewise there is a phonemic contrast between the voiceless fricative [ɕ, sʲ] and the voiceless affricate [tɕ, tʲsʲ] — [ɕikakɯ, sʲkakɯ](/sikaku/(square)) and [tɕikakɯ, tʲsʲkakɯ] (/cikaku/(perception)), but none between the voiced fricative [ʑ, zʲ] and the voiced affricate [dʑ, dʲzʲ]. They too are nothing but positional variants or are in free variation.

Distributions of allophones of /s, z, c/ before /yV/ are also suggestive:

1. /s/: [ɕa, sʲa]/sya/ — [ɕakai, sʲakai]/syakai/(society), [ɕo, sʲo] /syo/ — [ɕomotsɯ, sʲomotsɯ]/syomocu/(book), [ɕɯ, sʲɯ]/syu/ — [ɕɯdai, sʲɯdai]/syudai/(theme).

⁷ [ʲ] stands for palatalization; [˜] stands for nasalization.

2. /z/: [(ḍ)ẓa, (dʲ)zʲa]/zya/ — [dai(ḍ)ẓa, dai(dʲ)zʲa]/daizya/
(big snake), [(ḍ)ẓo, (dʲ)zʲo]/zyo/ — [ço(ḍ)ẓo, sʲo(dʲ)zʲo]
/syozyo/(virgin), [(ḍ)ẓɯ, (dʲ)zʲɯ]/zyu/—[te(ḍ)ẓɯy̆, te(dʲ)zɯy̆
/tezyuṇ/(procedure).

3. /c/: [t̠ça, tʲsʲa]/cya/ — /cya/(tea), [t̠çe, tʲsʲe]/cye/ — t̠çeko,
tʲsʲeko]/cyeko/(Czecho(slovakia)), [t̠ço, tʲsʲo]/cyo/ — [t̠ço:çi,
tʲsʲo:sʲi]/cyo:si/(tune), [t̠çɯ, tʲsʲɯ]/cyu/ — t̠çɯ:ciy̆, tʲsʲɯ:siʲy̆]
/cyu:siṇ/(center).

/sye/ and /zye/ do not usually appear in Standard Japanese. From
this we see that allophones of /s, z, c/ before /y/ are the same as those
before /i/.

Examination of all the allophones of /s, z, c/ listed above reveals
that there are very interesting phonetic correlations between the three
phonemes:

1. Allophones of /s/ and those of /z/ make a pair of the voiceless
   fricatives and the corresponding voiced affricates (with the corresponding voiced fricatives as free variants):

   /s/ — [s] before /e, a, o, u/, [ç, sʲ] before /i, y/.

   /z/ — [(d)z] before /e, a, o, u/, [(ḍ)ẓ, (dʲ)zʲ] before /i, y/.

2. Allophones of /c/ and those of /z/ make a voiceless-voiced pair
   (though the latter sometimes drop the [d] or [ḍ, dʲ] and become
   the corresponding voiced fricatives):

   /c/ — [ts] before /a, u/, [t̠ç, tʲsʲ] before /i, y/.

   /z/ — [(d)z] before /e, a, o, u/, [(ḍ)ẓ, (dʲ)zʲ] before /i, y/.

3. Allophones of /s/ and those of /c/ make a pair of the voiceless
   fricatives and the corresponding voiceless affricates beginning with
   [t] or [t̠, tʲ]:

   /s/ — [s] before /e, a, o, u/, [ç, sʲ] before /i, y/.

   /c/ — [ts] before /a, u/, [t̠ç, tʲsʲ] before /i, y/.

Thus we obtain a triangular correlation between /s/, /z/ and /c/.

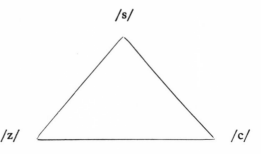

/s/

/z/   /c/

On the other hand, there seems to be the following correlation in English:

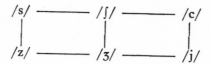

3.4 There is not a noticeable difference between Japanese [s, z, ts, dz] and English [s, z, ts, dz], though a slight difference can be observed by a trained phonetician.

The nearest English sounds to Japanese [ɕ, sʲ], [ʑ, zʲ], [tɕ, tʲsʲ] and [dʑ, dʲzʲ] are [ʃ], [ʒ], [tʃ] and [dʒ]. However, Japanese [ɕ] and [ʑ] differ from English [ʃ] and [ʒ] in that the point of articulation of the former is a little more retracted than the latter. It should also be noted that Japanese [ɕ] and [ʑ] are not accompanied by lip-protrusion as is usually the case with English [ʃ] and [ʒ]. Impressionistically, English [ʃ] and [ʒ] sound noticeably "darker" or "deeper" than Japanese [ɕ, sʲ] and [ʑ, zʲ], which are "sharp" according to Jakobson-Fant-Halle's terminology.[8] A similar difference exists between English [tʃ], [dʒ] and Japanese [tɕ, tʲsʲ], [dʑ, dʲzʲ].

With all these differences, we can find the following rough correspondence between Japanese /s, z, c/ and English /s, z, ʃ, ʒ, c, j/.

JAPANESE	ENGLISH
[s] in /se, sa, so, su/	[s] in /se, sa, sæ, sə, so, su/
[z] (intervocalic) in /-ze, -za, -zo, -zu/	[z] in /-ze, -za, -zæ, -zə, -zo, -zu/
[ɕ, sʲ] in /si (sye), sya, syo, syu/	[ʃ] in /ʃi, ʃa, ʃæ, ʃə, ʃo, ʃu/
[ʑ, zʲ] (intervocalic) in /zi) (zye), zya, zyo, zyu/	[ʒ] in /(-ʒe, -ʒa, -ʒæ, -ʒə, -ʒo), -ʒu/
[tɕ, tʲsʲ] in /ci, cye, cya cyo, cyu/	[tʃ] in /ci, ce, ca, cæ, cə, co, cu/
[dʑ, dʲzʲ] in /zi (zye), zya, zyo, zyu/	[dʒ] in /ji, je, ja, jæ, jə, jo, ju/

However, English /si/ and /zi/ are not matched in Japanese; hence Japanese difficulty in pronouncing *sea, sit, zeal, zinc* or in distinguishing *seat* from *sheet*, z from ʒ. They substitute for /si/ and /zi/ [ɕi, sʲi] and [(d̪)ʑi, (dʲ)zʲi]). As there is no English initial

[8] Cf. R. Jakobson, C. G. M. Fant and M. Halle: *Preliminaries to Speech Analysis* (The M. I. T. Press, Cambridge, Mass., 1961), p. 33.

consonant cluster /dz/, the Americans usually pronounce Japanese initial /z/([dz]) as [z]. But since there is no contrast between [z] and [dz] in Japanese, the [z] does not cause any ambiguity. English also lacks initial /ts/ and many Americans seem to have more or less difficulty in pronouncing Japanese /cu/, especially if it stands initially as in /curu/(crane), /cunami/(tsunami).

3.5 Japanese /h/ and English /h/ differ but little except when they stand before /i/ and /u/. The Japanese allophone [ɸ] of /h/ before /u/ is already discussed in 3.1. Before /i/ as in /hito/(man) or /hima/(leisure) Japanese /h/ has more friction and is more palatalized. The allophone in this position is [ç]. This also appears before /y/ as in /hyaku/[çakɯ](hundred) or /hyo:ban/[ço:bay̰](reputation). English too has [ç] before /yuw/ as in *huge* or *human*.

It should be noted that the allophones of Japanese /h/, i.e., [h], [ç], and [ɸ], are the only non-sibilant voiceless fricative consonants in the language. Thus in Japanese there are two voiceless fricative phonemes; one being the sibilant /s/ and the other the non-sibilant or vocal tract fricative /h/.

4.1 Japanese /m, n, ŋ/ differ little from English /m, n, ŋ/ except that /n/ is usually dental like Japanese /t, d/. Japanese /n/ is considerably palatalized (to be represented with [nʲ]) or even becomes palatal [ɲ] before /i/. Thus /nisi/[ɲiçi, nʲisʲi](west), /niku/[ɲikɯ, nʲikɯ](meat), /kani/[kaɲi, kanʲi](crab). [ɲ] or [nʲ] before /a, o, u/ is phonemically analyzable as /ny/: /nya:/[ɲa:, nʲa:](mew), /nyo:/ [ɲo:, nʲo:](urine).

Japanese long syllable [m, n, ŋ] are phonemically /ɳ/, which will be treated in 7.2 and 7.4. As for the Japanese mispronunciation of English final /n/, see 7.3.

4.2 Japanese /ŋ/ is structurally quite different from English /ŋ/ in that it is not an established phoneme in all speakers and that it is psychologically identified with /g/ by most Japanese.

The fact is that in Standard Japanese /g/ appears initially and /ŋ/ occurs intervocalically and after /ɳ/: /gasu/(gas), /giŋko:/(bank), /guci/(complaint), /ge:mu/(game), /go/(five); but /kaŋaku/ (science), /tamaneŋi/(onion), /suŋureta/(excellent), /miyaŋe/(souvenir), /saɳŋo/(coral). Moreover there is usually an alternation of /g/ and /ŋ/ in "compound" words: /gaqko:/(school) but /zyoŋ-aqko:/(girls' school), /go/(word) but /taɳŋo/(simple word), /guɳ/ (army) but /kaiŋuɳ/(navy). It might be maintained that [ŋ] is merely an intervocalic allophone of the phoneme /g/, were it not for the following few contrasts in intervocalic positions: /tabiŋarasu/ (wanderer), /surigarasu/(frosted glass), /saŋŋo/(coral), /saŋgurasu/ (sunglass), /inoci karaŋara/(with bare life), /garagara/(rattlingly).

There seem, however, to be a growing number of young people who do not have the /ŋ/ phoneme at all. They use [g] or fricative [ɣ] instead of [ŋ] in intervocalic positions cited above.

Most Americans seem to have difficulty in using [ŋ] in proper positions in Japanese. They usually replace it with /g/. Because English /g/ is less lenis than Japanese (see 2.2) and because in Japanese even those who do not employ [ŋ] tend to weaken the explosion of [g] or to use fricative [ɣ] intervocalically, English [g] in this place sounds rather "strong" to the Japanese ear, though it does not cause any unintelligibility.

5.1 The Japanese language has only one liquid consonant phoneme /r/, which seems to share nothing with the /r/ of American English but its symbol. Phonetically Japanese /r/ is much more consonantal than American /r/ and includes various allophones or diaphones. In initial positions most speakers use retroflex alveolar plosive [ɖ], the explosion of which is weaker than that of /d/. Others use retroflex lateral [ɭ] and still others employ flapped [ɾ]. While in intervocalic positions flapped [ɾ] seems to be the most frequent but [ɖ] and [ɭ] are also used.

As Japanese has no phoneme which exactly corresponds either to English /r/ or /l/, the Japanese learners of English naturally find it very hard to discriminate between English /r/ and /l/. Thus they cannot usually distinguish *road* from *load, read* from *lead, write* or *right* from *light, pray* from *play, brew* from *blue, grass* from *glass, berry* or *bury* from *belly,* etc. Actually many homonyms of loan words from English have resulted in present-day Japanese from the confusion of English /r/ and /l/: /raito/ (from *right field(er)* in baseball and from *light*(lamp)), /re:su/ from *race* and *lace*), /rokeqto/ (from *rocket* and *locket,* /hurai/ (from *fry* and *fly* (in baseball)), /kurosu/ (from *cross* and *cloth*).

5.2 To make matters still worse, many Americans use a kind of flapped [ɾ] intervocalically as the "voiced t." This [ɾ] is quite similar to Japanese [ɾ] which is the most prevalent intervocalic allophone of /r/ in the language as noticed above. Thus the Japanese students of American English have to discriminate three phonemes /r/, /l/ and /t/ in intervocalic positions where they have only a single phoneme /r/. They are often puzzled by the "curious" fact that "Americans pronounce *t* like *r.*" The following sets are quite confusing to the

Japanese ear:[9] *berry* (*bury*)—*belly*—*Betty, parley*—*party, mealing*—
meating, marrow—*mallow*—*matter.*

/r/ and /l/, however, become less confusing in final positions, where
/r/ is fairly vocalic. Thus Japanese do not find it so difficult to distinguish *four* from *fall, bear* from *bell, appear* from *appeal.*

The Americans should be advised to apply their /l/ rather than /r/
to Japanese /r/. American /r/ is vocalic and it sometimes sounds like
weak /u/ or /a/ to the Japanese ear. /l/ would hardly cause any ambiguity when used for Japanese /r/, though it might sound somewhat strange in some positions, especially when it is pronounced by
those who use a very "dark" variety.

6.1 Both Japanese and English /y/ and /w/ are semivowel phonemes. They are phonetically nonsyllabic vocalic glides, but they
function as consonant phonemes. Japanese /y/ is phonetically not so
different from English /y/. Both Japanese and English prevocalic /y/
are glides which start from the tongue positions higher and more advanced than the following vowels, lips being usually spread. As for distribution, Japanese /y/ stands before /a, o, u/ but not before /e, i/.
It is not so difficult for most Japanese to pronounce English /ye/ but
very hard to pronounce /yi/. They find it difficult to distinguish *yeast*
from *east, year* from *ear, yield* from *eel.* In English, on the other hand,
the combination /Cy/ occurs only before /uw/ and /ur/ in stressed
syllables. Thus Americans seem to have some difficulty in pronouncing
Japanese /Cya/ as in /myaku/(pulse), /haŋŋyaku/(revolt) and
/Cyo/ as in /nyoronyoroto/(wrigglingly), /ryo:siṇ/(conscience).
Tokyo(/to:kyo:/) and *Kyoto*(/kyo:to/) are very often pronounced
by many American visitors as ['toukiou] and [ki'outou]. Americans
should especially be warned against confusing the following minimal
pairs of /CyV/ and /CiyV/. The former are more difficult for most
Americans, who tend to replace them with the latter.

/kyaku/(two syllables)(guest)—/kiyaku/(three syllables)(rule)

/ryo:si/(three syllables)(hunter)—/riyo:si/(four syllables)
   (barber)

/byo:in/(three syllables)(hospital)—/biyo:iṇ/(four syllables)
   (beauty parlor)

---

[9] An acquaintance of mine, who is a physicist, once went to hear
a lecture on nuclear physics by a visiting American scientist. When
the speech began he wondered if he had entered a wrong room, because the lecturer repeatedly used the word *alum.* Actually, he mis-
heard the speaker's *atom* for *alum.*

6.2 Japanese /y/ as well as /i/ palatalizes the preceding consonant more strongly than English /y/ and /i/ do. Thus /p, b, m, n, r/ are noticeably palatalized in /py, by, my, ny, ry/. /k, g, ŋ/ have allophones with fairly advanced points of articulation before /y/ (see 2.6). In some consonant phonemes the situations go still further. /y/ combines with the preceding consonant to form a palatal sound. Thus:

/cy/: [ʦɕ] in /cye, cya, cyo, cyu/
/sy/: [ɕ] in /sya, syo, syu/
/zy/: [(d)ʑ] in /zya, zyo, zyu/ (see 3.3)
/hy/: [ç] in /hya, hyo, hyu/ (see 3.5)
/ny/: [ɲ] in /nya, nyo, nyu/ (see 4.1)

6.3 Japanese /w/ differs from English /w/ both phonetically and distributionally. The phonetic difference between Japanese and English /w/ is correlated with that between Japanese /u/ and English /u/ or /uw/. /u/ in Standard Japanese is an advanced variety of back vowel [ɯ]. It is not accompanied with any lip-rounding. In some speakers the lips are even somewhat spread especially after /h/. It should be noted that Japanese /w/, too, lacks lip-rounding.

Distributionally, Japanese /w/ stands only before the vowel /a/ in present-day Standard Japanese as in /wa/(ring), /watasi/(I), /kowasu/(break), /kaiwa/(conversation). Furthermore, there is no combination /Cwa/ in Standard Japanese. Formerly, however, there existed combinations /wi, we, wo/ and /Cwa/ (at least /kwa, gwa, ŋwa/) and they still survive in some dialects. As for the new combination /hwV/, see 3.1.

7.1 /n̥/ and /q/ are unique phonemes of the Japanese language. Not only do they cause considerable difficulties in learning the language but also they present very interesting problems to phoneticians and phonemicists.

Before treating the two phonemes in question it is necessary to notice the peculiarity of Japanese syllables. They are characterized by their fairly constant isochronicity. Every Japanese syllable is approximately of equal duration. For example, words of three syllables are pronounced about three times as long as monosyllabic ones. Thus /uniŋame/(sea turtle) (four syllables) is twice as long as /umi/(sea) (two syllables) and four times as long as /me/(eye) (one syllable). By stating that /n̥/ and /q/ are syllabic we mean that their duration approximates the average length of a syllable in Japanese. Thus trisyllables like /tenki/(weather) and /teqki/ are about one and a half as long as the disyllabic /teki/(enemy).

7.2 /ŋ/ seems to be a rather elusive phoneme to Americans. It is very much influenced by the nature of adjacent (especially following) phonemes. The allophones of /ŋ/ in Standard Japanese are as follows. Notice that all these sounds are long enough to be syllabic:

1. [ɣ̃][10] in final positions: /udoŋ/(noodle), /kyoneŋ/(last year).

2. [n] before /ta, te, to/, /da, de, do/, /cu/, /za, ze, zo, zu/, /na, ne, no, nu/ and /r/: /kaŋtai/(fleet), /hoŋto:no/(true), /seŋdeŋ/ (propaganda), /baŋzai/(hurrah), /geŋzo/(photographic development), /oŋna/(woman), /heŋna/(strange), /kaŋri/(management), /seŋro/(rail).

3. [ɲ] or [nʲ] before /ci, cy/, /zi, zy/ and /ni, ny/: /seŋci/(centimeter), /keŋcyona/(conspicuous), /heŋzi/(answer), /gaŋzyo:na/ (strong), /haŋnin/(criminal), /siŋnyu:/(invasion).

4. [m] before /p, b, m/ and /hu/:[11] /kiŋpacu/(blonde), /meŋba:/ (member), /aŋma/(massager), /iŋhure/(inflation).

5. [ŋ] before /k, g, ŋ/: /saŋko:syo/(reference book), /guŋguŋto/ (rapidly), /beŋŋi/(convenience).

6. [ɨ̃] before /s/: /keŋsecu/(construction), /zyuŋsa/(policeman), /deŋsya/(electric train).

7. [ĩ] before /i, y/ and /hi, hy/: /hiŋi/(dignity), /paŋya/(bakery), /seŋhyaku/(one thousand and one hundred).

8. [ũ] before /o, u/, /ho/ and /wa/: /keŋo/(hatred), /aŋuŋ/(dark clouds), /deŋwa/(telephone).

9. [ẽ] before /e/ and /he/: /seŋeŋ/(one thousand yen), /siŋheiki/ (new weapon).

10. [ə̃] before /a/ and /ha/: /daŋacu/(oppression), /haŋhaŋ/(fifty-fifty).

The distinctive feature common to all the allophones mentioned above is the retention of nasal resonance of enough duration to constitute one syllable. On the other hand oral passages are stopped in [n, m, ŋ], constricted in [ɣ̃] or become quite passive or neutral in nasalized vowels like [ɨ̃, ĩ, ũ, ẽ, ə̃]. It should be noticed that phonemes /n, m, ŋ/, like other Japanese consonant phonemes, always stand before vowels and their allophones [n, ɲ, nʲ], [m] and [ŋ] are short and al-

----

[10] [ɣ̃] differs from [ŋ] in that there is a narrow passage between the posterior part of the velum and the back of the tongue.

[11] To put it more exactly, the lip-position of /ŋ/ before /hu/ is that of [ɸ].

ways orally released (see 1.3), while considerably long [n, ɲ, nʲ], [m] and [ŋ], which are the allophones of /n̩/, are never released orally. Thus the first [m] in [amma](/an̩ma/)(massager) is unreleased like the first [m] of English *home-made*, and the second [m]'s of both words are orally released. There is noticeable decrease of energy between the first and the second [m]'s in [amma] and *home-made*. The sequence of the double [m]'s in both languages are phonetically similar but their phonemic treatments are quite different. The case holds good in Japanese [anna](/an̩na/)(like that) and English *penknife*. Whether the nasal consonant in question is released orally or not is the crucial point in Japanese phonology.

7.3   The Japanese apply their /n̩/ instead of /n/ to English final /n/, because /n/ does not stand finally but /n̩/ does in Japanese. As the allophone of /n̩/ in a final position is not [n] but [ɣ̃], the Japanese tend to pronounce *pin, pen* like [piɣ̃, peɣ̃] (the preceding vowels are also slightly nasalized). The English word *pan*, when pronounced by a Japanese, sometimes sounds like French *pin*.

7.4   English speakers have difficulties of varying degrees in pronouncing Japanese /n̩/ correctly. The easiest cases are 2, 3, 4, 5, mentioned in 7.2, where as long as the nasal consonants are pronounced fairly long, the results would sound natural to the Japanese ear.

English speakers, however, tend to pronounce /-n̩n-/ and /-n̩m-/ not [nn] and [mm] but simply [n] and [m] as in *banner* and *summer*. They should be advised to double the [n] and [m] as in *pen name* and *dumb man*. There are minimum contrasts between /-n̩n-/ and /-n-/ and between /n̩m-/ and /-m-/ like the following:

{ /kan̩na/(plane, a carpenter's tool)
{ /kana/(kana-letter, Japanese syllabary)

{ /sono ban̩ni/(in that evening)
{ /sono bani/(at that spot)

{ /gan̩ma/(gamma)
{ /gama/(toad)

{ /kon̩morito/(thickly)
{ /komorito/(with a nurse)

7.5   In case 1, that is, when /n̩/ is final, English [n] or [ŋ] would do if it is pronounced lightly. But if [n] or [ŋ] is considerably long or released with a weak [ə], then the sound would be taken not as /n̩/ but as /nu/ or /ŋu/ by the Japanese.

7.6   In case 6 where /ŋ/ stands before /s/, the Japanese do not touch the tip of the tongue to the upper teeth or the gums. They do not use [n] but a kind of nasalized high central vowel. Yet the alveolar [n], if employed, will cause little ambiguity if speakers are warned not to insert a glide [ᵗ] between [n] and the following /s/. Thus the word *Honshu*(/hoŋsyu:/) (the main island of Japan) is pronounced by many Americans as [hantʃu:], which would possibly be taken for /haŋcyu:/(category). There are the following minimum contrasts between /s/ and /c/ in Japanese, and the special way of pronouncing [-ns-] and [-nʃ-] as [-nts-] and [-ntʃ-] make them quite confusing.

$\left\{ \begin{array}{l} \text{/keŋsi/[kei̯çi] (swordsman)} \\ \text{/keŋci/[keɲtçi] (viewpoint)} \end{array} \right.$

$\left\{ \begin{array}{l} \text{/toŋsu/[toi̯sɯ:] (tonnage)} \\ \text{/toŋcu/[tontsɯ:] (dots and dashes)} \end{array} \right.$

$\left\{ \begin{array}{l} \text{/kaŋsyo:/[kai̯ço:] (interference)} \\ \text{/kaŋcyo:/[kaɲtço:] (ebb tide)} \end{array} \right.$

$\left\{ \begin{array}{l} \text{/reŋsyu:/[ɖei̯çɯ:] (training)} \\ \text{/reŋcyu:/[ɖeɲtçɯ:] (party, company)} \end{array} \right.$

7.7   In cases 7, 8, 9, 10, that is, when /ŋ/ stands intervocalically or between a vowel and /h/ (except /hu/) or /y, w/, English speakers find great difficulties in pronouncing the correct sounds. If they use /n/ which will be suggested by the romanized spelling for the /ŋ/ in question (though /ŋ/ in these positions is sometimes spelled *n'* or *n-*), the results will be extremely puzzling to the Japanese. There are the following contrasts between /ŋ/ and /n/ in these positions:

/hiŋi/[çiĩi] (three syllables) (dignity)
/hini/[çiɲi] (two syllables) (into fire)

/keŋecu/[keẽetsɯ (four syllables) (inspection)
/kanecu/[kanetsɯ] (three syllables) (overheating)

/siŋai/[çiə̃ai] (four syllables) (intimacy)
/sinai/[çinai] (three syllables) (do not do)

Speakers should try to apply the proper nasalized vowels to the /ŋ/-phoneme in these positions.

8.1   Just as /ŋ/ is characterized by the retention of nasal resonance long enough to make it syllabic, so /q/ is characterized by the retention of occlusion or constriction in anticipation of the following voiceless plosive or fricative or affricate consonant phonemes. The retention is also characterized by noticeable laryngeal tension and is long enough to constitute a syllable by itself. The occurrence of /q/ is as follows. It appears only before voiceless consonants:

before /p/: /saqporo/[sapporo] (a city in Hokkaido), /suqpai/ [suippai] (sour).

before /t/: /kiqto/[kitto](certainly), /baqtarito/[battarʲito](with a thud).

before /k/: /roqka:/[dokka:] (locker), /seqken/[sekkey̌] (soap).

before /c/: /miqcu/[mʲttsui] (three), /iqci/[ittɕi] (agreement), /keqcyaku/[kettɕakui] (conclusion).

before /s/: /beqso:/[besso:] (villa), /keqsaku/[kessakui] (masterpiece), /giqsirito/[gʲiɕɕirʲito] (closely), /iqsyoni/[iɕɕoɲi] (together).

As the phonetic transcriptions above show, /q/'s before /p, t, k, c/ are actualized phonetically by unexploded long stops and /q/ before /s/ as a long [s] or [ɕ]. The phenomena are apparently like the double consonants in Italian. However, it should be noticed that the first unreleased members of the double consonants (which correspond to the phoneme /q/) are not only fairly long (i.e., syllabic) but also begin crescendo and end decrescendo and that there is a noticeable decrease in energy between the first member and the second.

/q/ rarely occurs finally as in interjections like /aq/(oh), /eq/(eh), where it is actualized by glottal stops or laryngeal tensions or contraction.

8.2   As there are no double consonants in English simple words, English speakers seem to have more or less difficulty in pronouncing /q/. Double consonant letters in English words do not represent actual double consonants but single ones, and speakers tend to drop /q/ in reading romanized spelling of Japanese which usually represent /q/ with the doubling of the following consonant letters. As is the case with /-nn-/ and /-nm-/ discussed in 7.4, they very often drop /q/'s in the words listed above. This would cause ambiguity or sometimes even misunderstanding. There are, in Japanese, the following minimum pairs of words with and without /q/'s:

/suqpai/ (four syllables) (sour).
/supai/ (three syllables) (spy).

/haqto/ (three syllables) (surprisedly).
/hato/ (two syllables) (pigeon).

/seqken̦/ (four syllables) (soap).
/seken̦/ (three syllables) (world).

/syuqcyo/ (four syllables) (business trip).
/syucyo/ (three syllables) (assertion).

/kaqsai/ (four syllables) (applause).
/kasai/ (three syllables) (fire).

TWO ANTHROPOLOGICAL STUDIES IN SPEECH

H. S. WISE, M.D.

Director, Norfolk City Health Department, Virginia

I. NAVAJO CONCEPTS OF ETIOLOGY AND THERAPEUTICS IN DYSPHEMIA AND OTHER DISORDERS OF SPEECH.[1]

INTRODUCTION

In his cultural setting, persuasive speech is of great importance to the tribal Navajo;[2] decision-making in the family, clan, and "outfit" is by absolute consensus.

> Navajo is an excessively literal language, little given to abstractions and to the fluidity of meaning that is so characteristic of English. . . . Most things can be expressed in Navajo with great exactness by manipulating the wide choice of stems in accord with the multitudinous alternatives offered by fusing prefixes and other separable elements in an almost unlimited number of ways.[3]

Under these circumstances of language, the "totally democratic" decision by "consensus of a committee of the whole" makes the manner and presentation of speech as important as its content. There is, therefore, great pressure on the individual to speak well, influence widely, and present problems in such a way that each member of the group can find the proposed solution acceptable. In this milieu, defects of speech become more important than they are to the less democratic "agreement by majority" Anglo groups.

Living on the Navajo Reservation for five years, in a medical setting, the writer noted that speech disorders do occur. However,

---

[1] As reported to the author during 1962 and 1963 by two Navajo medicine men (Hosteen Slinkey, an Eastern Navajo, as given in English, and Hosteen Bilagody, a Western Navajo, himself a stutterer, as translated to the author from Navajo by Mrs. Goldtooth, a trained interpreter).
At the time of this study, the author was Medical Officer in Charge of the Tuba City Indian Hospital, Division of Indian Health, U. S. Public Health Service, D. H. E. W., Tuba City, Arizona.

[2] Harry Hoijer, "Cultural Implications of Some Navajo Linguistic Categories," *Language in Culture and Society: A Reader in Linguistics and Anthropology*, Dell Hymes, ed. (New York: 1964), pp. 142-153.

[3] Clyde Kluckhohn and Dorothea Leighton, *The Navajo*, rev., Lucy H. Wales and Richard Kluckhohn (Garden City: Anchor Books, Doubleday and Co., 1962), p. 273.

exact statistics on incidence are not available since almost no non-Navajo becomes sufficiently acute to hear the nuances of the speech of the "Diné" nor do the efforts of the Navajo to speak English make evaluation of speech defects easy. Thus, school data is found to be inaccurate and almost non-existent; it is only recently (since W.W. II, in fact,)[4] that nearly universal school attendance has occurred. In consequence, for the speech pathologies, the epidemiological picture is very inadequate. The present data is for informational purposes only and does not represent, in any way, a definitive study of the speech problems of this generally multilingual ethnic group.

BACKGROUND

As a tribe, the Navajo is the largest (100,000+ members) and probably as pure, in bloodline, as any Indian group remaining in the mainland United States. It is situated on a desert and mountain reservation of 18,000,000 acres (equivalent in size to New Hampshire, Vermont, and Rhode Island) in three states—Arizona, New Mexico, and Utah—at elevations between 3,500 and 10,000 feet. Most of the land is severely eroded and almost non-productive;[5] some is individually owned but most is owned by the tribe. The sub-soil, on the other hand, contains a veritable treasure trove of wealth and is largely tribally-owned. Excluding those detribalized persons who have left the Reservation, the majority of the Navajo live and earn their living from this land. As a tribe they are divided, roughly, into three fairly equal groups: (1) a more anglicized Eastern segment, (2) a more traditionally Indian western segment, and (3) several small, southeastern hispanized splinter segments (the Ramah and Canyon-cito).[6]

Linguistically an Athabascan derivative, the tribal Navajo[7] is traditionally widely scattered, semi-nomadic, herd-dependent, matri-local, and clan-oriented. The individual's economic resources tend to be extremely limited, weather-dependent, and tribally—or federally—determined. His religion is animistic, witch- and ghost-ridden, yet has a sun-centered core concept. It has an organized and rich mythology, ritual, and art form which is less demanding of time or ethic than the surrounding pueblo and mountain tribal religions, yet has a

[4] Martin A. Link, ed., *Navajo, A Centcry of Progress, 1868-1968* (Window Rock, Arizona: K. C. Publications, in cooperation with the Navajo Tribe, 1968), pp. 82-83.

[5] Kluckhohn and Leighton, *op. cit.*, pp. 45-58, 68-71.

[6] *Ibid.*, pp. 36, 117.

[7] Ruth M. Underhill, *The Navajo* (Norman, Oklahoma: University of Oklahoma Press, 1956), pp. 3-16.

strong and satisfying hold on the people. In his religion all things are good *and* evil, not good *or* evil as in the Christian religion.[8]

The power structure of the Navajo is extremely dispersed, both historically[9] and currently. The type of control exercised varies with the situation involved,[10] i.e., by the medicine-man at a sing, the head-man at a community meeting, the councilman in government sessions, the elder in clan or "outfit" get-together, and the grandmother or uncle in a family or extended family discussion. Leadership is not, or ever has been, constant or hereditary, but rather is based on individual exercise of initiative, power, and personality which in turn is based primarily on the person's ability to convince and justify. Good speech, as with any democratic group, is of critical importance to upward escalation in status.

In the framework of his spoken language at least three forms of speech pathology are recognized by the Navajo. These are (1) dialectal difference, (2) tonal problems, and (3) dysphemia (stuttering). Others exist but were never clearly identified by the author's informants. To the Navajo, there is little causal relationship among these problems, nor are the means of cure identical. Unlike the Hopi, the Navajo has less certainty as to the causes of speech disorders, though in general, he believes they lie in personal impropriety and, more usually, in evil external influences. Of the disorders identified, however, only dysphemia has any real body of theory surrounding it.

DIALECTAL PROBLEMS

Since the language of the Navajo has no traditional written form[11] to help stabilize it, it has had a tendency to shift (migrate, undergo sound change).[12] Only the retarding factor of the "sing" and the necessity for maintaining the purity and accuracy of the "old way" have worked against an even more rapid change in its form and sound. In consequence, there have grown up a number of dialectal subgroups. While there is general understanding among the five major groups of Navajo, there is sufficient dialectal variation to make communication difficult on many occasions. In addition to the traditional changes which occur in any orally transmitted language, Navajo dialectal problems rest

---

[8] Kluckhohn and Leighton, *op. cit.*, pp. 176-252.

[9] L. R. Bailey, *The Long Walk, A History of the Navajo Wars, 1847-1868* (Los Angeles: Westernlore Press, 1964), pp. 108-109.

[10] Kluckhohn and Leighton, *op. cit.*, pp. 100-140.

[11] Linguists have created several written forms but it has never had wide acceptance among the Diné.

[12] Claude Merton Wise, *Applied Phonetics* (Englewood Cliffs, New Jersey: Prentice-Hall, Inc., 1957), pp. 146-168.

. . . in the fact that small phonetic differences . . . can not be bypassed. There is no leeway. In the language of the Sioux Indians there are also long vowels; one can, however, communicate quite effectively without rendering them very accurately. But there is nothing slouchy about Navaho. Sounds must be reproduced with pedantic neatness. . . . The language of The People is the most delicate known for phonetic dynamics.[13]

The talk of those who have learned Navaho as adults always has a flabby quality to the Navaho ear. They neglect a slight hesitation a fraction of a second before uttering the stem of the word. They move their lips and mouths too vigorously.[14]

Tone, stress, juncture, and time are phonemic, i.e., are "suprasegmental,"[15] and minute changes make major dialectal differences, thus making dialectal defects of speech easy. The only treatment used by the Navajo for this type of disorder appears to be shame and an attempt at teaching improvement by imitation.

TONAL PROBLEMS

Like Chinese, Navajo is a tonal language having four identified tonal types: 1) high, 2) low, 3) rising, and 4) falling.[16] Like Chinese, Navajo tones attach to the vowels. "Tones can be ignored in Chinese for the sake of stress. Not so in Navaho."[17] . . . "The only difference between 'azee' (medicine) and 'azéé' (month) is that the final long vowel of the latter has a high pitch, as indicated by the accent mark. The same thing is true for the difference between 'anaa' (war) and 'anáá' (eye)."[18] Minor changes in the use of tone completely alter meaning.

Otitis media and mastoiditis are common disease entities among the Navajo, with varying degrees of deafness as a common aftermath; tonal distortion often follows. Deafness in the Navajo produces a more seriously atypical speech than among the Anglo because of the tonal requirements of the language. Surprisingly, however, he does not seem to relate the cause of the problem with the linguistic effects. In consequence, the Navajo's methods of cure, by "sing" or by shaming, have no apparent relationship to the physiological causative condition.[19]

[13] Kluckhohn and Leighton, *op. cit.,* p. 258.
[14] *Ibid.,* p. 259.
[15] Archibald A. Hill, *Introduction to Linguistic Structures* (New York: Harcourt, Brace and Company, 1958), pp. 68-69.
[16] Kluckhohn and Leighton *op. cit.,* p. 257.
[17] *Ibid.,* p. 257.
[18] Kluckhohn and Leighton, *loc. cit.,* p. 257.
[19] Link, *op. cit.,* pp. 46-53.

Dysphemia

Stuttering, to the Navajo, has most of the same emotional overtones as it does with the Anglo; its cause is just as obscure. Unlike the white American, he has developed a technique for handling it which has been almost universally adopted by the Eastern Navajo, even by the non-stutterer in emotional situations, i.e., the voluntary stutter. On the other hand, the author was never able to obtain a word or group of words which specifically meant "to stutter" or "stuttering" that was subsequently understood by other Navajos with any consistency. Apparently the Navajo has "no name for it." He can, however, describe it with exquisite accuracy.

The identified cause for stuttering varies with the part of the Reservation in which the reason is sought. In general, "cause" falls into three categories: 1) embryonic injury, 2) "wrong doing," and 3) changes in handedness.

Embryonic injury is a cause which has two traditional and one modern explanation, depending on the person identifying the presumed reason for the disorder. Of these, the modern is much less specific than the more traditional ones: stuttering is caused by "something" which happens to the child because the mother "gets sick." When pursued, this cause nearly always evaporates into some indefinite item such as: "eating the wrong way," "falling off a horse," or "getting cold," etc. The traditional causes fall into two categories: 1) that which is due to an overt breaking of taboo, and 2) those that are due to the inadvertent breaking of taboos, or, due to an offense to a witch, ghost, or the "Holy People." When the types of taboo which seem to be involved in the production of stuttering are more specifically identified, they fall into two major groups: 1) those having to do with abnormal sexuality or incest, and 2) those having to do with the "forbidden things" like touching some lightning-struck item, killing a snake, or coming in contact with the mother-in-law.

Wrong doing, as a cause, involves the stutterer himself. In this explanation of cause, the individual actively breaks a taboo, offends a witch or ghost, or in some way displeases the "Holy People." The most common taboos broken seem to be in coming in contact with menstrual discharge or breaking some obscure form of the incest code.

The third, and by far the most common cause identified by the Navajo, particularly among the Western group, is related to handedness. As with most peoples, left-handedness is considered to be in someway damaging to the individual; as a result, there is considerable pressure on the family of a child to assure his right handedness. Among the Western Navajo (the more traditional tribal group) many things are done to assure right-handedness. During the first year of the child's life, much of his time is spent on a cradle-board. For the child's welfare a squirrel's tail may be placed over his head; however, more often a piece of turquoise is attached to the bail of the board by a piece of buckskin. To assure right-handedness, the left hand is bound to the side while the right is left free. When the child is let off of the cradle board, he is further induced to use his right hand. He is handed things to the right; he is held so that his right hand is free. He is encouraged to use his right and sometimes punished when he uses his left hand. Further, on entering the Indian School, it has been traditional for the teacher to enforce the use of the right hand. It is evident that the Navajo have observed an apparent relationship between left-handedness, change of handedness, and stuttering; they usually advance this as a major cause when asked.

Therapy, among the Navajo, in the main consists of two alternative methods: 1) "the sing," and 2) controlled stuttering, i.e., slow, repeated voicing of the initial syllable until speech can be continued. The "sing" is the more common of the two by the Western Navajo, while, in the experience of the author, the Eastern group, both stutterer and non-stutterer, tend to use controlled stuttering in speech situations which cause tension.

The "sing" is not always the same one. The type of "sing" depends on the assumed cause of the condition. When the cause is not known, the stutterer may be taken to a diagnostician, a "handshaker." There, after an appropriate ceremony, the shaker's advice is given and the indicated "sing" is undertaken. Since Navajo medicine has a heavy psychological component, many stutterers are apparently cured. Of the remainder, many learn to handle their stuttering with little tension. In consequence, stuttering is less often seen and more rarely recognized or "negatively re-enforced" among the Navajo than among a comparable number of Anglos, though on occasion a brutally direct and public form of "fun" is made of a dysphemic.

CONCLUSION

In speech disorders observed over a five year period by the writer, as discussed in English with one medicine-man and through an interpreter with another who was a stutterer as well, it was revealed that at least three types of speech problems are identified by the Navajo: dialectal, tonal, and dysphemic. In as exacting a language as Navajo, with the heavy necessity to convince which a general concensus demands, each person is forced to attempt perfection in speech. In cases where the individual cannot succeed, generalizations as to causes and methods of cure have been identified. Unlike the

Hopi, no exact or universal methods of cure have apparently been developed by the Navajo.

II. HOPI CONCEPTS OF ETIOLOGY AND THERAPEUTICS IN DYSPHONIA AND DYSPHEMIA.[20]

Neither aphonia nor stuttering, in the experience of the author, appears to be a common disorder among the Hopi; however, they do exist.[21] Exact statistics on incidence are not currently available, since the Hopi's confidence in the "Anglo" reporting an honest and accurate picture of Hopi cultural characteristics is extremely low. School data, likewise, is not available, since it is only recently that fairly universal school attendance has been obtained. In consequence, for the speech pathologies, the epidemiological picture is very inadequate. As is true for the first of these studies, the following presentation of data is for informational purposes only and does not represent, in any way, a definitive study of the speech problems of this often multilingual ethnic group.

BACKGROUND

As a tribe, the Hopi divide, roughly, into the "Modern" and the "Traditional" groups. The "Traditional" Hopi, i.e., "those who hold to the old ways and keep to the old religious beliefs," is a member of an inbred, pacifist, theocratic culture which is village-centered, agriculturally-based, and clan-oriented. His economic resources are extremely limited, weather-dependent, and community-determined. His religion is highly organized, extremely demanding, time consuming, and markedly satisfying as a social institution. It has a well developed art form which makes traditional demands for stability (in

---

[20] As reported by "Grandpa Charlie" through his daughter, Daisy Albert, to the author on April 2, 1966.

[21] Wendell Johnson, "The Indians Have No Word for It: Part I. Stuttering in Children," *Quarterly Journal of Speech,* Vol. 30, 1944, pp. 330-337; "Part II. Stuttering in Adults," Vol. 30, 1944, pp. 456-465. See also:

J. C. Snidecor, "Why the Indian Does Not Stutter," *Quarterly Journal of Speech,* Vol. 33, 1947 pp. 493-495.

Edwin Lemert, "Stuttering Among the Northern Pacific Coastal Indians," *Southwest Journal of Anthropology,* Vol. 8, 1952, pp. 429-441.

Edwin Lemert, "Some Indians Who Stutter," *Journal of Speech and Hearing Disorders,* Vol. 18, 1953, pp. 168-174.

J. L. Stewart, "The Problem of Stuttering in Certain North American Indian Societies," *Journal of Speech and Hearing Disorders,* Monograph Supplement 6, April, 1960.

Edwin Lemert. "Stuttering and Social Structure in Two Pacific Societies," *Journal of Speech and Hearing Disorders,* Vol. 27, 1962, p. 3.

dance, design, hairstyle, and dress) yet allows for great individuality of creativity (in song, gift, and drama). The religious belief is centered around an "Almighty Spirit" who may be represented by natural phenomena (sun, moon, etc.), who has intermediaries in the form of Kachinas who can be represented by certain humans (in appropriate dress and state of spiritual preparedness) and who can act for or translate His will. From this "all-encompassing spirit" comes the good which attaches itself to the worthy (i.e., good earth, rain, sun, growing things, etc.). Such good is represented in the stylized art form of the Kachina's costume, the woven belt, and the gift doll (the hand-carved and painted Kachina) which is given to the deserving child. Government is by the respected elders whose election is greatly influenced by religious status and kiva politics.

In such a theocratic, clan-based, kiva-centered, village-oriented, apartment-housed culture, physical aggression has had to be modified in order to preserve the manpower base for its very tenuous existence on an arid, high-altitude, short-seasoned, desert area. To protect itself against more aggressive ethnic groups, it has withdrawn into a defensive social unit, closely packed into multi-storied houses, ranged about irregular plazas, atop high mesas, surrounded by sheer cliffs, near everflowing springs. Surrounding these defensive villages are the farms, orchards, and flocks which are primarily dependent for water on the sub-surface seeps found in the arid valleys. The Hopi "dry farm" and traditionally maintain a two-year reserve of dried food. Their mode of aggression, within the village, is verbal; gossip and psychodrama are the two prominent means of social catharsis. Within the kiva, religious, cultural, and historical tribal education is carried out on a memory-based, verbal level. Education is divided by sex, men teaching male knowledge to boys and women educating the girls in the female arts. Religious precepts modify all knowledge. The folk tale, song-story, and song-poem are highly prized speech-art forms. Language, and the ability to manipulate language, particularly for the male, are of supreme importance in the hierarchical progress of a Hopi on the status ladder of his society.

At least two forms of speech pathology are recognized by the Hopi in the framework of his spoken language. Others may exist, but were never identified for this writer in his contact with the people over a six-year period. The forms recognized are: muteness and stuttering. Both, to the Traditional Hopi, have a common etiology but require quite divergent treatments. Causally, it is believed that the two disorders result from foetal influence. If a mother, with child in-utero, is exposed to a "silent one," whether human or animal, the foetus may be marked. After birth the marked child may be mute or, more likely, will stutter. Depending on which condition appears, one of two therapies is undertaken (with a high rate of success, it might be added).

DYSPHONIA

For the mute child the following treatment is applied. In Arizona, near Marble Canyon, on a mesa between Page and Moenkopi is a layer of copper-bearing rock which contains green, yellow, and brown pigments. A man, more commonly a Kachina, goes there to obtain green pigment (copper ore). He searches for a particularly hard form of this color-bearing rock. On returning to his village, he grinds it into a fine grained, mildly soluble powder. To this is added a small amount of liquid (water) and after appropriate religious preparation it is dropped beneath the tongue or down the throat of the speechless child. "Sometimes only a drop is needed and the child will speak." To all accounts, only small amounts of the liquid are ever used, for the cure rate is very high!

DYSPHEMIA

For the stuttering child, the cause[22] is the same—maternal exposure to a "silent one"—but the cure is quite different. When the mother notices that the child is beginning to stutter she obtains "sacred pollen" (corn pollen) and a "prayer feather" (the down feather of the American Eagle). After appropriate prayer and preparation, she takes the child to a Kachina; any Kachina apparently is satisfactory. With the child present, the pollen and the prayer feather are placed in the Kachina's hand. He takes the pollen and feather and with a "backward motion" (counter clockwise) rubs the pollen over his face three times. This completed, and with proper prayers, he takes the remainder of the pollen and the prayer feather out onto the mesa where it is placed as a message to the "Almighty." Thereafter, the stutterer's speech begins to improve and eventually he is able to speak fluently.

CONCLUSIONS

The efficacy of the two treatments is attested to by the Hopi. In children who had dysphonia or dysphemia and were treated, it appears to work. Certainly, the incidence of these defects is extremely low among the people of the villages. Why it works is hard to explain.

---

[22] Unlike the Navajo, the Hopi has apparently never equated stuttering with handedness.

To the devout, it is proof of the "Spirit's" power; to the skeptical, it falls into the realm of psychotherapy. Whatever the cause, or the means of cure, to the Hopi a satisfactory and functional explanation of etiology and therapeutics has been devised and an organized and successful procedure for meeting these socially unacceptable speech forms has been developed.

THE FOURTH OF JULY REVISITED

Bower Aly*

University of Oregon

The Spirit of '76

On July 4, 1793, John Quincy Adams, scion of the famous Massachusetts family, fulfilled his obligation as orator for the Town Authorities of Boston with an oration deemed by his hearers to be a veritable model of eloquence. In a burst of fervor, the orator exclaimed, "Americans! let us pause for a moment to consider the situation of our country at that eventful day when our national existence commenced."[1] In his exhortation Adams adopted the view held generally in 1793, and for a century thereafter, concerning the observance of the Fourth of July. Of all the holidays, saints' days, and days of celebration, none has been observed throughout the United States of America with more enthusiasm or with greater consistency than Independence Day. The Fourth of July, celebrating, somewhat incongruously, an event that occurred on July 2, 1776, thus tended to unite Americans and to provide them with the occasion for their most characteristic epideictic oratory.[2]

In the nineteenth century, who delivered the Fourth of July orations? Who heard them? What was said? What were the circumstances? The answers to these and comparable questions provide an avenue to understanding the development of nationhood in the United States and the uniting of her people.

In some degree the Fourth of July oratory doubtless became the conscious instrument of nation-makers. Ebullient oratory, extolling

*Bower Aly (Ph.D., Columbia University, 1941), Professor of Speech, The University of Oregon, is the author of *The Rhetoric of Alexander Hamilton* and other works. He wishes here to express his indebtedness to the Huntington Library, and to the State Historical Society of Missouri, for courtesies extended during the preparation of "The Fourth of July Revisited"; and to innumerable students who have contributed to his understanding of the history of American public address.

[1] James Spear Loring, *The Hundred Boston Orators Appointed by the Municipal Authorities and Other Public Bodies, from 1770 to 1852; Comprising Historical Gleanings, Illustrating the Principles and Progress of Our Republican Institutions* (Boston: John P. Jewett and Company, 1852), p. 233.

[2] Carl Becker, *The Declaration of Independence: A Study in the History of Political Ideas* (New York: Random House, 1942), p. 3. See also Howard H. Martin, "The Fourth of July Oration," *The Quarterly Journal of Speech,* XLIV (December, 1958), 393-401. See also Merle Curti, *The Roots of American Loyalty* (New York: Columbia University Press, 1946), pp. 136-141.

Americans and viewing with disdain the effete nations of Europe, could and did on occasion make the judicious grieve; but it also served to voice the pride and to build the confidence of popular audiences in their institutions and in their destiny. To praise the Americans in America was not more difficult than to praise the Athenians in Athens. The Missouri editor admonishing his fellow-citizens may thus have written more shrewdly than he knew when he complained that a Fourth of July "passed off rather more silently than might have been expected. . . . we should think that in a town like ours the public spirit would speak from the mouth of a tolerable sized cannon on the anniversary day of our country's independence."[3] Surely the Missouri editor would have applauded the sentiments expressed in Wisconsin when, since the Fourth of July fell on a Sunday, no provision was made for its celebration:

> It should be taught to our youth as a part of their duty to themselves and posterity, to keep alive the 'vestal fires' of liberty,—to revive [the] spark which burned so steadily and strongly in the days that tried men's souls,—and it is a solemn duty, by orations, by reading the declaration—by patriotic speeches and toasts—to vivify and refresh the memory of all, of the great event it commemorates.[4]

THE FESTIVITIES

During the nineteenth century, Independence Day—almost invariably referred to as "The Fourth of July"—occasioned celebration in cities, towns, and countryside. Someone, perhaps the local schoolmaster or some exceptionally favored youngster, read the Declaration of Independence. Normally an invited orator spoke at length to a great public gathering; additional speeches were often scheduled throughout the day. Frequently the festivities took place in a grove, and in the early days of the republic the orator might literally speak from a stump. The militia were sometimes in evidence; parades, with floats and banners, appeared in the towns; and firecrackers and cannon fire were not unknown. In the countryside the people gathered to consume quantities of food served at rude tables in "brush arbors"; in the towns and cities the celebrating patriots were more likely to resort to hotel or tavern. In either case, the toasts drunk in any available beverage were not likely to be perfunctory. The toasts of two sorts—regular (or announced) and voluntary (ostensibly on the spur of the moment) were sometimes in such number as to place in question the ability of the celebrants, after the thirteenth libation, to give

---

[3] *Missouri Register* [Boonville], July 9, 1844.
[4] *The Argus* [Madison, Wisconsin], July 10, 1849.

thoughtful attention to any speaker. The voluntary toasts varied from year to year and from place to place; but for a hundred years or more the regular toasts conformed so fully to type as to be predictable. They are exemplified by some of those offered at a foregathering of Americans in Montreal on July 4, 1811:

Our country—May she never doubt the fidelity of her absent sons in the hour of danger.

Patriots of '76—Your children best know your worth when bore down by overbearing spirits.

Sojourning Americans—May you all be ready at your country's call.

Brother Jonathan—May his great gun be loaded with true American principles, wadded with traitors, and pointed at the enemies of liberty. Yankee doodle.

* * *

Many in one (epluribus Unum) the motto of the United States.

The American Constitution—The greatest piece of human ingenuity, the safeguard of our union, and the shield of our liberty.

Our native country—May she have a speedy and amicable adjustment with all nations.

Yankee doodle—More powerful than the shouts of rams' horns, which brought down the walls of ancient Jericho.[5]

THE ORATIONS

For the most part the Fourth of July orations might well have taken their cue from the toasts. In varying degrees of sophistication, the orators expressed pride in the past, satisfaction in the present, and confidence in the future of their country. These expressions of pride, satisfaction, and confidence permeated American oratory when the United States was a loose alignment of commonwealths along the Atlantic seaboard; they continued to characterize Fourth of July speeches of the continental nation emerging into the twentieth century. Moreover, certain phrases recurred so consistently as to become well-nigh ritualistic. They were heard eventually in Springfield, Oregon, as they had been heard in Springfield, Massachusetts; and in the state of Washington as well as in Washington, D. C. The language, the rhythms, the prosody can be observed to vary in time and place, but the views expressed by John B. Henderson on July 4, 1847, will be found over and over again in the Fourth of July orations:

Though all former governments have fallen and yielded to the corroding influences of time, and shared the fate of all other human concerns, yet there are principles, firm as the unchangeable

[5] *Niles Weekly Register* [Baltimore, Maryland], October 12, 1811, p. 103.

rocks of Adamant, upon which the fabric of government will stand, until human affairs shall have ceased and Heaven's Messiah shall fill the throne of peace. Those principles are founded upon the equality of mankind, upon truth, reason and justice; and the government whose foundations rest upon these, and whose strength is dependent upon the free will of a virtuous people, will only fail when time shall grow hoary with age, and nature herself shall decay.[6]

IV

The Exceptions

Not all the Fourth of July orations conformed to the pattern. As sometimes happens the variant speeches may prove more interesting, if less instructive about the general practice, than those conforming to custom. The sober discourse that Henry James (the elder) delivered in Newport, Rhode Island, although patriotic enough in its Jamesian way, could hardly be confused with the fustian of the backwoods orator whose sublimest art consisted in twisting the British lion's tail and making the American eagle scream. In distinctive phrases Henry James expressed on that fateful Fourth of July following Abraham Lincoln's first inauguration and the firing on Fort Sumter the perturbations that he shared with many of his countrymen:

> No doubt many men, whose consciences have been drugged by our past political prosperity, do fancy some such inevitable destiny as this before us,—do fancy that we may become so besotted with the lust of gain as to permit the greatest rapacity on the part of our public servants, the most undisguised and persistent corruption on the part of our municipal and private agents, without forfeiting the Providential favor. From that sort of spread-eagle-ism I told my friend that I hoped we were now undergoing a timely and permanent deliverance.

* * *

> As Americans, we love our country, it is true, but not because it is *ours* simply; on the contrary, we are proud to belong to it, because it is the country of all mankind, because she opens her teeming lap to the exile of every land, and bares her hospitable breast to whatsoever wears the human form.

* * *

> For my part, if I thought that our rulers were going to betray in this agonizing hour the deathless interest confided to them,— if I thought that Mr. Lincoln and Mr. Seward were going at last to palter with the sublime instincts of peace and righteousness that elevated them to power and give them all their personal prestige, by making the least conceivable further concession to the obscene

6 *Democratic Banner* [Louisiana, Missouri], August 16, 1847.

demon of Slavery,—then I could joyfully see Mr. Lincoln and Mr. Seward scourged from the sacred eminence they defile, yea more, could joyfully see our boasted political house itself laid low in the dust forever, because in that case its stainless stars and stripes would have sunk from a banner of freemen into a dishonored badge of the most contemptible people on earth; a people that bartered away the fairest spiritual birthright any people ever yet were born to, for the foulest mess of material pottage ever concocted of shameless lust and triumphant fraud.[7]

The Fourth of July orations of Henry David Thoreau are likewise atypical. In his speech delivered at Framingham, Massachusetts, on July 4, 1854, Thoreau, endeavoring to demonstrate the superiority of private conscience over public law, reported his discovery: "I did not know at first what ailed me. At last it occurred to me that what I had lost was a country." Six years later, on July 4, 1860, he was called to North Elba, Ohio, to deliver an address commemorating "Old John Brown of Osawatomie." There he spoke not for John Brown's life, for the old man had been hanged on December 2, 1859, but for John Brown's character, his immortality.[8]

Surely no Fourth of July oration—at least during the nineteenth century—could have run more directly counter to the prevailing lines of discourse than that delivered in Rochester, New York, by Frederick Douglass, a slave escaped from bondage, a black man of unconquerable spirit, who told to his white audience the story as it was in 1852:

This Fourth July is *yours* not *mine*. *You* may rejoice, *I* must mourn. To drag a man in fetters into the grand illuminated temple of liberty, and call upon him to join you in joyous anthems, were inhuman mockery and sacrilegious irony.

* * *

What, to the American slave, is your 4th of July? I answer; a day that reveals to him, more than all other days in the year, the gross injustice and cruelty to which he is the constant victim.

* * *

Go where you may, search where you will, roam through all the monarchies and despotisms of the old world, travel through South

[7] Henry James, *The Social Significance of Our Institutions: An Oration Delivered by Request of the Citizens at Newport, R. I., July 4th 1861* (Boston: Ticknor and Fields, 1861), *passim.*

[8] Henry David Thoreau, "Slavery in Massachusetts," *A Yankee in Canada, with Anti-Slavery and Reform Papers* (Boston: Ticknor and Fields, 1866), pp. 97-116. See also "The Last Days of John Brown," as published in *The Liberator,* July 27, 1860, and in *Anti-Slavery and Reform Papers by Henry D. Thoreau, Selected and Edited by H. S. Salt* (London: Swan Sonnenschein & Co., 1890), pp. 82-90.

America, search out every abuse, and when you have found the
last, lay your facts by the side of the every day practices of this
nation, and you will say with me, that, for revolting barbarity
and shameless hypocrisy, America reigns without a rival.[9]

THE OCCASIONS

To suppose that the speeches of Henry James, Henry David
Thoreau, and Frederick Douglass truly represent Fourth of July
oratory would be delusive. They do not. Almost equally delusive
would be the supposition that the celebration of Independence Day
was given over entirely to the celebration of independence. The
expectation of throngs of citizens suggested to many enterprisers of
varying degrees of private interest and public spirit that the Fourth
of July could be a good day for events somewhat extraneous to commemorating the birth of the United States of America.

The Fourth of July thus became an occasion for laying cornerstones.
In 1795 Massachusetts combined the celebration of Independence
Day with the laying of the cornerstone of the State House on
Beacon Hill.[10] In 1815 the city of Baltimore found "the Fourth" a
convenient day for laying the cornerstone of a monument to George
Washington.[11] With such good precedent, the citizens of Missouri did
not hesitate to lay the cornerstone of the new University of Missouri
on July 4, 1840;[12] and six years later the citizens of Springfield,
Missouri, thought it well to lay the cornerstone of the Southwest Missouri High School on July Fourth.[13] The precedent established in 1795 and 1815 was further confirmed in Washington, D.C.,
on July 4, 1851, with the laying of the cornerstone of the enlargement
of the Capitol.[14]

Doubtless the expectation of good summer weather in an era when
auditoriums, if available at all, could hardly accommodate throngs
of citizens, suggested the expediency of holding great public events
out of doors on the Fourth of July. The Fourth thus became the
great gathering day, and not only for the laying of cornerstones. In
1817, the chief stockholders in a superb bridge "now erecting over
the Susquehannah river, at a place called *Rock Run*" met to observe
the work in progress and to celebrate the day with "an elegant

---

[9] Frederick Douglass, *Oration, Delivered in Corinthian Hall, Rochester,
by Frederick Douglass, July 5th, 1852* (Rochester: Lee, Mann & Co., 1852),
passim.
[10] Loring, *The Hundred Boston Orators*, p. 254.
[11] *Niles Weekly Register*, July 8, 1815, p. 329.
[12] *Columbia Herald* [Missouri], February 11, 1892.
[13] *The Advertiser* [Springfield, Missouri], August 8, 1846.
[14] *The Oregon Statesman*, August 12, 1851.

entertainment."[15] In the years to follow, great crowds gathered on "the Fourth" to witness the breaking of ground for the new Erie Canal;[16] the commencement of the Cumberland Road westward of the Ohio;[17] the opening of the Croton Aqueduct into New York City;[18] the breaking of ground for the new railroad out of St. Louis to the West;[19] and the opening of navigation between Lake Erie and the Great Hydraulic Canal at Niagara Falls.[20]

The passing years saw the Fourth of July employed as an occasion to denounce the British and their high-handed actions at sea;[21] to aid the ladies of the Methodist church,[22] to promote the building of a railroad and telegraph to San Francisco;[23] to celebrate at Marquette, Michigan, the completion of the St. Mary Canal;[24] to dedicate before 20,000 spectators, in New York, the equestrian statue of George Washington in Union Square;[25] to organize a pioneer society for all who had lived in Greene County, Missouri, since 1838;[26] and eventually, in 1892, to plead on behalf of a Woman Suffrage Club that women be given the same rights as those accorded to four million slaves.[27]

As the years passed, the Fourth of July seemed to become more and more available to causes or private concerns even less related to Independence Day than the laying of a cornerstone or the breaking of ground for a new railroad. Temperance societies, seeing the temptations present even on the very grounds provided for the Fourth of July celebration, found the time and place auspicious for temperance sermons.[28] Candidates for public office, from Sheriff to Congressman, endeavored if not to speak then at least to see and be seen. The great day tended to become tainted, in the opinion of some dedicated patriots, by party politics. In Philadelphia, on July 4, 1838, John J. McCahen thus employed the national birthday to attack

[15] *Niles Weekly Register,* July 19, 1817, p. 336.
[16] Martha Lamb, *History of the City of New York* (New York: A. S. Barnes & Company, 1877), II, p. 676.
[17] *Missouri Republican* [St. Louis], August 15, 1825.
[18] Lamb, *History of the City of New York,* II, p. 730.
[19] Walter B. Stevens, *Missouri—The Center State: 1821-1915* (Chicago: The S. J. Clarke Publishing Company, 1915), I, pp. 132-133.
[20] *New York Tribune,* July 7, 1857.
[21] "Political Portraits with Pen and Pencil . . . ," *Democratic Review,* IX (October, 1841), 388.
[22] *Missouri Register,* June 11, 1844.
[23] *Fulton Telegraph* [Missouri], July 27, 1849.
[24] *Report of the Pioneer and Historical Society of the State of Michigan* (Lansing: Thorp and Godfrey, 1886), VIII, p. 156.
[25] *Tri-Weekly Messenger* [Hannibal, Missouri], July 17, 1856.
[26] *Tri-Weekly Patriot* [Springfield, Missouri], June 15, 1867.
[27] *The Express* [Springfield, Missouri], July 22, 1892.
[28] *Oregon Argus* [Oregon City], July 4, 1857.

the "activities of the Federal Party."[29] In Augusta, Georgia, a year later, Elijah Anglin sought to celebrate the day with a partisan toast:

> Gen. Jackson—He has whipped the British, he has out Gen-eralled the French, he has choked down the Bank, and gutted nullification.[30]

Perhaps less partisan and certainly more acceptable, the Fourth of July and Grief Meeting held six years later in Springfield, Missouri, permitted the delivery of not one but two lengthy orations "especially descanting upon the virtues . . . of the Hero of Orleans who had recently died."[31] The celebration held on July 4, 1849, in Orange-burgh, South Carolina, at which secessionist toasts were offered, could hardly qualify as a commemoration of the spirit of 1776;[32] and in Charleston on the same day the toast offered by T. S. Blanding might well have been suspect:

> Sacred to the memory of Thomas Hart Benton, who, in a feeble attempt to injure our right arm, has been crushed by our Foote.[33]

Despite all the causes served by the Fourth of July, however, great numbers of Americans doubtless attended the celebrations for the same reason that prompted Fisher Ames in 1794 not only to go hear the oration but also, as he said, "to see the bustle of the Boston frolic."[34] Often, as inveterate participants could report, "A good time was had by all."

Yet not every one had a good time at all of the many thousands of observances. Sometimes, as with the magnificent celebration planned by the Pilot Grove and Pisgah Rangers for July 4, 1844, the rains descended and the floods came to abort all plans.[35] Sometimes un-toward accidents occurred on the Great Day, as at Geneva and Auburn, in 1835;[36] and at Portsmouth, New Hampshire, in 1840, when a large pavilion erected in the form of an amphitheatre gave way and came tumbling down with a horrible crash, so that nearly a thousand persons were thrown to the ground amid "screams of

---

[29] The Southern Missouri Advocate [Jackson], September 1, 1838.
[30] Jeffersonian Republican [Jefferson City, Missouri], August 3, 1839.
[31] The Advertiser, July 5, 1845.
[32] Jefferson Inquirer [Jefferson City, Missouri], August 11, 1849.
[33] Fulton Telegraph, July 27, 1849.
[34] Seth Ames, ed., Works of Fisher Ames with a Selection From His Speeches and Correspondence (Boston: Little, Brown and Company, 1854), I, p. 146.
[35] Missouri Register, June 11, 1844; July 9, 1844.
[36] Jeffersonian Republican, August 15, 1835.

affright, and . . . groans of pain."[37] Even when no untoward event occurred, the day was sometimes solemn, as it may well have been at Old Fort Schuyler, when on July 4, 1796, General Philip Schuyler chose to announce his retirement:

> The last sands of my political life, as one of your representatives, are nearly run out; but whilst I continue in that honourable station, be assured that my best abilities will be exerted to promote the interest and happiness of the community at large, and that of my Fellow-Citizens of the Western Counties in particular; by whose industry a howling wilderness is reducing to smiling and fertile fields."[38]

Thirty years later both John Adams and Thomas Jefferson, with a felicity that did not go unobserved, died on Independence Day and thus gave themselves and the anniversary a certain unanticipated dignity.[39] The observances of the Fourth before, during, and after the Civil War often proved to be sobering and sometimes sombre. In Detroit, on Independence day, 1857, a fight occurred in which Deputy Sheriff Small was fatally injured.[40] In 1861, Captain Howell of the Canton Guards was shot and the troops were called out.[41] On the same day Ex-Senator Green, after reading the Declaration of Independence, was pursued and captured by Col. Palmer's troops.[42] Two years later the Fourth of July address delivered by Brigadier General Bartholow inveighed against the rebels and their sympathizers.[43] In 1866, the Civil War having been concluded, General John A. Logan, delivering the Fourth of July oration at Salem, Illinois, asserted that Independence Day belongs to loyal men and not to traitors, who have no civil rights except those specifically granted to them by the victors;[44] and at Hibernia, Missouri, in 1868, the people announced a Fourth of July meeting to raise funds for the widows and orphans of the Confederate dead.[45]

THE HEARERS

In Pontiac, Michigan, on the Fourth of July, 1854, Mrs. T. J. Drake declared, "Everybody has gone to the grove to hear the

[37] *Niles National Register* [Baltimore, Maryland], July 18, 1840, p. 307.
[38] *The Minerva, & Mercantile Evening Advertiser* [New York], July 30, 1796.
[39] *Tri-Weekly Messenger*, August 28, 1856. See also Lawton T. Hemans, *Life and Times of Stevens Thomas Mason—The Boy Governor of Michigan* (Lansing, Michigan Historical Commission, 1920), p. 31.
[40] *New York Tribune*, July 7, 1857.
[41] *Weekly Missouri Democrat* [St. Louis], July 16, 1861.
[42] *The Liberty Tribune* [Missouri], July 26, 1861.
[43] *The Macon Gazette* [Missouri], July 26, 1863.
[44] *The Loyal Missourian* [California], July 12, 1866.
[45] *The People's Tribune* [Jefferson City, Missouri], June 17, 1868.

speeches."[46] Her assertion could stand with but slight modification for innumerable communities throughout the United States for more than a hundred years. The audiences for the speeches on the Fourth of July included, as some of the old folks could say with slight exaggeration, "Everybody who *is* anybody."

Even in sparsely settled areas, the audiences often numbered thousands of persons, eager for sociability, amusement, and speechmaking of the kind that came to be expected on July Fourth. In days when men and women walked, rode horseback, or came in horse and buggy, the pioneers traveled from miles around on the Fourth of July to watch Adam Cobb walk to and fro on the platform, flourish his bandanna, and occasionally weep, as he gave his famous oration. Happily a text of his speech has been preserved; and inasmuch as some understanding of the hearers can be developed from a knowledge of the speeches they enjoyed, a portion of the text of Adam Cobb's oration is reproduced:

> I appear before you, at this time, in behalf of our beloved Washington and our forefathers. I have come to speak their praises, for it was them that bore the *brunt* of our sorrows and made us a free and a happy people.
>
> Yes, my friends and enemies, it was my forefathers and anchestors as well as yours that fit with our beloved Washington when he whipped the great battle of the cow pens in the State of old North Carolina. When the Red Jackets came to beguile us from our homes, besides the Red Man of our native land. Our forefathers and our *anchestors* had to work their *craps* the best they could, with the rifle in one hand and the Brazin seikle in the other, and the hot briling sun shining down on their backs.
>
> But our glorious, beloved Washington is no more, for he is buried way down on old Faginia shore. Whar the willows wave over his grave, and we see him no more, for he is buried way down on old *Faginia* shore, where the willows wave over his grave, and we see him no more. So *Sweet-Li* let him Lye, and sleep for ever more.[47]

Presumably the Wisconsin pioneers never heard Adam Cobb's oration; but Mrs. Gratiot's description of a Fourth of July audience in the early settlement of Wisconsin suggests that he might have been well received:

> The first insight I had in border society was at the Fourth of July celebration, of the same year. . . . Several very polished persons, of course, were present; but it was the contrast that made

[46] Letter, Mrs. T. J. Drake to Eddie Smith, Michigan Pioneer and Historical Society, *Historical Collections* (Lansing: Wynkoop Hallenbeck Crawford Company, 1907), p. 676.

[47] William S. Bryan and Robert Rose, *A History of the Pioneer Families of Missouri* . . . (St. Louis: Bryan, Brand & Company, 1876), p. 512, *et seq.*

it original: Capt. Comstock, Maj. Farnsworth, Dr. Newhall, Capt. Hardy, Mr. Meeker and others. Col. Strode delivered the oration. But of miners with uncut hair, red flannel shirts, and heavy boots drawn over their pants, there was a great number, all eager to dance and enjoy themselves to the worth of their money; but I must say to their praise, that they all behaved like gentlemen. The ladies were few.[48]

In 1825, in the new Marion County, Missouri, an estimated 500 persons assembled "'with all that enthusiasm which the remembrance of our birth-day as a nation so justly inspires" to hear the reading of the Declaration of Independence and the delivery of an oration.[49] On the same day in Licking Summit, Ohio, eight to ten thousand spectators heard "with universal satisfaction" an oration pronounced by Thomas Ewing, Esq.[50] At Springfield, Illinois, the "young men's convention and old soldier's meeting" held on July 4, 1840, attracted 5,000 delegates and 5,000 spectators.[51] On the same day at the Buttonwoods, Rhode Island, 10,000 people met for the Harrison celebration in conjunction with the Fourth;[52] at Concord, Massachusetts, 6,000 delegates attended a similar meeting;[53] and at Salisbury, North Carolina, 12,000 persons assembled in "the most immense crowd of people that ever was congregated in North Carolina."[54]

On July 4, 1851, 500 people met in Marysville, Oregon Territory, to celebrate the Fourth, with an appropriate anthem, a national prayer, the reading of the Declaration of Independence, an oration, a dinner, and numerous toasts.[55] On July 4, 1859, a crowd estimated at 4,500 people met at Syracuse, Missouri, in circumstances described in the following account:

> . . . by noon, the place seemed to be one living, moving mass of human beings, composed of old, young, middle aged,—grave and venerable sires and matrons, the young men, rigged out in their Sunday best—the handsome young ladies, *spreading* themselves, (we mean their hoops) arrayed in gaudy attire, their smiling and lovely faces beaming with pleasurable emotions—the young juveniles, intent upon the full enjoyment of the great day, with rosy cheeks and curly hair—and lastly a host of Africa's sable race, all looking sleek and happy; making up such a mass of human beings as is seldom seen on occasions of the kind, in country towns.[56]

[48] Ellis Baker Usher, *Wisconsin: Its Story and Biography 1848-1913* (Chicago: The Lewis Publishing Company, 1914), I, p. 42.
[49] *Missouri Republican*, July 18, 1825.
[50] *Independent Patriot* [Jackson, Missouri], August 13, 1825.
[51] *Niles National Register*, July 18, 1840, p. 309.
[52] *Ibid.*, July 18, 1840, p. 307.
[53] *Ibid.*
[54] *Ibid.*, August 1, 1840, p. 345.
[55] *The Oregon Statesman*, July 22, 1851.
[56] *California News* [Missouri], July 9, 1859.

The responsibility for celebrating the anniversary was normally placed with a committee whose members exerted themselves to accommodate different types of hearers. During the celebration held at Lucas Spring in St. Louis, Missouri, on July 4, 1819, the principal chiefs of the Osage Indians were in evidence, as was a "native American eagle in full life."[57] At Danby, Michigan, a generation later, whites and Indians joined in a celebration at which short addresses delivered by speakers of both races were interpreted for mutual edification.[58] At Atoka, Indian Territory, on July 4, 1875, some 3,000 Indians celebrated the anniversary for the first time. They heard, among others, their Chief, who spoke in the Choctaw language.[59]

A year later, at the centennial of American independence, Carl Schurz, the eminent Missouri statesman of German birth, spoke in Lafayette Park to a huge audience of Germans who throughout the day had celebrated the centennial with a procession that included marching bands, household illuminations, a liberal display of flags, banners, union lanterns, the bursting of rockets, and the glare of thousands of torches.[60]

Usually the audiences gathered for the Fourth of July could expect a meeting on dry land, a speech by a man to whom women were permitted to listen, and a season of merriment unclouded by sorrow. Anticipating the occasion at Carterville, Illinois, James A. Washburn described the circumstances, composition, and mood of a fairly typical Fourth of July audience:

> Our folks are preparing to celebrate the 4th hugely. At Marion "the old folks" have a big meeting, and at Carterville they propose to have an ebullition of Patriotism and spread Eagle Oratory, and possibly of beer and ice-cold lemonade with a spike in it— accompanied by a regular "Hoe down" or Barn-dance. They make things lively on the glorious Fourth, those Cartervillians do—even if it requires a regular "Knock-down" and Drag-out or so.[61]

Sometimes unexpected events intervened to defeat expectations and thus to create an unusual audience or unusual conditions. In 1875, General Sherman, in a party that included members of his staff as well as dignitaries from Iowa, Illinois, and Missouri, denied the force of custom. The party celebrated the Fourth not on dry land but

[57] *Missouri Gazette and Public Advertiser* [St. Louis], July 7, 1819.
[58] *Report of the Pioneer Society of the State of Michigan* (Lansing: W. S. George & Company, 1883), IV, p. 32.
[59] *The Advertiser* [Boonville, Missouri], July 9, 1875.
[60] *St. Louis Globe-Democrat,* July 4, 1876.
[61] Letter, James M. Washburn to S. A. Lancaster, June 11, 1882 (Private Collection).

aboard the excursion steamer *J. H. Johnson* on the Mississippi River
near Quincy, Illinois, and heard a speech in which General Sherman
complimented the young men of Iowa, Illinois, and Missouri.[62]

In Augusta, Maine, on July 4, 1834, Miss Green turned the world
upside down when she did the speaking to an audience including men
who were permitted to listen—and cheer:

> If I shall have been so happy as to gain the approbation of
> those for whose sake I have so far departed from the strict limit
> which ancient prejudices have too long prescribed to our sex, I
> shall be amply repaid for all the sneers of whitlings and fools.
> [Cheers] I have been only desirous of winning the approving
> smile of the nobler sex for my sentiments, not for myself. And I
> say unto you, lords of creation, as you call yourselves, if you doubt
> my sincerity, I proclaim it here in the face of all Augusta, now
> assembled around me, and you may believe me or not as you
> please—but there is not one among you, Tom, Dick, or Harry, that
> I would give a brass thimble to call 'husband,' tomorrow.[63]

On July 4, 1881, many Americans who had expected to celebrate a
day of joy were subdued to learn that on July 2 Charles J. Guiteau had
shot their President, James A. Garfield. When Samuel Odell in his
Fourth of July oration, paid tribute

> to the President and his dear, despairing wife, his aged mother and
> the loving kiss she gave to her beloved son on the 4th of March
> last, it was easy to see how earnestly the speaker felt what he was
> saying, and the tears that filled the eyes of young and old told
> how sincerely the vast audience felt and appreciated the dreadful
> calamity that now hangs over our republic.[64]

The 30,000 people gathered in Richmond, Virginia, in 1896, formed
an audience with little reason for the usual merriment. They listened
to General Stephen D. Lee deliver a eulogy on Jefferson Davis, late
President of the Confederacy;[65] and some of them heard General John
B. Gordon, addressing the United Confederate Veterans in their National Encampment, praise the state of Virginia and its people.[66]

THE CRITICISM

As Wichelns observed in 1925, "Histories of criticism, in whole or
in part, we now have, and histories of orators. But that section of the

---

[62] *The Canton Press* [Missouri], July 10, 1875.
[63] *Jefferson Republican*, August 30, 1834.
[64] *Springfield Express*, July 8, 1881.
[65] *Lexington Intelligencer* [Missouri], July 11, 1896.
[66] *Ibid.*

history of criticism which deals with judging of orators is still un-written."[67]

In 1969, the history of the criticism of oratory remains unwritten. Even so, the annalists and some of the newspapers of the nineteenth century took oratory seriously and endeavored to pass judgment on it. If the judgments disclosed an imperfect knowledge of rhetoric and a limited range of concepts, they nevertheless formed a body of folk-criticism revealing, as criticism so often does, as much of the prejudices of the critic as of the abilities of the criticized.

The popular critics of oratory tended to deal with delivery rather than with invention, except as the orator was observed to inculcate principles of morality. Although notable exceptions can be found, the folk-criticism tended toward generalized praise, particularly for moralistic or patriotic themes, rather than caustic comment. The critic of O. H. Travers' oration thus observed that it was "in all its essentials of the high character, and such as should be impressed upon the minds of the youth of the present age."[68] The oration of Prof. D. DeMott Woodmansee was "spoken of by those who heard it, and are compe-tent to judge, as an effort worthy of a scholar, a deep thinker, and a true orator."[69] On one anniversary Champ Clark was expected to "jerk tail feathers from the American eagle;"[70] but on another he de-livered to the Law Class of the University of Missouri an address stressing that young lawyers should not feel that they must be atheists to be successful.[71]

In an age that did not know microphones and yet sometimes re-quired the voice of the orator to compete with the wails of children and the barking of dogs, not to mention occasional outbursts from convivial cronies on the outskirts of a crowd, the most elementary of critiques—"I could hear every word"—might represent a triumph not lightly to be regarded. Even some practiced orators did not always attain it. When Dr. Pope Yeaman delivered a Fourth of July oration in 1892, he succeeded with a good-natured audience, even though one scrap occurred "and the police gathered in the combatants."[72] But when Dr. Yeaman spoke four years later, the hum of conversation was so loud that it finally forced him to stop speaking.[73] Even though

[67] "The Literary Criticism of Oratory," *Studies in Rhetoric and Public Speaking in Honor of James Albert Winans by Pupils and Colleagues* (New York: The Century Co., 1925), p. 181.
[68] *Springfield Express*, July 8, 1881.
[69] *The Press* [Carthage, Missouri], August 24, 1882.
[70] *Missouri Statesman* [Columbia], July 1, 1898.
[71] *The Paris Mercury* [Missouri], June 12, 1896.
[72] *The Brookfield Gazette* [Missouri], July 8, 1896.
[73] *The Paris Mercury*, July 10, 1896.

the oration delivered by Hon. W. W. Thayer on July 4, 1892, was adjudged to be a brilliant effort, "which contained a large amount of deeply interesting food for thought for all," great dissatisfaction was expressed "because the greater part of the audience was unable to hear it."[74]

The folk critic was much concerned with diction, voice, and delivery generally. Of Dr. Pope Yeaman one critic observed that his

words are each distinctly uttered, dropping from his lips like coins from the mint. His sentences are polished and rounded and full of thought. . . . It was thought by some that he approached perilously close to politics in certain parts of his speech, but as he left his hearers to make their own applications of the doctrine he preached on that occasion, each political party may apply the remarks to the other and no harm done.[75]

However, not every critic concerned himself exclusively with diction. For example, one country editor reported of a speaker (referred to as "colored") that

He raised himself above prejudice and above malice. Indeed, his speech was remarkable, and shows that Mr. Tandy has a well balanced head, a fine education, an excellent character and a pure heart.

Concerning a second speaker the editor opined that he "is not as pleasant a speaker as Tandy but a closer and better reasoner."[76]

The editor-critic of *The Oregon Oracle* found the oration of G. M. Miller to be not of the usual "spread eagle" style but one full of facts and practical suggestions.[77] The flamboyance that came to be expected of the Fourth of July orator appears to have been both enjoyed and deprecated. It could hardly have persisted without approval of some sort; yet deprecatory references to the "spread-eagle" style abound. One account has it that "the 'Eagle was spread' by so many orators (?) the 4th, that his birdship is as flat as a leather apron, and it will take him the rest of the season to organize himself into a rounded form again."[78]

Apparently fervent speeches for the Fourth of July were less objectionable prior to the Civil War. The oration delivered by John L. Blair at Madison, Wisconsin, on July 4, 1850, was adjudged to be "a beautiful and spirited composition, creditable alike to the head and heart of the author, and was listened to with intense interest by an

[74] *Corvallis Gazette* [Oregon], July 8, 1892.
[75] *The Brookfield Gazette,* July 8, 1892.
[76] *North Mo. Herald* [Huntsville], July 6, 1870.
[77] *The Oregon Oracle* [Philomath], July 9, 1885.
[78] *The National* [Memphis, Missouri], July 9, 1885.

immense audience."[79] At the Fourth of July celebration in Madison nine years later the

> oration was attentively listened to, and abounded with apt references to the history of the day and congratulatory allusions to the comparatively prosperous condition of the country. It was delivered in the forcible and attractive style that characterizes Hon. Arthur McArthur's oratory.[80]

For comprehensive criticism of Fourth of July oratory one must turn to *The Hundred Boston Orators,* a volume published before the Civil War. Unavoidably parochial, admittedly not without error, and couched in the phrases of another day, the work of James Spear Loring nevertheless takes oratory seriously. It provides texts and criticism of Fourth of July orations delivered in Boston from 1783 to 1851, together with an account of the orator and the occasion. The judgments rendered reveal a respect for oratory as a form of intelligence engaged in the expression and the forming of opinion.[81]

Although a noteworthy earlier work, perhaps by William Cullen Bryant, is not limited to Fourth of July speeches, it does formulate views applicable to their criticism. Some of these views are colored by an optimism to which a present-day critic of oratory might not subscribe:

> However people may be captivated with prettily turned speeches and holyday orations, and delight in the play they give to the fancy and taste, they will not be led by them to responsible action on important emergencies. There is an instinct, as it were, among the ignorant and vulgar, as well as those of better taste and sounder judgment, which prevents them from being imposed upon by these superficial and heartless speech makers. There is an earnestness and naturalness of manner in all those who speak from feeling and from just views of their subject, and who themselves participate in the passions they would communicate, which cannot to be put on. Such persons rarely fail to find forcible, if not elegant expressions, and to arrest the attention and influence the minds of their hearers. It is such oratory we wish to see encouraged in this country, and such only we believe is likely to succeed.[82]

The Apogee

On July 4, 1917, the Fourth of July and its observance came full circle; for on that memorable day, in London, by order of King George

[79] *The Argus* [Madison, Wisconsin], July 9, 1850.
[80] *The Daily Wisconsin Patriot* [Madison], July 5, 1859.
[81] Loring, *op. cit.*
[82] "Modern Oratory: A Review of *The Speeches of Charles Phillips, Esquire . . .* , *The North American Review,* VII (July, 1818), 225.

V, the British joined unreservedly in the celebration of the 141st anniversary of American independence. The Stars and Stripes flew from the Victoria Tower of the Houses of Parliament. The Welsh Guards played American airs at the Palace of St. James. Distinguished Englishmen, including the Rt. Hon. Arthur James Balfour, the British Foreign Secretary, attended the reception held by Walter Hines Page, the American Ambassador, in observance of the Great Day, and both the Ambassador and the Secretary made Fourth of July speeches. Ambassador Page said,

> This kingdom is the stedfast friend of freedom. In the celebration of this birthday we therefore dedicate ourselves not only to our own ideals but likewise to the additional task of strengthening our close friendship with this other great branch of the English-speaking world.

To this speech, Secretary Balfour replied:

> Are we not bound together for ever? Will not our descendants, when they come to look back upon this unique episode in the history of the world, say that among the incalculable circumstances which it produces the most beneficent and the most permanent is, perhaps, that we are brought together and united for one common purpose in one common understanding—the two great branches of the English-speaking race?[83]

Perhaps the Englishman and the American alike were bearing witness to the prescience of Otto von Bismarck, who—it is said—on being asked, "What is the most important fact for the twentieth century?" replied, "That North America speaks the English language."

On July 4, 1917, the Fourth of July may be said to have reached its apogee. Thereafter the Americans, as they became perhaps more sophisticated and certainly more urban in their civilization and its accompanying commitments, tended less and less to observe the Fourth of July at all; or if they observed it to do so not with the reading of the Declaration of Independence, which had become to many of them an antique relic of the long ago, nor with speeches in praise of their forebears and in recollection of their nationhood, but in frolics at the beaches or other playgrounds. It seemed that as the Americans became more and more involved in saving the world, they tended to become less and less appreciative of their own heritage and consequently, as they thought, had less need to be reminded of it. In gaining the world perhaps the Americans, like Henry David Thoreau, lost a country.

[83] *The Fourth of July in London* (London: Darling & Son, Ltd., 1917), *passim*.

RHETORIC AND POETIC IN MIMETIC DRAMA

HUBERT C. HEFFNER
Indiana University

Since drama is the rendering of an action by the agents of that action, as characters, actually doing the deeds and saying the sayings of which the action is composed, it includes events that happen to those characters, deeds done upon one another, changes occurring within individual characters, and the interactions of agents—their psychological responses one to another and to deeds done upon them. In such a construction characters, like all men in life, 'attempt to discuss statements and to maintain them, to defend themselves and to attack others'; in other words, they employ rhetoric in its basic sense. Rhetoric as it appears in drama is, as we must constantly bear in mind, only an analogous kind of rhetoric for a number of reasons. Rhetoric is the art of observing and using all of the available means of persuasion in order to influence or obtain conviction in an audience. Rhetoric is the art of public speaking and, as W. Rhys Roberts observes, "public speaking" is in many instances a better translation of the Greek word *rhetorica* than is the term rhetoric.[1] In drama, however, the act of persuasion is more often exercised upon one or a few individuals rather than upon an audience. Yet Clytemnestra's speech to the Chorus, after she has murdered Agamemnon, is an example of forensic oratory; and Antony's speech at the burial of Caesar is an excellent piece of political oratory. Rhetoric employs all of the available means of persuasion but is at its best when it relies largely upon the enthymeme, whatever its mode of persuasion may be. Rhetoric in drama, by contrast, is usually most dramatically effective when it relies upon feelings, emotions and passions, either as its genesis or its end. Further differences will appear as we advance our discussion of "Rhetoric in Mimetic Drama"; yet with these differences rightly understood, I believe it will become apparent through such an examination as I propose that rhetoric and poetic are complementary arts and that the critic who wishes fully to employ the instruments of poetics must also be a student of rhetoric.

For purposes of clarity I must now define these terms as I shall be using them. Rhetoric, as I have stated, is the art of discovering and using all of the available means of persuasion in order to influence or

---

[1] W. Rhys Roberts, *Greek Rhetoric and Literary Criticism* (New York: Longmans, Green and Co., 1928), pp. 22-23.

convince an audience. Its end is an action or a doing, though the action may be merely a change in men's opinions or it may be the incitement of a mob to violence and destruction. Rhetoric is then a practical art, as are politics and ethics. It therefore has its own principles and systems. Poetic, conversely, is a productive art, a constructive art, whose end is the formulation—the making—of an object. The tangible object which is the end of poetic art may be as humble and substantial as a loaf of bread or it may be as exalted and complex as a tragedy by Aeschylus or an epic by Homer. Poetics as the art of making is primarily concerned with formulation and hence with form. It is the form—that is, the way in which it is formulated—that gives the tangible object its peculiar powers or effects and serves to differentiate it from the many other objects of its kind. Every made thing has powers or effects. In the useful arts we designate these in terms of utility; in fine arts we designate them in terms of beauty. Both the useful art object and the fine art object differ from natural objects in their genesis. Art objects are artificial, requiring the artifice of a maker for their coming to be. Natural objects have with themselves their own power of generation and decay. The acorn genetically contains and generates the oak tree of the same species of which the acorn itself was generated by natural process. No picture or poem ever directly produced seeds in the same manner from which additional pictures and poems grew naturally. Art and nature are therefore different and an art object cannot be rightly judged as a natural object. But useful art objects, fine art objects, and natural objects can in theory be confused and analogized to each other. Plato, placing the likeness of things as primary in his philosophical quest for oneness, or unity, made just such an analogy; hence to him the final test of an object of art was not its beauty but its contribution to the goodness of the citizen and the welfare of the state. To him art was an instrument and its test was utility, its efficacious influence upon conduct. Thus the Platonists and their numerous descendants refuse to make a differentiation between poetic and rhetoric. They would add to Aristotle's famous definition of tragedy some such final clause as the following: "A tragedy, then, is the imitation of an action that is serious and also, as having magnitude, complete in itself; in language with pleasurable accessories, each kind brought in separately in the parts of the work; in a dramatic, not in a narrative form; with incidents arousing pity and fear, wherewith to accomplish its catharsis" *for the betterment of the citizen and the improvement of the state.*[2]

[2] I owe this distinction and the phrase added to Aristotle's famous definition to the late Dr. Ronald S. Crane. See also his *The Language of Criticism and the Structure of Poetry* (Toronto: University of Toronto Press, 1953), especially pp. 80ff.

In passing, let us note that the Platonist would have to drop out of that definition the phrase "complete in itself," for the completion, as in other types of rhetoric, must occur in the audience. As is well known, the Renaissance critics, failing to understand the Aristotelean idea of catharis, revived an instrumentalist conception of poetry. They turned back to Horace's famous statement: "The poet's aim is either to profit or to please, or to blend in one the delightful and the useful." With varying degrees of emphasis and interpretation, they made the ends of art delight and instruction, or as Dryden puts it, delightful instruction.[3] Such a conception of the ends, aims, or functions of art tends to make all art dominantly didactic, rather than strictly mimetic. To the extent that didacticism dominates the construction of an art object, to that same extent rhetoric rather than poetic becomes the source of its principles of formulation. From the seventeenth century to the present day the making of works of art and the theorizing about art have fallen increasingly in the domain of the rhetorician. But even a Soviet "agitprop" or a Bertholt Brecht imitation thereof, in so far as they are dramatic, have their mimetic elements despite the subordination of these to rhetorical principles.

To prevent misundertsanding I digress to say that I am not arguing that didactic poetry must of necessity be inferior poetry. Dante's *Divina Commedia* is a great didactic poem; so is Spencer's *The Faerie Queen*. Even a mimetic drama may be interpreted and staged didactically. *Hamlet* has twice been produced in Moscow as a purely Marxian document and I need not remind the reader that a host of modern critics have followed Ernest Jones in interpreting that great play as a Freudian exemplum.[4] I still do not believe, despite these instances, that Shakespeare read Karl Marx or was a disciple of Sigmund Freud. As Sam Smiley has well shown in his excellent study of the American

---

[3] Dryden's exact statement from *Of Dramatic Poesy; An Essay,* spoken by Lisideius, is as follows: *"A just and lively image of human nature, representing its passions and humours, and the changes of fortune to which it is subject, for the delight and instruction of mankind."* Lisideius had been asked by Eugenius to give a definition of a play to guide their discussion of dramatic poesy. The same end or function of poetry and especially drama appears in various other critical essays by Dryden. See John Dryden, *Of Dramatic Poesy and Other Critical Essays,* 2 vols., ed. with an Introduction by George Watson (London: J. M. Dent and Sons, Ltd.; New York: E. P. Dutton and Co., Inc., 1962), I, 25.

[4] The Freudian interpreters of Shakespeare's plays are far too numerous to mention individually. For a yearly account of these see "The Year's Contributions to Shakespearian Study" appearing annually in *Shakespeare Survey,* published by the Cambridge University Press. Freudian interpretations are by no means limited to Shakespeare's play; see, for example, Maud Bodkin, *Archetypal Patterns in Poetry* (London and New York: Oxford University Press, 1963) and Francis Ferguson, *The Idea of Theatre* (Princeton: Princeton University Press, 1949).

plays of social propaganda written during the nineteen-thirties,[5] the didactic play presents a host of problems in analysis and interpretation whose solutions are chiefly within the realm of rhetoric. I am excluding that kind of construction from what I have to say about rhetoric, in mimetic drama, though didactic drama to be dramatic must in part be mimetic. In didactic drama thought is the chief and controlling part in the sense that the thesis, propaganda, or doctrine which the piece is constructed to present determines the formulation of all of the other parts. Every didactic poem is in the general sense of the term an argument whose end or purpose is to persuade or to convince. In structure it may be well made (pièce bien fait) in the sense that its incidents are organized as antecedents and consequences and in the sense that its action has a beginning, a middle, and an end that are causally related. But the didactic play need not be well made since its unity is essentially a unity of thought rather than of action. The episodic plot is no detriment to the purpose or function of didactic drama, for its primary aim is not the arousal and purgation of specific emotions for the sake of wholeness and beauty. It is, as I have said, persuasion and conviction. Such didactic plays are strictly circumscribed in what they say or mean by the message or doctrine which they are constructed to convey. Conversely, what a mimetic drama says or means is analogous to what a great event in history may mean. To ask what the *Oresteia* means is like asking what the rise, triumph, and downfall of the Third Reich means. In truth, a mimetic drama does not "mean" in the sense that a didactic drama does. It *is* rather than it *means*. Or as H. D. F. Kitto puts it, if one asks what the *Antigone* means, the only adequate answer is that it means the *Antigone*, nothing less and nothing more.[6]

Though the operation of rhetorical principles may be observed in the various parts of the constructed form of mimetic drama, that operation is most readily apparent in two of the qualitative parts— thought and diction. A number of modern critics, especially some of the so-called New Critics, have given extensive examination to rhetoric in diction, often with informative results. Since these modern critics define rhetoric as any manipulation of language which designates, evokes, or conveys meaning, they often make no distinction between rhetoric and poetic; indeed, some of them—I. A. Richards and Kenneth Burke are examples—subsume poetic under rhetoric. Their discoveries and conclusions, informative as they may be in

[5] Sam M. Smiley, "The Structure of Didactic Drama as Represented in American Plays of the Depression Era." Unpublished Ph.D. dissertation, Indiana University, 1967.
[6] *Form and Meaning in Drama* (London: Methuen, 1964).

other respects, are of little help in our present inquiry. When drama is defined as a making with words, it is confused with literature in general, undifferentiated from epic, lyric, essay, or novel. Words formulated as discourse are merely a means in drama, formally subordinate to and determined by three other parts, plot, character, and thought. Elder Olson states the matter well in the following paragraph from his *Tragedy and the Theory of Drama:*

> We find, thus, further confirmation of our view that drama is not essentially a form of literature, but rather a distinct art which may or may not employ language as an artistic medium. It is literary only through its employment of dialog. . . . ; and while, beyond all doubt the highest forms of drama demand dialog, dialog itself cannot be regarded as the most important element, though it is frequently thought of as precisely that. On the contrary, it is a subsidiary part. Without it, certainly, a great number of subtle effects would be impossible; more than that, the profundity of great drama would be impossible; but these very considerations show that it is simply the medium through which these effects are achieved, under the governance of plot. The dialog exists to give the plot its quality and power; therefore it is subordinate to plot. Since the representation determines when dialog is proper and when it is not, and what the nature of the dialog shall be, the dialog is also subordinate to the representation. Indeed, in one respect, the dialog is simply an extension of the representation, detailing what words shall be said in what order.

Drama is not primarily a making with words; it is primarily a making with action, deeds, events, occurrences which are directly rendered by the agents themselves, not narrated. Though drama is a narrative art, it is not a narrated art; hence drama as narrative differs from the novel or short story and the rhetoric of drama differs from the rhetoric of fiction. The actions which the dramatist formulates are not merely the deeds and events done and happening; they are also the changes which go on within the characters. This so-called inner action may often be more important structurally than the outward action. It is both of these kinds of action which determine what words shall be spoken and how they shall be said; hence the immediate formal determinant of diction in drama is thought. In our inquiry into the operations of rhetoric in drama we will most readily find those in an examination of thought in drama.

Please note that I say thought in drama, not thought about drama, not even thought in the reader or audience; though thought in the drama, when adequately comprehended or rendered on the stage, may also be the thoughts in the reader's or the audienc's mind and imagination. Thought in drama appears in all that the characters say and all that the characters do. The deed may be as simple as a glance or the lifting of an eyebrow, which signifies consciousness or awareness. Consciousness or awareness is the basis of thought in drama, the first stage or gradation in a hierarchy of possible kinds of thought without which the other stages are impossible. Incidentally, this is why the first lessons in the training of an actor must be lessons in how to listen on the stage and to indicate that one is listening and responding or reacting. Such a signification of awareness as a glance or the lifting of an eyebrow will result in a simple general statement, such as "I (the character) am aware that that is a door or that another person is present." The action on the part of the character may signify more than simple awareness. It may say "I am aware of the presence of another that I dislike or that I fear." This is a signification of thought as feeling which may be so intensified by events and by interactions of characters that it becomes thought as emotion. If such a development of thought is to occur, it will depend upon two other elements, the kind of character and what we may loosely call the circumstances. Thus we see that thought in mimetic drama is formally controlled by character, which is in turn formally controlled by plot. To put the same matter in another way, in mimetic drama thought and character are devices for the making of plots and for making actions convincing. Plot, which is the structural organization of a completed whole, is in mimetic drama the marshalling or architectonic elements which governs all of the other parts. In didactic drama, conversely, thought takes over this architectonic function to a major degree. Because drama is an art with evocative powers, rather than a deliberation arriving dialectically at conclusions, thought in drama is essentially thought as feeling and emotion. Thus poetic is not, strictly speaking, a part of dialectic, as is rhetoric. Nevertheless, deliberative thought may and does occur in drama. When it does, it remains dramatic only when it arises out of and includes the arousing of emotions. Pure deliberative thought based strictly upon enthymemic and logical reasoning, divorced strictly from feelings and emotions, has no place in drama, though it may in oratory. Indeed, extended deliberative thought of this kind would, to the extent that it was employed, destroy the dramatic nature of a play.

In drama in which thought is a structural part of the whole that thought arises out of the consciousness or awareness of the agents. If the stimulus is sufficiently strong or continuous, if the agent is of such a character, and if the circumstances are of such a kind, the awareness will include or will develop into feelings and emotions. Feelings and emotions intensified or prolonged within the agent will result in desires and needs, which, if not easily or immediately satisfied, will force the agent to deliberate. That deliberation in drama may be either expedient or ethical; that is, deliberation about ways and means of attaining desired ends, or about the best instruments for the purpose, or it may be about the rightness or wrongness, the justice or injustice, of the purpose and the means of attaining it. Expedient deliberations can and frequently do appear in comedy but when the deliberation involves ethical questions and issues both the character and the action to that extent become serious. Note, however, that mock-ethical deliberation, such as Falstaff's deliberation on honor, is an excellent comic device.

In a play which involves the full range of formulated thought deliberation results in decision, an act of the will. Decision may result in change within the character, a change in attitude and outlook. It may eventuate in a speech and cumulatively it may result in a deed. Usually the three outcomes are the consequences of decisions; thus it is apparent that in a well-formulated mimetic drama thought is the antecedent of action. Decision may, of course, result directly from feelings and emotions without deliberation; indeed, in drama such is the kind of action that frequently occurs. Decision, whether it is deliberative or not, is the fullest or most complete kind of differentiation of one agent from another that is possible in drama; hence it is the highest stage in characterization. Two characters may do exactly the same deed. Action alone is not adequate to the characterizing of agents. Brutus and Cassius both plunge daggers into Caesar but they act from almost opposite motives. Cassius seeks to denigrate and destroy the man Caesar, whom he envies; Brutus acts solely for the good of Rome. Motive and hence understanding of character becomes apparent through the revelation of thought. Thought in the well-formulated mimetic play is the matter of character and character, along with plot, are the formal causes of thought.

It is possible to arrange an order in which thought operates in mimetic drama. On the lowest dramatic level we may find thought as general statement of an indifferent kind. Such a general statement may be a revelation of a state of being or of feeling. Such thought is on the lowest dramatic level because it is essentially static; but such a utilization of relatively static thought is often employed, especially in the early stages of the action. Thought becomes more dramatically operative when it appears as maximizing and minimizing (amplification and diminution, important and unimportant, serious and trivial, praise or blame). Such an operation of thought more actively involves agents interacting and hence makes the thought more dramatically a part of the whole action. In so doing it potentially leads to the next level of thought; that is thought as arousing emotion. In the quarrel scene in *Julius Caesar* as Brutus increasingly denigrates and condemns the past actions of Cassius, Cassius must increasingly defend and even extol those actions. Scorn, anger, and indignation are aroused thereby in the two characters, which is thought becoming dramatic action.

In contrast, a mere rendering of a state of feeling or emotion would be more in the nature of a general statement and hence less dramatic. As I have said, decisions and deeds may issue directly from emotions aroused and often do in drama; but thought is more fully exploited when general statement, maximizing and minimizing, and arousing passion result in an argument, as they do in the quarrel scene in *Julius Caesar*. Such an argument involves proof and refutation, charge and counter-charge, which must end in some kind of decision, even if the decision be merely to break off the argument. Under any eventuality, attitudes have been changed, motives have been exposed, psychological relationships have been altered and these constitute dramatic action even though the argument may result in no immediate deeds or additional events. This is the highest level of thought as it operates in mimetic drama because, since it must eventuate in decision, it results in the maximum differentiation of agents as characters and the fullest rendering of motives to action. In other words, thought as argument is the most complete rendering of thought as the material of character in action.

Each of these operations of thought can and do appear in the didactic play but appear with a degree of difference. The primary function of thought as argument in such plays is often not for the sake of formulating characters and motivating actions but is rather for the sake of thought itself; that is, at its worst dramatically speaking, it is the enunciation or promulgation of a thesis or a doctrine, which is essentially the thesis or doctrine of the playwright. In terms of diction such an operation results in speeches that are possible rather than speeches that are rigorously appropriate to a certain kind of character in a certain kind of action. The possible speech, for example, is often apparent in Restoration and eighteenth-century plays. In these the subject of love, or honor, or death arises; whereupon a character makes an extended speech on love, saying whatever is possible to him in that situation or on that subject. The action halts while the possible is being said. This kind of speech becomes most detrimental to drama when the character is obviously the mouthpiece of the dramatist. In the mimetic play, on the other hand, the speech must arise organically out of the thoughts and feelings of a certain kind of man in a specific situation and is controlled in its formulation by the character and the kind of action of which it is a part. Each type of speech involves to an extent rhetorical principles and practices but the possible speech is dominantly a rhetorical speech. If space permitted an examinaton of diction simply as diction, we would find rhetoric further involved in mimetic drama. An examination of the two criteria of dramatic diction—clarity and interestness or excitation—would illustrate further ways in which rhetoric and poetic are conjoint.

Instead of pursuing this analysis of diction, I wish now to examine briefly but somewhat more closely than we have done the relation of thought to an organized action; that is, to a plot. Substantively a plot is composed of three elements or parts, suffering, discovery, and reversal, though not all plots have plot reversals. Discovery may, and often does, substitute for reversal as a means of bringing a conclusion or ending to an action. The term suffering embraces all that goes on within a character, all that he experiences or undergoes, including his specific responses and reactions to what he experiences and undergoes. Suffering on its lowest level as spectacle is physical suffering: Prometheus being chained to the rock; the blinding of Gloucester; Lear biding the pelting of the pitiless storm; the agonies of countless stage deaths. On a higher formal level suffering is psychological and on this level becomes essentially an aspect of thought as I have defined thought.

In any well-formulated plot suffering is the material basis of discovery. A discovery in drama is a change from ignorance to knowledge. Discovery is therefore by definition dramatic action, for a dramatic action is change in the human condition. Discovery is also by definition dramatic action as thought, since any change from ignorance to knowledge must in some degree involve thought. There are in drama various kinds and types of discovery which may be arranged on an ascending formal order in terms of the interrelations of thought and action. The simplest kind in the sense of the least formally effective is discovery of a thing, which is nothing more than the recognition of an object or a place. A higher kind of discovery is an incidental discovery, one that belongs to and is confined to a single incident. This is a higher kind formally speaking because it potentially or actually involves persons discovering each other and thus involves thought and action. The highest kind of discovery is plot discovery; that is, a discovery of one character by another which affects their psychological attitudes one to another and the course of the action. Plot discoveries may in turn be arranged hierarchially in terms of their complexity in the relating of thought and action. A discovery by sign is the least formal. In such a discovery Character A discovers Character B by means of some identifying mark, token, or sign, which amounts to little more than a recognition brought about through spectacle;

though even in this type thought as a kind of recall or memory is present. A higher type is discovery through memory. Such discoveries require some device, some token or sign, to trigger the recall. Memory is nevertheless a kind of thought and is most adquately expressed, not in spectacle, but in diction. Above this type is discovery by right reasoning, which usually involves both sign and memory. Reasoning, however, represents a higher, more active level of thought and action than does mere memory and its effective rendering requires diction. In the manipulation of such discoveries all of the elements and devices of rhetorical reasoning, including analogy, enthymeme, and syllogism, are available to the playwright. Odd as it may seem, a more dramatically effective type of discovery is discovery by wrong reasoning, which employs the device of paralogism. Such a discovery is of a higher formal type because it requires a further discovery to correct the false discovery and thus involves more action and thought. These explanation should be ample to illustrate further the interrelations of thought and action and hence the inseparable relations of rhetoric and poetic in mimetic drama. The highest forms of discovery in drama lead not merely to characters discovering each other but result in self-discovery—the self-discovery of an Oedipus, a Hamlet, a Lear, and thousands of other great characters. Such self-discoveries account in a measure for the illumination of the nature of man and the human condition which drama so abundantly affords. Space permitting, I could show how the utilization of rhetorical elements and principles operates in each of these types of discovery but that would require an extensive examination of various examples from plays.

I conclude with merely mentioning some other ways in which thought operates in mimetic drama and thus involves rhetoric. The art of constructing a dramatic action is in part the art of arousing expectations, anticipations within the play which may lead to expected or to unexpected outcomes. Both the expected and the consequent unexpected are aspects of thought. The arousal of expectations within the play is brought about largely by the way in which the playwright establishes possibilities and probabilities in the action. Expectations within the play, properly established, may become expectations within the audience and again rhetorical methods and devices are important to the playwright.

Finally, a play may be viewed as a series of speeches and thought can be an element which unifies the whole. A speech is a single significative expression or word or a combination of significative words. Speeches in plays are unified by conjunction into larger units of episode or scene. These larger units are in turn conjoined into the unity of the whole; thus a play may be viewed in its entirety as a single speech. As such it makes significant statements which, as elements of thought, are designed to affect the thought of an audience. Even the mimetic play, then, is to this limited extent a rhetorical composition and rhetoric and poetic become, so to speak, twin servants of a single art. He who seeks to know poetic and *poiesis* must know rhetoric.

A MODERN VIEW OF DELIVERY

KARL R. WALLACE
University of Massachusetts

The endeavor to look anew at old concepts is often revealing and instructive. I hope to show that this is particularly true of a concept in rhetoric that has been variously, and sometimes loosely, called *delivery, pronuntiatio, actio, declamation,* and *elocution.* To some rhetoricians and teachers of speech, the "meaning" of *delivery* may be simple and self-evident; to others the word may be so vague and weasel-like that its significance can only be stipulated. For confirmation, each group may point to the same evidence, namely, that major theorists seem to avoid discussion of the nature of delivery—though most of them, like Cicero and Quintilian, are almost lyrical over *pronuntiatio* and *actio* as powerful influences in persuasion—or they omit mention of delivery altogether, as did George Campbell in his lectures on the philosophy of rhetoric.

I want to direct attention to the nature of delivery. Either its nature is not worth the trouble of thorough analysis and understanding, or delivery as a discernible part or component of a communicative act escapes analysis and upon probing vanishes into nothing of consequence. In looking at the concept anew, we shall first note briefly what the traditional rhetoricians and elocutionists have said, if indeed they said anything. We shall then proceed to see how delivery was understood when perceived in its original context as one of the five constituent parts, or divisions, or operations of rhetoric. Finally, we shall suggest that it can properly be viewed as utterance that objectifies one's response to a context in which the respondent is functioning as a communicator. The physical basis is vocal and gestural (or bodily) behavior. This behavior is modified and shaped by words and word combinations that are subject to, and are dominated and refined by, the meaningful aspect of the utterance.

I

The difficulties inherent in dealing with the concept of delivery may be swiftly indicated.[1] Aristotle sets the stage, for his "definition" of delivery as well as his attitude toward it are reflected in the long his-

---

[1] Doubtless some graduate student scholar should assemble and survey the evidence exhaustively. I hope that my choices from the historical record are

tory of rhetoric and still resonate in the pronouncements of modern teachers of English and speech.

> [Delivery] is, essentially, a matter of the right management of the voice to express the various emotions—of speaking loudly, softly, or between the two; of high, low, or intermediate pitch; of the various rhythms that suit various subjects. These are the three things—volume of sound, modulation of pitch, and rhythm— that a speaker bears in mind.[2]

In this passage it is clear that Aristotle recognized the physical aspects of *hypocrisis* and the regulation or management of those features of voice perceived as *megathos* ("volume," or the space-filling quality of utterance), *harmonia* (pitch and accentuation), and *rhythmos* (time and measure).[3] He is referring, too, to those meanings associated with the speaker's and listener's emotional state of being. He appears not to link vocal behavior with intellectual or mental activity; rather, words and word combinations are the primary carriers of meaning.[4] We are told by implication that a speaker does not manipulate or "manage" his voice so as to reveal the meanings of words.[5] Aristotle makes no mention of gesture, as Cope admits.

---

not unrepresentative. For penetrating criticism and helpful suggestions in the preparation of this paper, I am indebted to my colleagues, Professors Jane Blankenship and Herman Cohen.

[2] *Rhetorica* 1403 b 28-32, trans. by W. Rhys Roberts. *The Works of Aristotle Translated into English under the Editorship of W. D. Ross,* 12 vols., XI (Oxford: At the Clarendon Press, 1924). Roberts' translation should be compared with that of John Henry Freese in the Loeb Classical Library: *Aristotle: The "Art" of Rhetoric* (Cambridge: Harvard University Press, 1959).

[3] Perhaps E. M. Cope's interpretation and renderings of the Greek are sharper and more revealing to the modern student than the translation of others. See *An Introduction to Aristotle's Rhetoric* (London and Cambridge: Macmillan and Co., 1867), pp. 277-278. Cf. *The Rhetoric of Aristotle with a Commentary by . . . Edward Meredith Cope, Revised and Edited . . . by John Edwin Sandys,* 3 vols. (Cambridge, England: At the University Press, 1877), III, 1-3.

[4] Although today we would not care to distinguish sharply the meanings carried by words as they are used in utterance from those meanings borne by other features of utterance, we must understand that all learned men, as well as rhetoricians, once accepted such a distinction. Intellectual experience and an intellectual state of being were different from emotional experience and an emotional state of being; the indicative functions of language, attributed chiefly to what we call nouns, verbs, adjectives, and adverbs (i.e., the substantive aspects of utterance), and the indicative mood seemed obviously different from the non-indicative functions of language revealed in the other "moods" of utterance.

[5] This point emerges in part from Aristotle's treatment of style in the *Rhetoric* and in part from Aristotle's belief, explicitly stated in *De Interpre-*

Quintilian incorporates Cicero's view of delivery; so we shall be missing nothing if we let the *Institutes* speak for Cicero. Quintilian dutifully reports that "Delivery [*pronuntiatio*] is often called *action* [*actio.*] But the first name is derived from the voice, the second from the gesture. For Cicero in one passage speaks of *action* as being a *form of speech* and in another as being a *kind of physical eloquence.*"[6] Prompted by Watson's rendition of the Latin, we should have Cicero saying that *actio* is as it were the speech of the body or the eloquence of the body.[7] Watson has Quintilian using *actio* as a generic term synonymous with *pronuntiatio.* Its "parts"—voice and motion (or movement)—are constituent parts, not discrete elements. Functionally, *pronuntiatio* directly reveals emotional meanings which rouse corresponding emotional meanings in listeners.[8]

The Ramists, as is well known, split the theory of rhetoric into invention and judgment on the one hand, and elocution and utterance or pronunciation on the other. Abraham Fraunce's understanding of *pronuntiatio* seems to represent the Ramists. Following Omar Talon, Fraunce described it as a "fit deliuering of the speech alreadie beautified," and offers no more by way of definition.[9] He is obviously implying that in the prepared, premeditated oration the act of delivery follows composition. Fraunce implies darkly what Francis Bacon implies more plainly. In *The Advancement of Learning* Becon uses *elocution, tradition,* and *delivery* as virtually equivalent terms. They all refer to the transmission, the delivering over, of one person's thoughts to another. In employing these words, he has in mind the physical

tatione (16 a 4-5), that "spoken words are the symbols of mental experience" and that these bear "significance and meaning." Trans. E. M. Edgehill. *The Works of Aristotle* . . . , I (Oxford: At the Clarendon Press, 1928).

[6] *The Institutio Oratoria of Quintilian,* trans. H. E. Butler, 4 vols. (The Loeb Classical Library, Cambridge, Mass.: Harvard University Press, 1959), xi, 3; IV, 243. Cf. Quintilian's *Institutes of Oratory, or Education of the Orator in Twelve Books,* trans. John Selby Watson, 2 vols. (Bohn's Classical Library, London: George Bell and Sons, 1909), II, 344. The references are to Cicero's *De Oratore,* III, 59 and *Orator* xvii.55.

[7] Quintilian: Namque actionem Cicero alias *quasi sermonem* alis *eloquentiam quandam corporis.*

[8] The author of the *Rhetoric to Herennius* writes that *pronuntiatio* is "divided" "in vocis figuram"—vocal shape or figure, which Caplan translates, Vocal Quality, and "in corporis motum"—bodily movement, which Caplan englishes, Physical Movement. *Cicero ad C. Herennium, De Ratione Dicendi,* trans. Harry Caplan (The Loeb Classical Library, Cambridge, Mass.: Harvard University Press, 1954), III, 11, p. 191. In remarking that vocal flexibility may be achieved "by declamatory exercise," Caplan observes that this book contains the earliest appearance of *declamatio* as applied to delivery in extant Latin literature. *Ibid.,* fn.

[9] *The Arcadian Rhetorike,* edited from the Edition of 1588 by Ethel Seaton (Oxford, England: The Luttrell Society, 1950), p. 106.

basis of any act of communication, which for him meant speech, voice, gesture, and written characters.[10]

The better-known eighteenth-century rhetoricians and elocutionists either take no notice of delivery, as is true of Joseph Priestley and George Campbell, or regard it as the management of voice and body.[11] Hugh Blair devoted most of his discussion of "the pronunciation or delivery of a discourse" to voice, distinctness, slowness, and propriety.[12] In preparing the ground for his treatment of delivery, he reasserts that "tones and gestures" are the primary indicators of emotional experience. But he asserts, also, that the meanings embedded in ideas and words are enforced by vocal and gestural behavior. Thus Blair appears to imply that utterance possesses an intellectual quality as well as an emotional one.[13]

The father of the elocutionists, Thomas Sheridan, provides the significant evidence. "Elocution," he says, "is the just and graceful management of the voice, countenance, and gesture in speaking."[14] Sheridan's amplified version of this definition is more explicit:

---

[10] *The Advancement of Learning. The Works of Francis Bacon,* ed. James Spedding, Robert Leslie Ellis, and Douglas Denon Heath, 7 vols. (London, 1879), III, 384ff, 388ff, 399; *De Augmentis Scientiarum,* V,1; *Works,* 407, see K. R. Wallace, *Francis Bacon on Communication and Rhetoric* (Chapel Hill, N. C.: University of North Carolina Press, 1943), chs. I, IX.

[11] In his "scientific" treatment of rhetoric in general Campbell omits mention of delivery and of any of the roughly synonymous terms: action, pronunciation, gesture, and the like. But in his *Lectures on Pulpit Eloquence,* Campbell handles delivery in "Lecture III: Of the Expression," and "Lecture IV: Of Pronunciation" (London: John Bumpus, 1824). There is *"grammatical pronunciation,"* or the phonetic aspect of utterance, and *"rhetorical pronunciation."* This "consiseth in giving such an utterance to the several words in a sentence, as shows in the mind of the speaker a strong perception, or, as it were, feeling of the truth and justness of the thought conveyed by them, and in placing the rhetorical emphasis" on those words that give "the greatest energy and clearness to the expression." (Pp. 205-206.) Under pronunciation Campbell includes gesture. This is not the place to explore the complex, dependent relationships among *sentiment,* which is revealed most forcibly in delivery, and *expression, elocution,* and *pronunciation.* For Campbell style and delivery *must* reflect the sentiments as these were understood by mid-eighteenth century philosophers and rhetoricians; hence to him delivery could not be limited to purely physical events.

[12] *Lectures on Rhetoric and Belles Lettres* (New York: Richard Scott, 1815), pp. 365, 367.

[13] The relevant passages are somewhat ambiguous, but the key passage appears to be this: ". . . he who, in speaking, should employ bare words, without enforcing them by proper tones and accents, would leave us with a faint and indistinct impression, often with a doubtful and ambiguous conception, of what he had delivered." *Ibid.,* p. 366.

[14] *A Course of Lectures on Elocution* . . . (London: W. Strahan, 1762), p. 19.

A just delivery consists in a distinct articulation of words, pronounced in proper tones, suitably varied to the senses, and the emotions of the mind; with due observation of accent; of emphasis, in its several gradations; of rests or pauses of the voice, in proper places and well measured degrees of time; and the whole accompanied with expressive looks, and significant gestures.[15]

Although recognizing that *pronuntiatio* had "such a comprehensive meaning amongst the ancients, as to take in the whole compass of delivery, with its concomitants of look and gesture," Sheridan observed that the meaning of the word by his day had been narrowed to denote chiefly articulation and accent. In looking at the elocutionary movement broadly, Frederick W. Haberman has observed that by 1725 the significations of *style, elocution,* and *pronunciation* had changed markedly:

> Whereas pronunciation once embraced the whole field of delivery, it later signified the correct phonation of words in isolation. *Elocution,* which once meant the manner of artistic composition, became identified with the manner of artistic delivery. *Style,* once a subsidiary synonym for elocution, later comprehended the whole [art] of the choice and arrangements of words.[16]

In general it can be said that the elocutionists concentrated on bodily action, voice management, vocal production, and pronunciation, and that "delivery" referred to physical behaviors signified by these terms.[17] It can be said, also, that the elocutionists, like the ancients, assigned high value to vocal and gestural behavior because voice and bodily movement were charged with the power and revealed the subtleties of emotion and feeling. The vocabulary of those who write of the affective side of behavior varies somewhat, but the writers are all thinking of non-verbal meanings. James Mason, for example, speaks of "the full Sense and Spirit" and the "Sentiments" of the reader and speaker, and James Burgh of "the principal Passions and Humors."[18] Sheridan himself insisted that "the passions and the fancy have a language of their own, *utterly independent of words.* . . . [Italics mine.][19]

Until about the middle of the eighteenth century, then, the term "delivery" referred to vocal and gestural behavior that signaled the

[15] *Ibid.,* p. 10.
[16] "English Sources of American Elocution," *Background Studies in the History of Speech Education in America* (New York, 1934), p. 112.
[17] *Ibid.,* pp. 110-111.
[18] For Mason: *An Essay on Elocution, or Pronunciation* (London, 1728), p. 22; for Burgh: *The Art of Speaking* (London, 1762), title page.
[19] *Lectures on Elocution,* p. x.

speaker's state of emotion and feeling. Nothing seems to have been said about the intellectual or symbolic aspect of experience that is associated with the primary, indicative meanings of words. During the century some rhetoricians and elocutionists began to claim that delivery ought to be "natural" and sound like conversation. Certain qualities of vocal and bodily behavior were held to be unmistakable signs of what was going on when a speaker was *communicating* with someone. Between expressing and performing on the one hand, and communicating, or talking to and with, on the other, there was a real difference in voice or tone or style of utterance. Modern teachers of speech and rhetoric who know the history of their discipline are familiar with the controversy that boiled up over the proper way of achieving the conversational quality in delivery. The quality was evident in any mode of delivery open to the public speaker, the actor, and the interpretive reader. But how best to attain it? The controversy over method though it sheds strong light on the nature of delivery we cannot find space for here.[20]

Among teachers of public speaking in the twentieth century, James A. Winans was probably the first to probe searchingly into conversational quality. Even in the most formal circumstances, he said, speaking is an enlarged conversation in which the speaker's mental, vocal, and gestural activity reveal the meanings of utterance as directly and immediately as it does in the most impromptu and spontaneous conversation. There is a difference between being aware of "the sound and feel" of words as is usually evident in a "memorized," or "reading," or absent-minded, or declamatory mode of delivery and being fully aware of meaning at the moment of utterance. There is a difference between the feeling or sense of communicating *with* an audience and the aloofness that marks soliloquizing.[21] In a word, during delivery a speaker is dominated by meanings prompted by the desire to communicate something appropriate to his hearers and for their benefit.

Despite Winans's contribution and despite the scientific analysis of speech and language behavior by students of linguistics, psycholinguists, and experimental phoneticians, there is still no clear and commonly-accepted view of the nature of delivery. In support of this

[20] The beginning of the debate and its central concerns are presented judiciously in W. M. Parrish, "The Concept of 'Naturalness,'" *Quarterly Journal of Speech,* 37 (December, 1951), 448-454.

[21] *Public Speaking,* 2nd ed. (New York, 1917), pp. 34-35. Winans knew that Thomas Sheridan and Richard Whately before him had pointed to the conversational or natural mode as the proper standard of delivery. (See Winan's discussion of this point in his "Whately on Elocution," *The Quarterly Journal of Speech,* 31 (February, 1945), 1-8.) But it remained for Winans to build it into the concept of delivery, rather than let it stand apart to be used only as a standard and guide for teacher and pupil.

statement, I shall reproduce a few "definitions" by the better known textbook writers on public speaking, speech fundamentals, communicative speaking, and the like. None of the quotations is earlier than 1951:

> Delivery can be regarded as the whole of the speaker's overt behavior.

> [Delivery] is the vital, physical means by which ideas are transmitted to a listener.

> [Delivery] is *delivered* language.

> Delivery is a comprehensive term for all aspects of a speaker's mental, audible, and visible behavior while addressing an audience.

> Delivery is the total management of mind, voice, and body in the act of speaking. [And from the same page:] It is the moment of consummation of the communicative act.

> [Delivery involves] the utterance of a message in the presence of other people. . . .

The amplification of the last of these definitions follows the Winans line. Involved in delivery is "a keen sense of communication and a vivid realization of your idea at the moment of utterance, and . . . control [over] all the channels of action—mental, physical, and vocal —to support and re-enforce ideas." The student is told that during delivery "you reactivate a subject and ideas to support it, that you regenerate the enthusiasm that led you to speak in the first place." The "full and sharp realization of content . . . includes more than bare meaning; the implications and emotional content must also be realised." Moreover, "the reference here is not merely to . . . striking emotions . . . but to those attitudes and significances constantly present in lively discourse . . .—the sense of one moment of meaning as being more important than another, awareness of query as opposed to assertion, concern as different from indifference," etc.[22]

II

The original rhetorical context in which *delivery* appeared may help in understanding our problem if not in solving it. The classical rhetoricians probably held that creative and analytical activity took place primarily, and perhaps entirely, within the speaker and that he resorted to voice and gesture in order to transmit to others what had been going on inside his head. The divisions or parts of rhetoric were *inventio, dispositio, elocutio, memoria,* and *pronuntiatio* (delivery).

[22] The quotations are from *Public Speaking as a Liberal Art* by John F. Wilson and Carroll C. Arnold (Boston, 1968), pp. 320, 321.

Concerned with the teaching of formal speechmaking and with the conditions that made an oration effective, the theorists saw the "parts" of rhetoric as operations indispensable to the production of a speech. Invention involved the finding of the materials of the speech, specifically the discovering of arguments, from the well of one's experience and from the circumstances calling for persuasion. Disposition was the selecting and ordering of the fundamental materials of the speech and thus the forming of it. Elocution was the wording, the putting into verbal symbols, of what had been invented and arranged, and memory involved the recalling of words in a sequence. Left to delivery, then, was the making of the vocal sounds associated with words and the indicating of the emotional context of words.

The five operations had a psychological basis. Their processes were categorized in terms of faculties or powers of the mind and soul. To see, if only briefly, what faculties were responsible for what operations is to see that delivery involved the emotional responses of the speaker, not the intellectual. When a speaker was said to invent and to dispose, two faculties were primarily at work: understanding and reason. The understanding, the abstracting power, searched about in man's storehouse of experience for materials having the simplest of abstract forms. The reason, closely allied with the understanding, was engaged in combining and synthesizing the simplest forms discovered and apprehended by the understanding; reason conducted the activities of composition and division. In these processes reason was also judging the consistency, the relevance, and perhaps the appropriateness, of what it was forming. The understanding was revealed in nondiscursive mental activity as intelligence, wit, and insight; reason was revealed in discursive activity. It was the mind disposing, i.e., the mind engaged in moving about from one position to another the simple forms supplied by the inventive powers of the understanding. Thus the understanding and reason functioning together were held to account for discovering, selecting, and shaping that which was to be spoken. What was spoken were words and word patterns. Within the speaker—may we say, within the speaker's mind?—words were images, both auditory and visual. These were originally learned through sense experience and whenever man had to employ sensory channels through which to reach others he pulled on the language experience available to him. Reproducing words, so the classicists held, was the joint responsibility of memory and imagination. The symbolic, or meaningful, aspect of words was due to the joint efforts of the understanding and reason.[23] What we know about these operations, then, coupled with what is known

23 The imagination of course had functions other than that of reproducing sensory experience. It could be inventive in its own right and in cooperation

about the habits of preparation of the great orators who illustrated the classical tradition—their occasional writing of the complete speech, their protracted oral practice and rehearsing, and the committing of the whole to memory—all suggest that composition was one thing and delivery another. A speech could exist, and did exist, undelivered orally, although it might be built for a definite audience, as were John Milton's speeches to Parliament. A speech, then, lived for its audience through print or through voice and gesture. Either channel of transmission revealed the speaker's intellectual operations, his linguistic meanings, equally well, but *pronuntiatio* and *actio* supplied power that print could not match, for they revealed the full emotional and affective experience of the orator. In post-classical times, the elocutionist was alive to this fact and his efforts to exploit it occasionally produced marvels of vocal and gestural gymnastics. Attention to the emotional resources of voice and gesture rather than to the meanings of words and word structures served to keep alive the notion that composition was one kind of thing and delivery another. Prior to the elocutionists, Peter Ramus and his followers claimed for logic the intellectual operations involved in inventing, disposing, and judging and relegated to rhetoric the activities of styling and delivering. The first three operations were sufficient to produce a composition in words; the last two provided ways of enhancing and embellishing speech and language for purposes of delighting and persuading. Perhaps it is not too extreme to say that in the hands of Ramean theorists delivery became quite unintellectual indeed.

Although the difficulties of interpretation are many, I think that rhetoricians in the classical tradition saw speechmaking as two different acts or events, the one bringing about a composition, the other transmitting the composition, the one consisting of the intellectual activities essential to the creating of a verbal product, the other consisting of vocal, gestural, and emotional behavior in response to what had been composed. Possibly the theorists regarded the external, palpable event as something more than the motor behavior necessary for conveying the inner impalpable event to the ears and eyes of an audience. Was the outer event the counterpart, or perhaps the correlative, of the inner event? Were vocal and gestural behaviors representing what had taken place internally? The historical evidence is too meagre to cope with these problems. It is true that Aristotle clearly stated the

with the understanding. The second kind of imaginative activity was prized by the rhetoricians, the first by the poets. A full account of the faculty psychology as understood by an Elizabethan can be found in my *Francis Bacon on the Nature of Man: The Faculties of Man's Soul: Understanding, Reason, Imagination, Memory, Will,* and *Appetite.* Urbana: The University of Illinois Press, 1967.

presumption that is still central to any theory of communication, namely: ". . . spoken words are the symbols of mental experience . . . [and] the mental experiences which these directly symbolize are the same for all. . . ." On this evidence, the spoken word is an integral part of the mental experience it symbolizes. Yet the same statement implies that speech does not symbolize nonmental experience. The implication would appear to be inconsistent with Aristotle's definition of delivery as the management of the voice in ways that reveal emotion. The definition, however, may be intended to suggest that vocal qualities, overtones, intonations, inflections, and the like directly address the senses of the hearer and that the response to such stimuli is direct rather than mediated through symbols. So one would regard the phenomena of delivery as body speaking to body rather than mind speaking to mind.

III

The underlying reason for the historic difficulties in characterizing delivery is a psycholinguistic one. In what way, or ways, does one regard and describe the relationship of speech heard or language seen on the one hand, to the communicator's inner experience and activity, impalpable and unobservable by the exterior senses, on the other? Prior to committing this "sentence" to the eyes of others, something has gone on inside me. I need not here tackle that baffling question, *what* has gone on inside me. I need only say that something has occurred. So we can ask: How is the outer, observable event linked with the inner, unobservable event? Are we dealing with two events or with a single one? Is what is uttered and gestured a complete act with its own beginning and ending? Does the interior event immediately prior to it comprise a complete movement with its proper beginning and ending? Suppose we regard a speech act, or a communicative act, as a single event. And suppose outer behavior is simply the *objective* feature of the event—that which is the actualization, the culmination of an experience whose origin resides in the contextual situation to which the event is the communicative response. If this were the case, utterance is an aspect of an act, an integral feature of creative activity, and not a separate sensory event. A speech act is then an element, not further divisible into units.[24]

A modern view of delivery would regard vocal and gestural events

[24] If the speech act be not an element, it may comprise two units or elements. But to bifurcate the speech act poses unnecessary problems. If there be a sensory event (A) and an inner event (B), how are they related? Is (A) the "counterpart" of (B)? Is (A) a "translation" of (B)? Is (A) the "objective correlative" of (B), as T. S. Eliot would hold? Are the two events connected by some mediating process, as Charles Osgood believes? Does one follow the other because of a learned dispositional tendency, as Charles Morris

and words uttered in communicative settings as integral parts of a single act. It is an act dominated by meaning and meaning therefore tinges every part of the act. In informal, dialogue-type circumstances, which classical theorists grossly neglected, the act can appropriately be called the speech act; in circumstances calling for formal discourse it can be called the rhetorical act, or perhaps rhetorical action. The essentials of the two acts are alike; so here we shall focus on the speech act. This act begins in a communicative setting that calls for an oral response. The oral response and accompanying gestures constitute the final and culminating stage of the response. Let us see.

In a setting calling for utterance, anyone who chooses to speak rather than not to speak has a reason. The speaker may or may not be aware of what prompts his utterance. In conversation he is typically unaware of what led him to speak, and if pushed to account for his choice he may be able to do no more than to say, "It was the thing to do." The reason for utterance, technically speaking, lies chiefly in the concept of purpose. In some settings a more accurate term than *purpose* is *intention*, or *goal*, or perhaps *motive*. The notion of purpose —and of related but not synonymous concepts—is a property or feature of a communicative context shared by speaker and hearer. The contextual feature is that which invites speech and determines the direction or goal of utterance. The goal in turn prompts the selection of the materials and means by which the speaker expects to achieve his purpose. That is, there comes to the fore a segment of experience that is felt to be relevant and appropriate. The shaping of such a segment of experience under the influence of purpose constitutes the form of the act. Or perhaps one can say that internally a configuration of purpose and experience takes place. The configuration issues, or is figured, and is perceived by the speaker and his hearer as meaningful utterance. If this be the nature of an act of speech, it is evident that vocal and gestural behavior is functionally a part of the act. It is the culminating or terminal feature. If the act be thought of as a whole or a unit, it is the kind of whole to which utterance is essential. There is no speech act without utterance, and no utterance without events logically and naturally prior to it.[25]

holds? Is the connection to be attributed to some purely mental event or thought as I. A. Richards would maintain?

[25] I do not mean to rule out internal acts of speech. Undoubtedly there are such. Sometimes we can even be aware of linguistic formulation as in silent rehearsing and editing. As a rule the internal act seems less complete—and less "clear"—than the external. On this kind of phenomenon, Edward Hulett, Jr. offers interesting speculations. See his "A Symbolic Interactionist Model of Human Communication. Part One: The General Model of Social Behavior: The Message-Generating Process," *AV Communication Review*, 14 (Spring, 1966), 16-21.

Another property or essential quality of the speech act is meaningfulness, and delivery as a part of the speech act is marked by meaning. To define meaning is unnecessary here. It is important to recognize only that whatever we mean by meaning it appears as a function of the speech act as a whole. One does not speak unless the context of the communicative situation is in some way meaningful to him. It must make sense to him. Further, in his expectation and appraisal of the communicative moment, what he chooses to say must be likely to make sense, not nonsense, to his hearer. Meaning is roused, like the past itself, whenever a bit of experience is put to use and becomes active. In communicative speech that is indeed what happens; our experience works for us. In utterance, experience and its climate of meaning come into play precisely because the conditions of context, purpose, material, and form combine to utilize a portion of the speaker's past. It has often been said that we speak out of our experience to the experience of others; it makes deep sense also to say that we speak out of our meanings to the meanings of others. Hence a modern view of delivery must hold that vocal and gestural behavior is dominated and guided by meaning. Winans was close to the mark when he said that a speaker is engaged in the realization of ideas during the moments of utterance. If one objects to "idea," it might be better to say that a speaker is actualizing meaning. Or to say that experience that is potential, specific, and directed to the utterance of the moment is becoming actual and real to the speaker. And present during communicative utterance is always an edge of meaning revealed in the quality or "tone" of vocal behavior, saying that the speaker is talking *to* and *with* his auditor and not merely to himself. This quality, as Winans said, is identical with a *sense of communication,* something that is experienced by a speaker as a feeling-tone that pervades the utterance. A speaker who sounds the tone of communication is aware, in the fringes of his attention field, that his success depends upon the understanding, respect, and good will of his listeners. He knows that *by* saying something he is trying to satisfy both himself and others.[26]

If it be true that informal, extempore utterance and that the prepared utterances of public speeches no matter how simple or elaborate are the final stages of creative, communicative acts and are the objective actualizations of inner, communication-directed activity, it is equally, though less obviously, true that the vocal and gestural behaviors of the oral reader and the actor are the culminations of creative acts. It is commonly held that a poem is incomplete unless read

---

[26] For this short way of saying much I am indebted to J. L. Austin's *How To Do Things With Words* (Cambridge, Mass.: Harvard University Press), pp. 94, 108, 109.

aloud. The reader who is other than the poet brings his experience to to the understanding and interpretation of the text. Thus to some extent he shares in a creative enterprise that is completed and actualized by his utterance. Actors and director actualize through the resources of theatre the script of the playwright. The term, "living theatre," is apt.

The speech act and the rhetorical act are unitary wholes. They exist for the sake of meaning-to-be-communicated. They are indivisible except for purposes of analyzing, teaching, and learning. As one of the parts or aspects of such acts, delivery is permeated with the meaning of these acts.

That meaning must be regarded as an integral feature of delivery is an idea that is recognized more or less clearly by some students of speech behavior. They may, or may not have been directly influenced by the Winans tradition. S. S. Curry, for example, asserted that "expression is subjective as well as objective . . ." and that "the objective phenomena are manifestive of subjective experience."[27] Without caring to define delivery, Parrish said:

> We have held steadily before us the conception that one speaks not merely to express himself, but to accomplish some purpose with relation to a given audience, and *this conception must determine the nature of the speaker's delivery*, just as it must determine his choice of a subject and his selection of materials. [Italics mine.][28]

Waldo Braden and Giles Gray deplore the notion that a speech and its delivery have been considered two different things.[29] Keith St. Onge writes that "delivery is the total management of mind, voice, and body

[27] From Curry's language it is difficult to tell whether an act of speech was viewed as a unitary whole. ". . . expression is not of the body but through the body; we feel that there is something mystic and and hidden, unseen and unheard by our fellow-men and often only vaguely felt by ourselves; but it is made manifest by the motions and actions of the body, and the tones and modulations of the voice." "Inward emotion causes an outward motion; inward condition, an outward *position*. [Italics mine.] Thus expression is, 'the motion of emotion,' the presentation of a vast complexity of physical actions which are directly caused by psychic activities." Again, "Matter itself is but force in a state manifest to sense; it may be called the expression of force." The quotations are from *The Province of Expression* (Boston, 1891), pp. 23-25. The whole section, pp. 21-36, should be pondered.

[28] Wayland Maxfield Parrish, *Speaking in Public* (New York, 1947), p. 184. Opposite the title page Parrish places a quotation from William Ellery Channing: "Speech is not merely the dress . . . , but the very body of thought. It is to the intellect what the muscles are to the principle of physical life. The mind acts and strengthens itself through words. It is chaos, till defined, organized by language." Parrish was an admirer of Winans.

[29] *Public Speaking: Principles and Practices* (New York, 1951), p. 476.

in the act of speaking." It marks "the moment of consummation of the communicative act."[30] William P. Sandford and W. Hayes Yeager are aware of the difficulties of definition, and allude to the views of Winans, Charles H. Woolbert, James M. O'Neill, Andrew Weaver, and Ray K. Immel, and then remark: "Delivery is obviously something more than the mere manipulation of external movements of the body and management of tones and inflections of the voice."[31] Huber Ellingsworth and Theodore Clevenger, Jr. state their position unequivocally: " 'Delivery' is not an object or an event, but is instead an aspect of the speech act. It never occurs outside the context created by a speaker addressing an auditor on some occasion in certain language concerning a particular idea."[32]

Surely today delivery cannot be properly described nor defined in terms that are exclusively physical. Nor can it be associated primarily or exclusively with the "expression" of emotion. It is saturated with the meaning for which a particular act of speech exists.

[30] *Creative Speech* (Belmon, Cal., 1964), p. 183. It should be observed that the author's treatment of delivery is hardly in keeping with this conception.

[31] *Principles of Effective Speaking* (New York, 1929), p. 263. But their definition, emphasizing the oral communication of ideas "contained in the speech," reminds one of the position of the classical rhetoricians. A psychological monist and behaviorist, Woolbert insisted upon the oneness of body and mind and understood the mutuality of meaning and the physical bases of communicating it. In *The Fundamentals of Speech* (New York, 1920), he made much of the phrase, "carrying the meaning." For some pivotal passages see pages 60, 83-84, 100, 288.

[32] *Speech and Social Action: A Strategy of Oral Communication* (Englewood Cliffs, N. J., 1967), p. 148.

THE STATUS OF /r/ AMONG NORTH CAROLINA SPEAKERS

LUCIA C. MORGAN

University of North Carolina

INTRODUCTION

The speech of native North Carolinians is usually labeled *Southern* by individuals from other speech areas. The untrained listener may not be able to identify all of the characteristics of the speech which are associated with the so-called Southern Accent, but he will invariably point to the treatment of /r/ as a major clue to the identification of the speaker's regional accent.

Wise, who spent the last 35 years of his life among Southern people, describes the speech of the South in the following manner:

> The speech of the South, like any other regional speech, is characterized by many subtle nuances of duration, pitch, tempo, and rhythm, which defy easy symbolization. These shadings must be heard to be appreciated. Such characteristics are not regarded as violations of standard Southern practice, so long as they remain relatively small. If such small differences are disregarded in the three major American dialects, it will be seen that standard Southern speech bears a close kinship with standard Eastern American speech in respect to the treatment of unstressing, and in the use of the various allophones of /r/ and of the combination *o* plus *r* plus vowel, as in *horror*. In respect to the distribution of many of the English phonemes, it bears a close relation to General American speech.

> But these statements apply well only to the standard forms of regional speech. As soon as the substandard forms are compared, it will be seen that the /r/-systems of the Southern and Eastern areas diverge considerably, and that the distribution and use of the other phonemes in Southern and General American diverge very greatly indeed.[1]

One concludes, therefore, that a speaker from one of the New England states might omit /r/ in the very same words as does a Southerner, but his speech would not be labeled southern. On the other hand, a North Carolinian might treat the /r/ in the same manner as does a speaker from the midwestern area (i.e., Michigan or

---

[1] Claude M. Wise, *Applied Phonetics* (Englewood Cliffs, New Jersey, 1956) p. 205.

Ohio) and his speech would remain identifiable as speech of the South. The presence or absence of specific allophones of /r/ is not the final basis for judgment of a regional accent, but it is one of the major clues. A trained investigator will evaluate the treatment of /r/ as he collects his data.

This report is concerned with the treatment of /r/ in specific positions as observed among native North Carolina speakers during the period 1960-68. The studies[2] upon which the report is based were structured in such a way as to permit the observation of changes in /r/ since the investigations of Lowman and McDavid during the period 1934-48.[3]

SUMMARY OF LOWMAN AND MCDAVID FINDINGS[4]

Postvocalic /r/ After Stressed Vowels

Postvocalic /r/ after the stressed vowel in *ear, care, door* and *poor* is preserved and fully constricted in those areas of North Carolina designated by Kurath as South Midlands.[5] (This includes the western counties comprising the geographic areas known as the Mountains and the Piedmont. Asheville, Greensboro, Winston-Salem and Charlotte are the largest cities within the South Midlands speech area. Raleigh and Durham are border cities since they are nearer the eastern counties.)

Postvocalic /r/ is preserved to a considerable extent in the coastal counties of North Carolina, but the trend toward the use of [ə] is spreading throughout the eastern half of the state, particularly in the north central counties bordering the Virginia Piedmont.

Postvocalic /r/ after the stressed vowels in *corn* and in *barn* was preserved in the South Midlands, but it was usually dropped in the areas designated by Kurath and McDavid as the South.[6] The portions of North Carolina considered to be in the South speech area are the northeastern counties of the Albemarle Sound and the Neuse River valley and the southeastern counties of the Cape Fear River and the Peedee River valleys.

Postvocalic /r/ in the north central counties followed the treatment of /r/ in the Virginia Piedmont.

---

[2] These studies were supported by an Alumni Grant, (1-198, 1959-60) and a Faculty Grant (485, 1968) University of North Carolina at Chapel Hill.

[3] Hans Kurath and Raven I. McDavid, Jr., *The Pronunciation of English in the Atlantic States* (Ann Arbor: University of Michigan Press, 1960), p. vi.

[4] Kurath and McDavid. This summary was compiled from data on pages 18-19, 107-108, 112-113, 115-122, 170-172 and maps 25, 151, 156 and 157.

[5] Kurath and McDavid, p. 18 and map 2.

[6] Kurath and McDavid, map 2.

Postvocalic /r/ After Unstressed Vowels

Postvocalic /r/ after the unstressed vowel in *father* is preserved in those areas where postvocalic /r/ is preserved after stressed vowels. In areas where the postvocalic /r/ is not preserved after stressed vowels, the final syllable in *father* is pronounced [ə]. In the South this pronunciation is spreading, particularly among the better educated and the younger people.[7]

The Stressed Vowel /ɜ/ in Thirty

In all areas of North Carolina the constricted vowel was used. The degree of constriction was observed. The western counties showed greater constriction than did the eastern counties. Varying degrees of lip rounding were noted, with the eastern counties showing the greater tendency toward rounding. The [ɜɪ] which is common in the Lower South was observed in areas bordering South Carolina.

There was no apparent relationship between the use of [ɜ] and [ə] or [ɝ] and [ɚ]. A comparison of Maps 25 and 151 indicated that there were more speakers using the constricted [ɝ] than there were speakers using the constricted [ɚ].

Current Studies on North Carolina Accents

The highly diversified speech patterns of the University students indigenous to North Carolina were the motivation for the series of continuing studies of accents within the state.[8] To one who is not intimately familiar with the regional pecularities of speech in North Carolina, the phonemes, allophones and word usages become a kaleidoscope of sounds—shifting, reappearing and disappearing at unpredictable intervals. Some system of identification of the speech patterns had to be devised if adequate communication was going to be maintained with the students. During my first year of teaching in North Carolina, many words defied immediate translation. The following sentences are composites of the words recorded in 1958-59.

He set dine boy a stell will in the cryin' station.

Translation: He sat down by a steel wheel in the Crown station.

---

[7] Kurath and McDavid, p. 169.

[8] Lucia C. Morgan, "The Speech of Ocracoke, North Carolina: Some Observations," *Southern Speech Journal*, XXV (Summer 1960), pp. 314-322; "North Carolina Accents," *North Carolina Journal of Speech* (Vol. I, No. 1, November 1967), pp. 3-8; "North Carolina Accents," *Southern Speech Journal*, XXXIV (Spring 1969), pp. 174-182.

He locks his frin who is a quat top.
Translation: He likes his friend who is a quiet type.

Ah fink Mizriz Brine wint to the sell in Grim.
Translation: I think Mrs. Brown went to the sale in Graham.

The first step in a systematic plan for sorting out the accents was the use of a 5 x 7 card for each student in lieu of the customary roll book. At the beginning of each semester the names and home towns (or counties) were recorded on the cards. The birthplaces of the parents were noted, as well as extended periods of residence in other areas. As the semester progressed and students spoke before the class, pertinent pronunciations were recorded phonetically on the cards. Gradually, patterns began to emerge and the larger dialect areas could be noted. After ten years of listening to some 4,000 students, the minute deviations were clear cut and smaller speech areas could be established.

The second step involved recordings of the students on tapes and audio discs. Two grants from the University of North Carolina made possible the expansion of the recordings to include adults and children throughout the state. The socio-economic level, as well as the educational level, of some of these informants differed considerably from that of the University students.

The task of building a recorded library of North Carolina Accents is an on-going process. Graduate students in phonetics are contributing immeasurably to the project.

This study of the status of /r/ among North Carolina speakers is a part of the total project. The data presented here represent the findings to date. Subsequent recordings and investigations may support or invalidate the findings presented in this report.

Procedure

The need as described above, dictated the procedure. The data to be analyzed in this report came from five major sources:

1. University students at Chapel Hill:
   Class speeches, class recordings and recordings of structured sentences were used.
2. Adults in all major dialect areas:
   Recordings were collected of impromptu conversations and of the structured sentences.
3. Children in public schools:
   Recordings were collected of impromptu conversations.

A simplified group of sentences and words was constructed. When the children were in the lower grades pictures were substituted for the printed words.

4. Radio and Television:

   Phonetic transcriptions were made of speakers during political campaigns. Another valuable source was the daily news reports of the activities of the State Legislature when it was in session. The daily programs of women in the news were also used.

5. Casual conversations with individuals who were unaware that their speech was being analyzed.

The structured sentences afforded the best opportunity for comparison of specific sounds in varying positions. The sentences prepared for this particular report included the treatment of /r/ in all positions and in the specific words used by Lowman and Kurath in the 1934-48 investigations. Ample words using the /ɜ/ were provided as well as opportunities for the linking r and the intrusive r. An examination of the sentences given below will reveal that words containing postvocalic /r/ in both stressed and unstressed positions were frequent.

Test Sentences:

1. Fern and George were very thirsty before they reached their parked car.

2. Please close the door, but only after you leave your overshoes on the floor.

3. There! That is better. Now ask your mother how to reach Mr. Parker's farm.

4. The horse was standing quietly in the bright warm sunshine.

5. Where in the world have you been? Arthur has been waiting for hours.

6. The light from our house was gone when we returned.

7. I am certain her skirt was purple, but I do not remember the color of her blouse.

8. Tell Mr. Turner that Mrs. Martin wants to get some oil from the Crown Station.

9. Your aunt is on the porch.

10. If you do not care for your ears now, you will soon have poor hearing later on.

11. Tobacco is barned before the corn is harvested.

12. The idea is to observe law and order.

13. Here is the route on the map. Follow it to Raleigh and turn right on Carver Street.

14. The sermon on Thursday concerned Noah and the Ark.

The data from the structured sentences were compiled on large charts arranged according to speech areas and to word groups. The speech areas were designated as the South Midlands, the South and the Virginia Piedmont. The Virginia Piedmont included the north central counties along the Virginia border. The South was subdivided into the northeastern counties of the Albemarle Sound and of the Neuse River Valley, and the southeastern counties of the Cape Fear and Neuse River Valleys.

The word groups concerned the postvocalic /r/ after stressed vowels, the postvocalic /r/ after unstressed vowels, and the central vowel /ɜ/ as in *thirty*.

Data from the recorded interviews and from radio and television transcriptions were compiled as separate case studies, but the material on /r/ was arranged so as to afford a comparison with the findings on the structured sentences.

SUBJECTS

Between December 1967 and January 1969, samples of the speech of one hundred and twenty white and fifteen black North Carolinians were collected for this specific project. Any data collected prior to December 1967 were considered as background information. The subjects were all born in North Carolina. All but ten of the parents were also born in North Carolina; the other ten were born in adjacent southern states.

The ages of the subjects ranged from five to eighty-seven years. Twelve of the group were over sixty-five. Thirty-four were enrolled in colleges and universities and sixteen were in public schools. Thirty-five held degrees from institutions of higher learning, two of which were at the doctoral level.

Seventeen of the subjects held elected positions in the state or federal government. Fifteen were school teachers, two were newspaper men, eight were farmers, one was a retired university chancellor, and one was a well-known minister.

The speech samples were collected in four ways as stated above: (1) tape recordings of structured material; (2) tape recordings of free

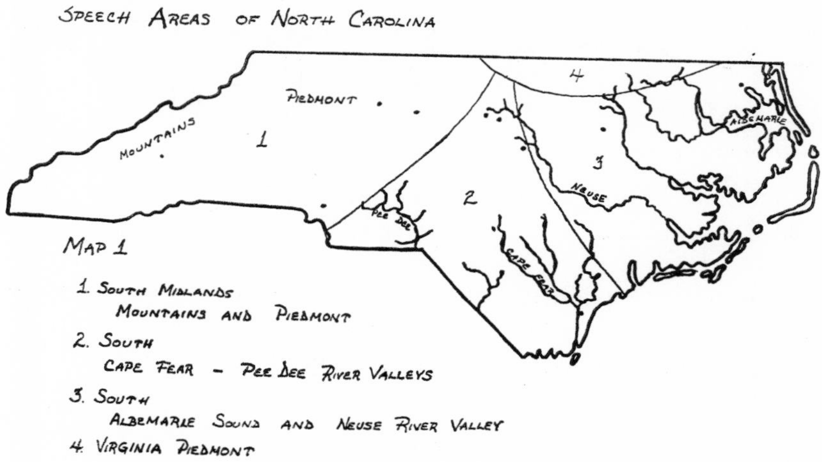

SPEECH AREAS OF NORTH CAROLINA
PIEDMONT
MOUNTAINS
1
2
3
4
ALBEMARLE
NEUSE
PEE DEE
CAPE FEAR
MAP 1
1. SOUTH MIDLANDS
MOUNTAINS AND PIEDMONT
2. SOUTH
CAPE FEAR – PEE DEE RIVER VALLEYS
3. SOUTH
ALBEMARLE SOUND AND NEUSE RIVER VALLEY
4. VIRGINIA PIEDMONT

NORTH CAROLINA
MOUNTAINS
Asheville
Winston Salem
Greensboro
Chapel Hill
Durham
PIEDMONT
Raleigh
Rocky Mt.
Elizabeth City
ALBEMARLE
PAMLICO
NEUSE
COASTAL
PLAIN
Charlotte
PEE DEE
Fayetteville
CAPE FEAR
New Bern
Morehead City
Wilmington
MAP 2
PHYSICAL FEATURES
AND
LOCATIONS OF MAJOR CITIES

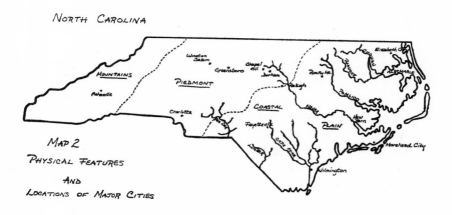

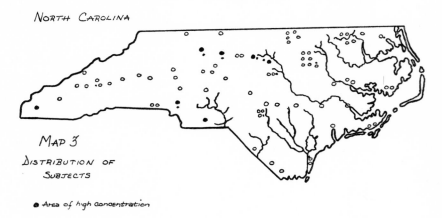

NORTH CAROLINA

MAP 3

DISTRIBUTION OF
SUBJECTS

● Area of high concentration

conversation; (3) phonetic transcription of speakers on television and radio; and (4) face to face conversations.

Map 3 shows the distribution of the subjects.

FINDINGS

Treatment of /ɜ/

All of the western counties of the South Midlands speech area showed a stronger /r/-system than did the remainder of the state. Among the speakers recorded, those from the mountain counties were more consistent than were the speakers in the Piedmont. There were no marked differences between the age groups in the mountains, but there were differences between the age groups in the Piedmont.

In the larger industrial areas of the North Piedmont, Winston-Salem, Greensboro and Burlington, the speakers had more constriction on the /ɜ/ as in *thirty* than did the speakers in the industrial areas nearer the South Carolina line. The general bodily tensions of the speakers seemed to make an observable difference in the degree of constriction used on the /ɜ/.

Only three subjects in the South Midlands area used the [ɜɪ] and then it was used infrequently and inconsistently. One subject was over sixty-five and the other two were in the late thirties. All three were in the Piedmont. The words in which the sounds appeared were *first, work, learn* and *early*. In a period of five minutes one subject used [ɜɪ], [ʌ] and [ɝ] in *first*, but in a conversation recorded ten days later [ɜɪ] and [ʌ] did not occur at all.

The three speech areas of eastern North Carolina had a weaker /r/-system than did the western counties. There were marked differences between the age groups. Individuals under twenty-five had a much stronger /r/-system than did the group between twenty-five and fifty-five. Those over fifty-five retained many of the variants common in a comparable generation in the Lower South. Variants were more numerous in the speech of all individuals in the eastern counties than in the South Midlands.

The variants of [ɜ] were particularly noticeable in the over fifty-five group. Several speakers used [ɝ], [ɜ̜ ~ ɜ ~ ɜᵘ*], [ɜɪ], [ʌɪ ~ ʌ ~ ʌə] in the same conversation. The choice of sound depended upon the particular word used and the stress placed upon that word in the sentence. The greatest variety was recorded on *work, first, learn, search, early,* and *person* or *personally.*

Again, as was the case in the South Midlands, the general bodily tensions of the individual and his rate and aggressiveness as a speaker seemed to make an observable change in the degree of constriction used on /ɜ/.

Maps 4-8 show the state-wide distribution of the treatment of /ɜ/ in *turn, thirsty, world, skirt* and *first.* Maps were not included for *work, learn, search, early* and *person* or *personally* since state-wide samples have not yet been collected for these specific words.

Postvocalic /r/ After Stressed Vowels

In the South Midlands and in the southeastern counties of the Cape Fear Valley, postvocalic /r/ was retained after the stressed vowel /ɑ/ in *parked, car, farm, barned* and *harvested,* but it was retained less frequently in the Peedee Valley, in the northeastern counties and in the Virginia Piedmont.

The majority of speakers in all areas dropped the postvocalic /r/ after the stressed vowel in *Arthur.*

Maps 9-12 show the distribution for the postvocalic /r/ after the stressed vowel [ɑ].

Considerable variance on a state-wide basis was observed in the treatment of /r/ after the stressed vowel /ɔ/ in *horse, George* and *warm.*

The /r/ was retained in *horse* by the younger speakers in the mountains and in the northern Piedmont and to some extent in the Cape Fear Valley, but it was either dropped or pronounced as [ə] by the

---

* A fully rounded form of [ɜ].

Stressed /ɜ/

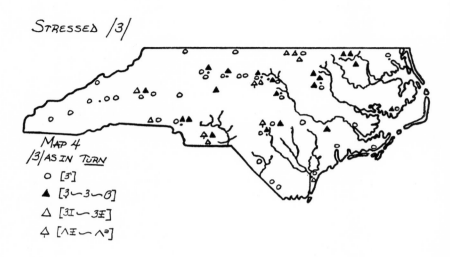

Map 4
/ɜ/ as in *Turn*

   o   [ɜ˚]
   ▲   [ɜ⌣ɜ⌢ɒ]
   △   [ɜɪ⌣ɜɨ]
   ⟁   [ʌɨ⌣ʌᵊ]

Stressed /ɜ/

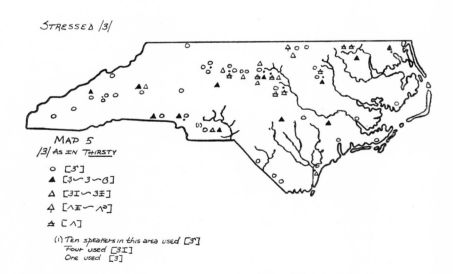

Map 5
/ɜ/ as in *Thirsty*

   o   [ɜ˚]
   ▲   [ɜ⌣ɜ⌢ɒ]
   △   [ɜɪ⌣ɜɨ]
   ⟁   [ʌɨ⌣ʌᵊ]
   ⩑   [ʌ]

     (1) Ten speakers in this area used [ɜ˚]
       Four used [ɜɪ]
       One used [ɜ]

STRESSED /ɝ/

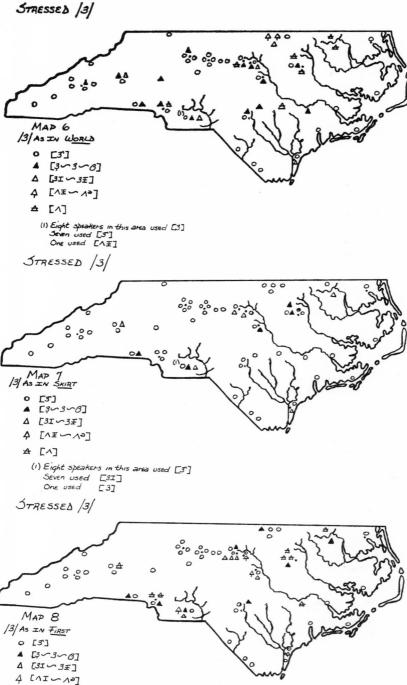

MAP 6
/ɝ/ AS IN WORLD

o   [ɝ]
▲   [ɝ‿ɝ‿ɵ]
△   [ɝɪ‿ɝɪ]
⟁   [ʌɪ‿ʌə]
⊿   [ʌ]

(1) Eight speakers in this area used [ɝ]
    Seven used [ɝ]
    One used [ʌɪ]

STRESSED /ɝ/

MAP 7
/ɝ/ AS IN SKIRT

o   [ɝ]
▲   [ɝ‿ɝ‿ɵ]
△   [ɝɪ‿ɝɪ]
⟁   [ʌɪ‿ʌə]
⊿   [ʌ]

(1) Eight speakers in this area used [ɝ]
    Seven used [ɝɪ]
    One used [ɝ]

STRESSED /ɝ/

MAP 8
/ɝ/ AS IN FIRST

o   [ɝ]
▲   [ɝ‿ɝ‿ɵ]
△   [ɝɪ‿ɝɪ]
⟁   [ʌɪ‿ʌə]
⊿   [ʌ]

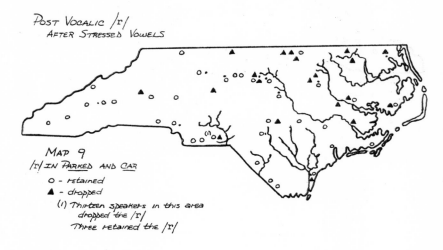

Post Vocalic /r/
After Stressed Vowels

MAP 9
/r/ in Parked and Car

   O - retained
   ▲ - dropped
     (1) Thirteen speakers in this area
       dropped the /r/
       Three retained the /r/

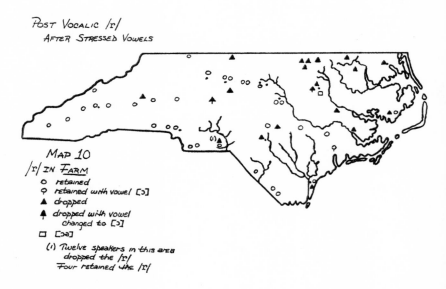

Post Vocalic /r/
After Stressed Vowels

MAP 10
/r/ in Farm

   O   retained
   Q   retained with vowel [ɔ]
   ▲   dropped
   ♠   dropped with vowel
      changed to [ɔ]
   □   [ɔə]
     (1) Twelve speakers in this area
       dropped the /r/
       Four retained the /r/

POST VOCALIC /r/
  AFTER STRESSED VOWELS

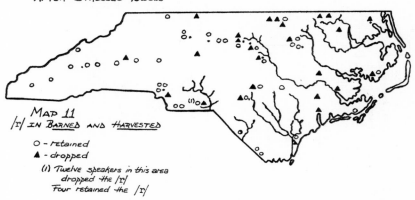

MAP 11
/r/ IN BARNED AND HARVESTED

  O – retained
  ▲ – dropped

  (1) Twelve speakers in this area
     dropped the /r/
     Four retained the /r/

POST VOCALIC /r/
  AFTER STRESSED VOWELS

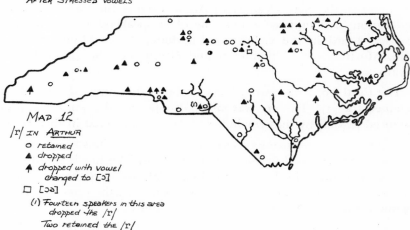

MAP 12
/r/ IN ARTHUR

  O retained
  ▲ dropped
  ⬆ dropped with vowel
     changed to [ɔ]
  ☐ [ɔə]

  (1) Fourteen speakers in this area
     dropped the /r/
     Two retained the /r/

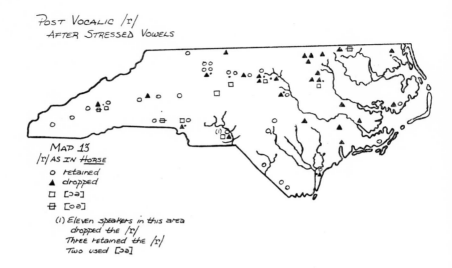

Post Vocalic /r/
After Stressed Vowels

Map 13
/r/ as in Horse
o retained
▲ dropped
□ [ɔə]
⊟ [oə]

(1) Eleven speakers in this area
  dropped the /r/
  Three retained the /r/
  Two used [ɔə]

majority of speakers in the Peedee Valley and in the northeastern counties. See Map 13 for details.

The variants were more numerous on *George*. The /r/ was retained by the majority in the South Midlands and northern Piedmont, but in the remainder of the state three additional pronunciations were heard. The /r/ was dropped in the Virginia Piedmont. Isolated instances of omission were found near Morganton, Statesville, Charlotte and in the Neuse Valley. In Anson County the [ɔə ∼ ɔwə] pronunciation predominated among the older speakers. The diphthong [ɔɪ] was heard in the vicinity of Charlotte, Rocky Mount, Chapel Hill, Murfreesboro, Wilmington and Greensboro. See Map 14 for details.

The third word was *warm*. Map 15 shows that only eight speakers retained the /r/. The /r/ was either dropped or the word was pronounced [wɔəm] by the remainder of the speakers used in this study.

Observations were made of postvocalic /r/ after the stressed vowels in *there* and *care,* and in *poor, door* and *floor*. The words *before* and *your* were included in the structured material, but since they appeared in a relatively unstressed position in the sentence, the results of these pronunciations were not tabulated in this study.

The /r/ was retained by a few speakers in the areas where /r/ had been retained after other stressed vowels. The /r/ was retained more often on *there* and *care* than it was on *poor, door,* and *floor.* The frequency of the use of [ə] in all of these words was far greater than had been expected.

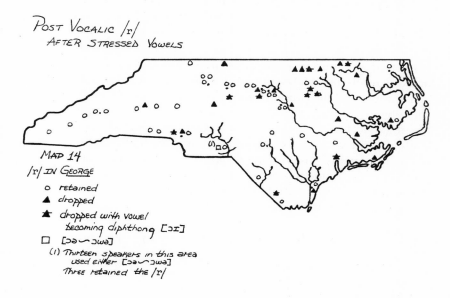

POST VOCALIC /r/
AFTER STRESSED VOWELS

MAP 14
/r/ IN GEORGE

o   retained
▲   dropped
★   dropped with vowel
     becoming diphthong [ɔɪ]
□   [ɔə～ɔwə]
  (1) Thirteen speakers in this area
        used either [ɔə～ɔwə]
     Three retained the /r/

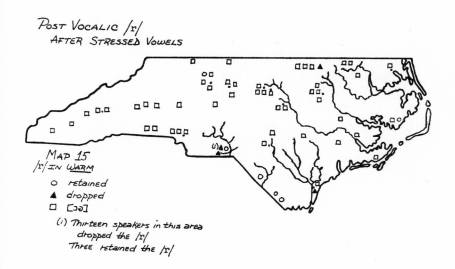

POST VOCALIC /r/
AFTER STRESSED VOWELS

MAP 15
/r/ IN WARM

o   retained
▲   dropped
□   [ɔə]
  (1) Thirteen speakers in this area
        dropped the /r/
     Three retained the /r/

Lowman and McDavid observed that the trend toward the use of [ə] was spreading in the eastern half of the state, particularly among the younger cultured speakers. Maps 16-18 show that the [ə] has now spread throughout the state, even into the remote areas of the mountains.

A third pronunciation of *poor, door, floor, before* and *your* was noted. Kurath and McDavid note that in Southern folk speech the [ə] is often lost and the pronunciations become [po], [do], etc.[9] They continue by saying that these pronunciations have some currency among the middle class, but they are avoided by cultured speakers. This study showed that the loss of [ə] was not limited to folk speech or to the educationally disadvantaged, but that the pronunciations [po] [do], etc. were numerous among university students, professors, teachers, newspaper men and high ranking government officials.

See Maps 16-18 for details.

Postvocalic /r/ After Unstressed Vowels

Postvocalic /r/ was retained in the South Midlands and to some extent in the rest of the state on words which contained a postvocalic /r/ in the stressed syllable. When the /r/ was retained after stressed vowel, as in *Parker, order* and *Carver,* it was usually retained in the unstressed position. But when there was no postvocalic /r/ in the first syllable, the /r/ after unstressed vowels was dropped, as in *after* and *remember.*

In the other three speech areas the /r/ was retained infrequently and there seemed to be less relationship between the presence or absence of /r/ in the stressed syllable.

The overall impression of North Carolina speech is that there is no /r/ after unstressed vowels. This may be due in part to the frequency of words in the average vocabulary which do not have *r* in the stressed syllable, e.g., *mother, father, sister, wonder, weather, better.* Further investigation is indicated in this specific treatment of /r/.

See Maps 19-21 for details.

Miscellaneous Observations

The extensive data on North Carolina accents have not been analyzed and tabulated in their entirety, but a few observations have been made which are pertinent to this study of the status of /r/ in North Carolina.

The linking /r/ as in *your aunt, color of, here is,* and *far along* was

---

[9] Kurath and McDavid, p. 171.

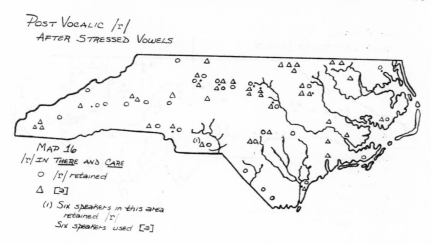

POST VOCALIC /r/
  AFTER STRESSED VOWELS

MAP 16
/r/ IN THERE AND CARE
  ○ /r/ retained
  △ [ə]

  (1) Six speakers in this area
        retained /r/
      Six speakers used [ə]

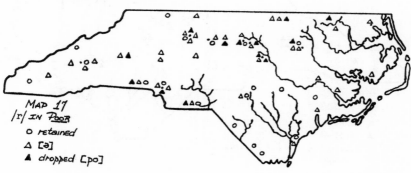

POST VOCALIC /r/
  AFTER STRESSED VOWELS

MAP 17
/r/ IN POOR
  ○ retained
  △ [ə]
  ▲ dropped [po]

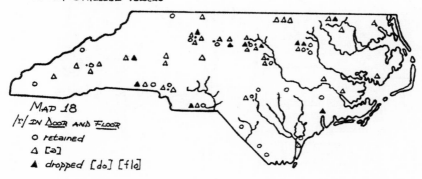

POST VOCALIC /r/
  AFTER STRESSED VOWELS

MAP 18
/r/ IN DOOR AND FLOOR
  ○ retained
  △ [ə]
  ▲ dropped [do] [flo]

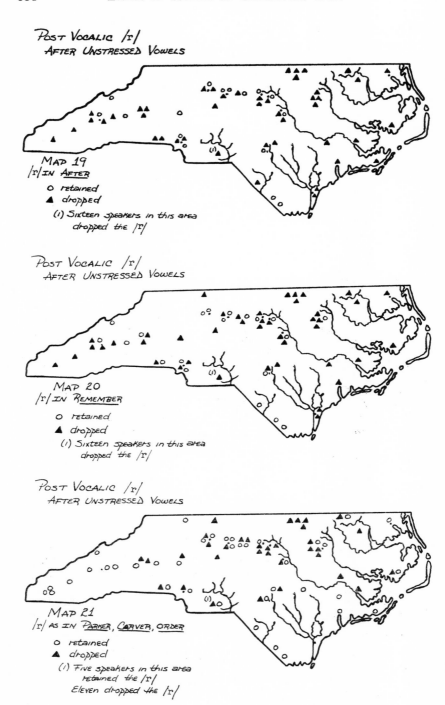

POST VOCALIC /r/
AFTER UNSTRESSED VOWELS

MAP 19
/r/ IN AFTER

o retained
▲ dropped

(1) Sixteen speakers in this area
     dropped the /r/

POST VOCALIC /r/
AFTER UNSTRESSED VOWELS

MAP 20
/r/ IN REMEMBER

o retained
▲ dropped

(1) Sixteen speakers in this area
     dropped the /r/

POST VOCALIC /r/
AFTER UNSTRESSED VOWELS

MAP 21
/r/ AS IN PARKER, CARVER, ORDER

o retained
▲ dropped

(1) Five speakers in this area
     retained the /r/
     Eleven dropped the /r/

used by a few speakers, but the trend was toward an /r/-less treatment of these words if the speaker habitually dropped the postvocalic /r/ (or used [ə]) when these words occurred in other positions.

The intrusive linking /r/ was heard in *following, swallow it* and *Cuba is* but it did not occur in *law and order* among the subjects used in this study. The intrusive /r/ was not a major characteristic of North Carolina speech.

A recording of a state legislator showed mixed usage of the linking /r/ and the intrusive /r/. He said, "We should certainly be aware of every area." [wi ʃʊd sʌtn̩lɪ bɪ əwærəv ɛʌə eɪrɪəˑ]

Numerous instances of the omission of /r/ in *cherry, very, minority, encourage, periodically, considerable, carry,* etc., were recorded during the political speeches of the 1968 campaigns. Similar omissions were noted among the university students. The omissions were not limited to those speakers who dropped postvocalic /r/ after stressed vowels. As a matter of fact, they frequently occurred in the speech of individuals who otherwise had a strong /r/-system.

The use of [ɝ] in *where* persists in the mountains, but it was not recorded among the university students from the mountain counties.

Both [ɝ] and [ɜɪ] were heard in the proper name *Jordan.*

A government official from the northern Piedmont used [ɜɪ] in *judge* and *judgment.*

A common pronunciation among the elderly blacks was [pɔɪtʃ] for *porch.*

The use of [ʌ] instead of [ɝ] or [ɜ] in *further* had much currency in the state, but since the word was not included in the controlled materials of this study, its frequency was not noted on maps.

Conclusions

The /r/-system in North Carolina is unstable. There are important regional differences and age differences. There is a trend toward stability among the younger speakers who have been exposed to teachers from other areas of the country and to the speech on radio and television.

At the time of this study the greatest stability was found on /ɜ/ in the mountains and in the northern Piedmont.

The [ɜɪ] is disappearing. It can still be heard among the older speakers, but it is unknown in the age group of twenty-five or less.

Postvocalic /r/ after the stressed vowels /ɑ/ and /ɔ/ is retained by more speakers than is postvocalic /r/ after other vowels.

Although the use of [ə] after the stressed vowels [ɪ], [ɛ], [æ], [u] and the diphthong [ou] is heard in all sections of the state, this pronunciation is more frequent in the eastern counties than it is in the Piedmont and the mountains.

Postvocalic /r/ after unstressed vowels varies somewhat in accordance with the presence or absence of /r/ in the stressed syllable, but the trend toward the use of [ə] in the unaccented syllable has spread throughout the state.

AN ALPHABET FOR THE HAWAIIANS

WESLEY D. HERVEY
University of Oregon

In 1951 while Claude M. Wise was a visiting professor in the Department of Speech at the University of Hawaii, he and the author became intrigued with the history of how an alphabet was introduced into the Hawaiian culture. One of the first articles to be published on the subject of Hawaiian orthography resulted from the collaboration of Wise and Hervey.[1] Since that time, this writer has completed additional research on the same subject.

The history of orthographic adaptations to the Hawaiian language began with the first voyages to the Sandwich Islands by James Cook and others and ultimately would encompass the history of Hawaii to the present time. This article has as its focus, the first attempts of missionaries to adapt an orthographic system to the writing and printing of the Hawaiian language. The two men who played leading roles in this early history were Elisha Loomis and Hiram Bingham.

Loomis, Printer In Paradise

Elisha Loomis was a printer by trade and a Christian missionary by faith, who had married Maria Sartwell and sailed to the Sandwich Islands on the *Thaddeus* with the rest of the first company of missionaries. The journals left by Maria and Elisha Loomis present an intimate picture of their reactions to Hawaii and Hawaii's reactions to them, during those crucial years from 1820 to 1826.[2] This journal begins with the simple statement, "Here begins the journal of Elisha and Maria (Loomis), October 2, 1819 to November 11, 1820."[3]

The specific purpose of the mission to the Sandwich Islands was to

---

[1] Claude M. Wise and Wesley D. Hervey, "The Evolution of Hawaiian Orthography," *Quarterly Journal of Speech*, XXXVIII (October, 1952).

[2] "Elisha and Maria Loomis Journal, October 23, 1819 to November 11, 1820," (Handwritten copy by Albertine Loomis), (MS in Hawaiian Mission Children's Society Library, Honolulu, Hawaii), p. 146.

[3] This copy from which these facts have been taken, was prepared by Albertine Loomis from the original received September 30, 1957 by the Hawaiian Mission Children's Society Library. Because of the fragile state of the original journal, this copy was used for research purposes, although this writer had access to the original which reads, "October 23, 1819, Elisha Loomis Journal."

teach the Hawaiians the Gospel; in order to realize this goal it was necessary to teach the people how to read in their own language. Since there was no written language, the first task of the missionary workers was to adapt an alphabet to the spoken language and then to print translations of the religious materials available. These translations were then to be distributed to the people, to be used in conducting the religious services, and later to be used in the newly established schools.

It was fortuitous that certain members of the nobility were accepting of the innovations introduced by the missionaries. King Liholiho (Kamehameha II) was well disposed toward them, as demonstrated by a favorite phrase which he used in the presence of Elisha Loomis, "nooe nooe miti, nooe allohah Amerika," which translated into the revised orthographic system of 1826 would read, "nui nui maika'i, nui aloha Amerika" (Very good, much love [affection] for America).[4] King Kaumualii of Kauai was also receptive to the new teachings, being pleased with the Bible sent him by the American Bible Society and anxious to understand its contents. When select portions of it were read in English and interpreted to him, he told the brethren (missionaries) that they must make haste and learn the Hawaiian language fast, so that they could tell him all about the Good Book. The King's desire to learn to read was so strong that he indicated to the missionaries that he was willing to devote ten years to its accomplishment, and from that day on "lest he should lose time while bathing," the King of Kauai took his Bible with him and studied while in the water. He told the missionaries that if they would come and settle on Kauai, he would build them houses and furnish them with lands and that all of his people would observe the Sabbath and worship the Christian God.[5]

The *palapala* (printed and/or written word) held great fascination for the *alii* (nobility) who came into close contact with printed Bibles and the mysteries of penmanship. The high chiefs and their wives were so eager for the new skills of reading and writing that they learned these skills with remarkable facility. Elisha Loomis writes that the King of Hawaii (Liholiho), was able to read "intelligibly" in the New Testament.[6] This would mean that he had learned to read English in about three and a half months. While the *alii* were eager to master these new skills, they wished to do so to the exclusion of the common people. For instance, in July, 1820, Maria Loomis indicated that the King objected to the missionaries teaching any to

4 *Ibid.*, p. 138.
5 *Ibid.*
6 *Ibid.*, p. 152.

read "except chiefs and the families of white men."[7] This tendency was later relaxed under pressure exerted by the missionaries. However, the attitude of the chiefs, concerning the question of equal educational opportunity, created cross-currents producing stress in the relations between the missionaries and those of high rank.

In August, 1820, Elisha Loomis mentioned in his journal that he "employed" the day putting together the Ramage Press, and found it was in good order and "but little damaged by the rough usage which it had received on the voyage."[8] He wished to prepare the press for printing a few alphabets for the use of the scholars.[9] What "alphabets" are referred to here? This whole matter is particularly interesting from the standpoint that January 7, 1822, is traditionally celebrated as the date of the first printing in the Hawaiian Islands. Is it possible that Mr. Loomis ran off several copies of an alphabet as early at August, 1820? At about the same time, another entry indicates that the govern-

TABLE 1

GRAPHEME-PHONEME RELATIONSHIP RECONSTRUCTION
BASED ON THE SPELLING BOOK BY HIRAM BINGHAM

Graphemes	Phonemes
a	/ɑ
e	e
i	i
o	o
u	u
ou	o-u
oi	ɔ-i
ai	ɑ-i
au	ɑ-u
oe	ɔ-e
ae	ɑ-e
ao	ɑ-o/
h	/h
k	k
l	l
m	m
n	n
p	p
r	r
t	t
v	v
w	w/

[7] *Ibid.*, p. 151.
[8] *Ibid.*, p. 164.
[9] *Ibid.*

ment had requested that some printing be done, but that this request could not be fulfilled because the press was not ready for use.[10]

Throughout the Hawaiian Islands, one of the most important topics of conversation concerned reading and writing.

Hiram Bingham, Alphabet Maker

From an examination of "Spelling Book and Select Scriptures" it is possible to reconstruct the working alphabet in use by this student of Hawaiian at this particular period. This orthographic system is essentially the first worked out in Bingham's own handwriting found in the unpublished material entitled "Spelling Book and Select Scriptures and Materials for Spelling Book."[11] The line drawn across the lower third of the sheet of paper of the original seemed to indicate that the (b), (d), (f), (g), (s), and (z) were to be used when writing foreign words. These notes by Bingham may well have represented his earliest thoughts on the subject of an alphabet. The following quotation of Hiram Bingham serves to clarify his philosophy so far as a choice of an alphabet for use in writing Hawaiian was concerned.

> To make the spelling and reading of the language easy to the people, and convenient to all who use it, was a matter of great importance, almost indispensable to our success in raising the nation. It was, therefore, a part of our task to secure to the people a perfect alphabet, literal or syllabic, of all the sounds which were then in use, and which would need soon to come into use in the progress of the nation.[12]

These words were prophetic when the sounds which would soon need to come into use were mentioned. Bingham must have known how many terms from the Christian religion would be introduced into the culture of the Hawaiians in a short span of time. How could these proper nouns be adapted to the phonology and orthography of the Hawaiian language? These new terms would include place names, proper nouns, the names of the books of the Bible as well as the names of foreign places throughout the world appearing with increasing frequency in the Hawaii of 1822. The following words in Table 2 were included in the list in Bingham's notes.

Several words in this list have not been positively identified either because of uncertainty in reading the handwriting on a discolored, time-ravaged manuscript and/or failure to find the referent for the

[10] *Ibid.*, p. 172.
[11] Bingham, "Spelling Book and Select Scriptures and Materials for Spelling Book." Manuscript prepared by Bingham, Oahu, Hawaii, 1822 (MS in Hawaiian Mission Children's Society Library, Honolulu, Hawaii).
[12] *Ibid.*, p. 18.

TABLE 2
PLACE NAMES SPELLED IN THE HAWAIIAN AND ENGLISH ORTHOGRAPHIES

Place Names: Bingham's Hawaiian Spelling*	Place Names: Current English Spelling
Amerika	America
Afrika	Africa
Asia	Asia
Europa	Europe
Rusia	Russia
Beretania	Britain
Franca	France
Hipaniola	Hispanola
Itali	Italy
Judea	Judea
Benigale	Bengal
Tahiti	Tahiti
Nuiorika	New York
Benigala	Bengal
St. Peteroboro	St. Petersburg
Lonedona	London
Roma	Rome or Romans
Jerusalema	Jerusalem
Kalakuta	Calcutta
Kep Horn	Cape Horn

*Ibid., p. 4.

proper noun as rendered by Bingham. A second list, also found among his notes, included the most frequently used proper nouns from the Bible as Bingham spelled them in the newly adopted orthography. These pages clearly represented the first notes of a scholar working out the problems of an orthography for a language with a number of characteristics unique to the experience of a New Englander. In the case of Cape Horn, Bingham wrote both words with closed syllables, although it is clear from a study of the other entries that he was making an effort to include only open-syllables. Table 3 displays Biblical names selected from Bingham's notes.

The listing of some words more than once in the original manuscript may indicate variant spelling trials engaged in by Bingham as he pronounced the words himself and attempted to record the pronunciation he thought to be most consistent with the phonology of spoken Hawaiian as he perceived it. At other times it seems that the appearance of a particular word more than once in the list may have been an attempt on the part of Bingham to test how the given word looked in written form in relation to how it was being pronounced on a trial basis.

TABLE 3

BIBLICAL NAMES SPELLED IN HAWAIIAN AND ENGLISH ORTHOGRAPHIES

Biblical Names: Bingham's Hawaiian Spelling*	Biblical Names: Current English Spelling
Davida	David
Iesu	Jesus
Kraist	Christ
Iaone	John
Mataio	Matthew
Luka	Luke
Paulo	Paul
Mose	Moses
Noa	Noah
Aberehama	Abraham
Isaka	Isaac
Jekoba	Jacob
Daniela	Daniel
Isaia	Isaiah

Ibid.

Bingham was explicit in his own writing concerning the lack of an adequate model for either the spoken or the written language of the Hawaiians, feeling that those who had attempted to write the names and places in the Hawaiian Islands had materially failed even in the case of the most common terms.[13] No foreigner or native was able to illustrate or explain the peculiarities and intricacies of the language, according to Bingham.[14] This statement simply underscores the situation then as now, that men using a language in the marketplace seldom stop to speculate on the nature of that language, beyond whether it satisfies the most pressing of mundane needs.

Though we obtained a few words and phrases from William Moxley and others, we found the dialect in use by foreigners often materially misled us, so that none could be trusted as to accuracy, and it required time to detect and unlearn errors. In the oft' recurring names of the principal island, the largest village, and the king of the leeward islands, 'Owhyhee, Hanaroorah, and Tamoree,' scarcely the sound of a single syllable was correctly expressed, either in writing or speaking, by voyagers or foreign residents. Had we therefore, followed the orthography of voyagers, or in adopting an alphabet, made a single vowel stand for as many sounds as in English, and several different vowels for the same sound, and given the consonants the ambiguity of our c, s, t, ch, gh, etc., it would have been extremely difficult, if not impractica-

13 Bingham, *A Residence of Twenty-One Years in the Sandwich Islands or the Civil, Religious, and Political History of those Islands, op. cit.,* p. 153.
14 *Ibid.*

ble to induce the nation to become readers, in the course of a whole generation, even if we had been furnished with ample funds to sustain in boarding-schools, all who would devote their time and labor to study.[15]

What Reverend Bingham was saying was that the pronunciation of major place names and proper nouns differed widely among the persons he had used as informants. Had there been a linguistic geographer, these variations could have been plotted for the individual islands and for districts on the various islands. The second inescapable point was that Bingham wished to adapt an orthographic system to writing Hawaiian that would not have included the same ambiguities inherent in the English alphabet. As will be seen, this philosophy eventually pervaded the entire discussion among the missionaries as to which symbols they were to choose for the Hawaiian alphabet and which they were to delete. A further observation of Bingham's was that through the course of two centuries American philologists demonstrated the difficulty of inducing the aboriginal tribes of the North American continent to use the European literature, and that the major cause of the failure in this regard was the "anomalous, intricate, and ever dubious orthography."[16] Following this general philosophy, the missionaries' expressed aim was to avoid an ambiguous, erroneous, and inconvenient orthography by assigning one certain sound to every character, thus representing with "ease and exactness the true pronunciation of the Hawaiian language."[17] The alphabet finally advocated by Bingham was (a), (e), (i), (o), (u), (h), (k), (l), (m), (n), (p), (w). Bingham indicated in his discussions of the subject that these twelve letters, and possibly eleven, omitting either u or w, "will express every sound in the pure Hawaiian dialect."[18]

TABE 4

AN ANALYSIS OF THE ORTHOGRAPHIC SYSTEM FOR THE VOWELS PROPOSED BY HIRAM BINGHAM

Graphemes	From Bingham Pronunciation Key	Phonemes Suggested by Hervey
a	as in "art" or "father"	/ɑ
e	as in "pale" or "they"	e
i	as in "machine"	i
o	as in "no"	o
u	as in "too"	u/

[15] *Ibid.*
[16] *Ibid.*
[17] *Ibid.*
[18] *Ibid.*

Table 4 is an analysis of the vowels of the orthographic system proposed by Hiram Bingham.

"The vowels were called so as to express their power by their names."[19] Accordingly, (a) was called [ɑ], (e) was called [e], (i) was called [i], (o) was called [o], and (u) was called [u].[20] The consonants also had names which would suggest their "power" (phonemic character); as such, Hiram Bingham was grappling with the basic concepts of phoneme, grapheme, and fit. When he used the term "power," he did so to describe the phoneme associated with the grapheme, or to discuss the relationship of the printed symbol with the associated phoneme. Referring to the vowels as [eɪ], [i], [ɑ], [o], [u] was undoubtedly an attempt to aid the native speakers of Hawaiian in recognizing the nature of the fit introduced to them.

Bingham identified the following consonant sounds to which the writer has added a phonetic transcription, e.g., "He"-[he], "Ke"-[ke], "La"-[lɑ], "Mu"-[mu], "Nu"-[nu], "Pi"-[pi], "We"-[we]. When the consonants were introduced to the Hawaiian pupils, they learned each consonant in a syllable with every possible combination of vowels, e.g. (ke), (ki), (kɑ), (ko), (ku), (he), (hi), (ha), (ho), (hu), and so forth.[21]

The alphabet in Figure 1 is illustrative of the alphabet after the revision of 1826, although no date has been established for this particular printing.

The alphabet in Figures 2, 3 and 4 was printed on a replica of the original Ramage Press used by Elisha Loomis. It can be recognized that this alphabet is an early one, since (b), (d), (r), (t), and (v) are included, although these symbols were omitted from the orthographic system after the revision of 1826. The diphthongs (ae), (ai), (ao), (au), (ei), (eu), and (ou) were included. Although the descriptive term for these vowel combinations was "diphthongs," a careful reading of the accompanying pronunciation key gives the impression that the missionaries had a developing understanding that these orthographic combinations were not articulated as diphthongs by the Hawaiians.

The First Alphabets

In Table 5, the first column includes the orthographic adaptations taken from the reproduction of the original imprint. Column two includes the descriptive commentary employed by the missionaries. The third column contains the key words employed in the original alphabet sheet together with a translation of the Hawaiian. The fourth column presents a phonetic analysis of the description found in the

[19] *Ibid.*
[20] *Ibid.*
[21] *Ibid.*

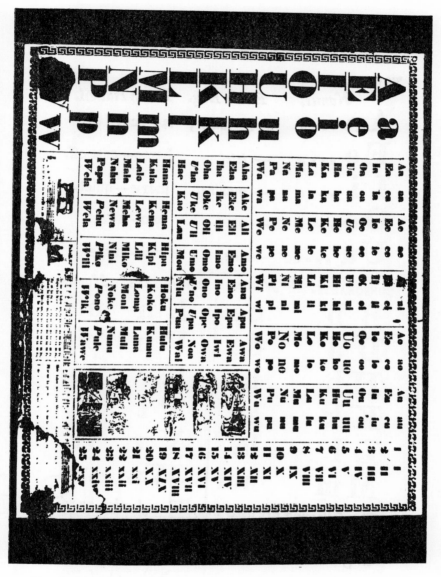

FIG. 1. Hawaiian alphabet on cloth, original in Hawaiian Mission Children's Society Library, Honolulu, Hawaii.

THE ALPHABET.

VOWELS.		SOUND.	
	Names.	*Ex. in Eng.*	*Ex. in Hawaii.*
A a ...a		as in *father,*	la—sun.
E e ...a		— *tete,*	hemo—cast off.
I i ...e		— *marine,*	marie—quiet.
O o ...o		— *over,*	ono—sweet.
U u ...oo		—*rule,*	nui—large.

CONSONANTS.	*Names.*	CONSONANTS.	*Names.*
B b	be	**N n**	nu
D d	de	**P p**	pi
H h	he	**R r**	ro
K k	ke	**T t**	ti
L l	la	**V v**	vi
M m	mu	**W w**	we

The following are used in spelling foreign words:

F f	ſe	S s	ſe
G g	ge	Y --	yi

FIG. 2. Page one of the first alphabet printed in Hawaii. Original in Hawaiian Mission Children's Society Library, Honolulu, Hawaii.

TABLE 5

PHONETIC ANALYSIS OF VOWELS SHOWN IN FIGURE 2

Graphemes	Description	Hawaiian Key Words and English Glossary	Column 2	Phonetic Analysis of: Pukui & Elbert
ae	as a in ayee	*ae* yes	ɑ-ɪ	ɑ-e
ai	as in aisle or idol	*ai* food	ɑɪ⊥	ɑ-i
ao	as a in far followed closely by o	*ao* bread	ɑ-o	ɑ-o
au	like ow in vow	*pau* all	ɑʊ	ɑ-u
ei	as in eight	*lei* beads	eɪ	e-i
eu	as a in late followed by oo	*weuweu* grass	e-ʊ	e-u
ou	as o followed closely by oo	*lakou* they	o-ʊ	o-u

second column, using the symbols of the International Phonetic Alphabet. The fifth column of the table presents the phonetic analysis of the graphemes according to Pukui and Elbert.[22] At times, as in the case of the grapheme (ae), the articulation as described in column two differs from the analysis presented by consulting Pukui and Elbert.[23]

The use of the descriptive phraseology in Figure 3, "as 'a' in 'far' followed closely by 'o,' " may indicate an attempt to discriminate the diphthong [ɑɪ] from the vowel combination [ɑ-i]. "Followed closely by" may have been the only way that the New Englanders knew of indicating that the Hawaiian diphthong [ɑ-i] was different from the English [ɑɪ].

"Double vowels pronounced separately," were listed separately as (aa), (ee), (ii), (oo). The (uu) combination was omitted from this list even though it is found in any number of place names such as "Punuluu." In reference to another aspect of the phonology of Hawaiian, there is evidence that the missionaries recognized the presence of the glottal stop but did not realize it was a phonemic element in the

---

[22] Mary Kawena Pukui and Samuel H. Elbert, *English-Hawaiian Dictionary* (Honolulu: University of Hawaii Press, 1964), pp. x-xi.
[23] Pukui and Elbert, *Hawaiian-English Dictionary, op. cit.,* p. xxix.

2

DIPTHONGS.

Ae as in *ayes*, - • - - ae—yes.

Ai as in *aisle*, or *idol*, ▪ ▪ ai—food.

Ao as *a* in *far*, followed closely by *o;* ao—bread,

Au like *ow* in *vow*, - - - pau—all.

Ei as in *eight*, nearly, - ▪ lei—beads.

Eu as *a* in *late*, followed by *oo;* weuweu—grass.

Ou as *o* followed closely by *oo;* lakou—they.

TABLE I.

LESSON 1.

Ba	be	bi	bo	bu
da	de	di	do	du
ha	he	hi	ho	hu
ka	ke	ki	ko	ku
la	le	li	lo	lu
ma	me	mi	mo	mu
na	ne	ni	no	nu

FIG. 3. Page two of the first alphabet printed in Hawaii. Original in Hawaiian Mission Children's Society Library, Honolulu, Hawaii.

3

pa	pe	pi	po
ra	re	ri	ro
ta	te	ti	to
va	ve	vi	vo
wa	we	wi	wo

LESSON 2.

Double vowels pronounced separately.

| Aa | ee | ii | oo |
| waa | kee | lii | hoo |

LESSON 3.

Dipthongal syllables,

Ae	lae	nae	pae
ai	hai	kai	mai
ao	hao	kao	mao
au	mau	nau	rau
ei	lei	nei	pei
eu	heu	peu	teu
ou	kou	hou	mou

FIG. 4. Page three of the first alphabet printed in Hawaii. Original in Hawaiian Mission Children's Society Library, Honolulu, Hawaii.

language. "There are, on the other hand, abrupt separations or short and sudden breaks between two vowels in the same word."[24] One characteristic of spoken Hawaiian which could have induced such a description is the double and triple vowel grapheme combinations which are pronounced not in the diphthongized manner of English, but separately. The second characteristic is the sudden break between two vowels in the same word which could have been descriptive of the glottal stop, although it was not recorded as such.[25]

Bingham made another observation of interest to those conversant with phoneme theory.

> The slight variation in quantity, though not in quality, of sound in the vowels requires no mark of distinction, any more than in the variations of the sound of a in the English words 'art' and 'father.' Here the quantity may differ slightly though it is not necessary to put a distinctive mark, or make a different character.[26]

Along these lines Pukui and Elbert have denoted both stressed and unstressed vowels in the pronunciation of Hawaiian. The phonetic analysis in the right-hand column of Tables 6 and 7 is the writer's interpretation of the descriptions used by Pukui and Elbert.

It is documented that the missionaries recognized variations in vowel length as manifested by speakers of Hawaiian. That they may not have been aware of the nuances discussed by Pukui and Elbert is not at all surprising. It becomes clear also from Bingham's observations that what he called diphthongal combinations were the vowel combinations recognized today as associated with the graphemes (ae), (ai), (ao), and (au). Bingham's description of how these combinations were spoken is explicit: "Whether more close or more open, each letter retains its original monosound."[27] This writer infers from the following statement that these vowel combinations may have been articulated in fluent speech in a manner resembling diphthongs as recognized in American English Speech. At other times they may have been articulated with varying degrees of separation between the vowel phonemes. "In the name of the island second in size in the group, whether pronounced Mau-i or Ma-u-i, there is no such difference as to cause a mistake in a native hearer."[28]

[24] Bingham, *A Resident of Twenty-One Years in the Sandwich Islands or the Civil, Religious, and Political History of those Islands, op. cit.,* p. 154.
[25] *Ibid.* (It is a moot point as to whether Hawaiian pronunciation has changed significantly since the 1820's.)
[26] *Ibid.*
[27] *Ibid.,* p. 154.
[28] *Ibid.*

TABLE 6

UNSTRESSED VOWELS*

Graphemes	Description	Phonetic Description from Hervey
a	like a in *above*	ə
e	like e in *bet*	ɛ
i	like y in *city*	ɪ
o	like o in *sole*	oʊ
u	like oo in *moon*	u

* Pukui and Elbert, *Hawaiian-English Dictionary, op. cit.,* p. xxix.

TABLE 7

STRESSED VOWELS*

Graphemes	Explanation	Phonetic Description from Hervey
ā	like a in *far*	ɑ
ē	like ay in *play*	eɪ
ī	like ee in *see*	i
ō	like o in *sole*	oʊ
ū	like oo in *moon*	u

* Pukui and Elbert, *Hawaiian-English Dictionary, op. cit.,* p. xxix.

Bingham felt that it would not be possible to write any language with a more simple or limited orthographic system, and at the same time have it equally intelligible to the children who would be using it. A syllabic alphabet of ninety-five characters would have accommodated the phonology of Hawaiian, but would not have been so simple or convenient as the alphabet adopted by the missionaries.[29]

Though five vowels and seven consonants would have been sufficient in expressing the phonemes of the Hawaiian language as recognized by the missionaries, there were other reasons for including the possibility of other graphic symbols. As communications among the peoples of the Pacific were accelerated through an increase in marine traffic, the spelling of other dialects of Polynesian became a more frequently encountered problem. There was the growing need for introducing to the Hawaiians the names of persons, places, and things from other countries.[30]

Bingham and others realized that eleven or twelve letters would have resulted in an orthographic system far too limited for a general

[29] *Ibid.*
[30] *Ibid.,* p. 155.

knowledge of the world in printed and written form. It also seemed important to preserve the identity of foreign and Biblical names. They could not have deleted consonant graphemes from the spelling of foreign names of persons and places simply because such symbols could have been dispensed with in writing the strictly Hawaiian words. The following additional consonants were therefore incorporated into the expanded orthography: (b), (f), (g), (r), (s), (t), (v), and (z).[31]

The Influence of John Pickering

According to Bingham, the compound consonants recommended by John Pickering for writing the Amerindian languages of North America were not included in the Hawaiian system, though the principles followed by him with respect to the vowels were followed also by the missionaries in their work.[32] At this point in this history we must acknowledge our indebtedness to Cj Stevens for calling attention to the fact that not only had Bingham read John Pickering's essay on a uniform orthography for the North American Indian languages but he (Hiram Bingham) and Thomas Hopu had paid Pickering a visit in the year 1819, before setting off for the Sandwich Islands.[33]

First of all, it appears that John Pickering wrote to Hiram Bingham on October 19, 1819 indicating, among other things, the desirability that some common orthography should be adopted for the unwritten language of the Hawaiians. It is interesting to note that Bingham took Pickering's advice and did compare the language of the Hawaiians with those of Tahiti and elsewhere. The use of the so-called "foreign sounds" of the vowels became a basic criterion followed by the missionaries in adapting an orthography to the unwritten language of Hawaii.

Later, Pickering included this same principle for the vowels, with a discussion of consonant graphemes in his essay on a uniform orthography.[34]

> I have always thought, therefore, that it would be best to adopt as the basis of our Indian orthography, what we call the foreign sounds of all the vowels. . . .

[31] *Ibid.*
[32] John Pickering, "An Essay On A Uniform Orthography For The Indian Languages of North America." *Memoirs of The American Academy of Arts and Sciences* (Cambridge: Cambridge University Press, 1820).
[33] Cj Stevens, "Early American Phonology" (Unpublished dissertation, Louisiana State University. August, 1954).
[34] *Ibid.*

a as in father
e as in there
i as in machine
o as in note
u as in rule
y as in you
B as in English and French
D the same
E as in there
F as in English
G English g hard as in game
H as aspiration as in English
K as in English
L same
M same
N same
O as in English robe, some, among
P as in English
R the same
S as in English at the beginning of a word
T as in English
U as English (oo), both long and short
V English (v) or German (w)
W as in English. French (ou)
Y as in English in words yet, you
Z as in English

. . . in the languages of the American Indians, we have only to ascertain, in the first place, every elementary sound, and to arrange the letters, by which we may choose to represent those sounds, in order of our own alphabet.[35]

When writing a foreign word in which there was a compound consonant which could not have been omitted, the practice was to retain one grapheme of the two, such as (p) for (ph), (t) for (th), and (k) for (ch).[36] When both consonant graphemes had to be preserved, the procedure was to insert an (e) and after a final consonant an (a) was used as in the word "Boston," which was spelled "Bosetona."[37] Thus, allowances were made for the introduction of loan words into the language of the Hawaiians at a time when the incidence of such innovations was increasing.

Summary

The final revision of the alphabet was not affected until 1826 and it was with this specific phase of the history that Wise and Hervey

[35] *Ibid.*, p. 2.
[36] Bingham, *A Resident of Twenty-One Years in the Sandwich Islands or the Civil, Religious, and Political History of those Islands, op. cit.*, p. 155.
[37] *Ibid.*

were concerned in their original research in this area. It must be remembered that the missionaries were not phonemicists, nor linguists of any sort except in a practical, self-taught manner. The only professional help they had came from another practical linguist, William Ellis, and from the more contemplative John Pickering, behind whom stood the philosophical Duponceau. It must be said with no more than a minimum of reservation that Bingham and his colleagues did astonishingly well. Anyone who has had the occasion to experience the relative ease of reading and writing Hawaiian will testify that the missionaries applied phonemic principles with remarkable success to the devising of an alphabet for a language that had none.

BIBLIOGRAPHY

UNPUBLISHED MATERIAL

Books

Bingham, Hiram. "Spelling Book and Select Scriptures and Materials for Spelling Book." Manuscript Prepared by Bingham, Oahu, Hawaii, 1822. MS Hawaiian Mission Children's Society Library, Honolulu, Hawaii.

Journals

Bingham, Hiram. "Journal of Mr. Bingham's Four to Mooi," Novmber 10, 1821. MS ABC 180-193. Houghton Library, Harvard University, Cambridge, Massachusetts.

Loomis, Elisha and Loomis, Maria. "Elisha and Maria Loomis Journal October 23, 1819 to November 11, 1820." MS Hawaiian Mission Children's Society Library, Honolulu, Hawaii.

Theses

Newbrand, Helene Luise. "A Phonetic Analysis of Hawaiian." Unpublished Master's Thesis, Department of Speech, University of Hawaii, 1951.

PUBLISHED MATERIAL

Alphabets

"Hawaiian Alphabet Printed on Cloth," n.p., n.d., Hawaiian Mission Children's Society Library, Honolulu, Hawaii.

"Hawaiian Alphabet Printed on Replica of the Original Ramage Press," Honolulu, 1907. Possession of the Writer.

Articles

Pickering, John. "An Essay on a Uniform Orthography for the Indian Languages of North America," *Memoirs of the American Academy of Arts and Sciences.* Cambridge, Massachusetts: Cambridge University Press, 1820. Ayer Collection, Newberry Library, Chicago, Illinois.

Wise, Claude M. and Hervey, Wesley D. "The Evolution of the Hawaiian Orthography," *Quarterly Journal of Speech,* XXXVIII (October, 1952), 311-325.

Books

Bingham, Hiram. *A Residence of Twenty-One Years in the Sandwich Islands, or the Civil, Reiglious, and Political History of those Islands.* New York: Sherman Converse, 1847. Possession of the writer, a gift from Professor Alfred G. Smith, University of Oregon.

Duponceau, Peter S. *English Phonology*. Philadelphia: Abraham Small, 1817. Ayer Collection, Newberry Library, Chicago, Illinois.

Ellis, William. *Polynesian Researches During a Residence of Nearly Six Years in the South Seas Islands*. London: Fisher, Son and Jackson, Newgate Street, 1829. Hawaiian Historical Society Library, Honolulu, Hawaii.

Dictionaries

Pukui, Mary Kawena and Elbert, Samuel H. *Hawaiian-English Dictionary*. Honolulu: University of Hawaii Press, 1961. Hawaiian and Pacific Collection, Sinclair Library, University of Hawaii, Honolulu, Hawaii.

Pukui, Mary Kawena and Elbert, Samuel H. *English-Hawaiian Dictionary*, Honolulu: University of Hawaii Press, 1964. Hawaiian and Pacific Collection, Sinclair Library, University of Hawaii, Honolulu, Hawaii.

CHANGING PATTERNS OF SOUTHERN DIALECTS*

RAVEN I. McDAVID, JR.

University of Chicago

I

The times have never been more favorable for analyzing the patterns of Southern speech. First, we now have massive quantities of data, which we never had before; some of it is already accessible to scholars, whatever their residence, and there will be more to come as the *Linguistic Atlas of the Middle and South Atlantic States* finds its way into print. Second, there is nationwide concern with some of the varieties of Southern speech; as the less-educated Southerners flock to Northern and Eastern cities in search of new opportunities, their pronunciation seems out of place in their new habitat, and their grammar stands in the way of their getting as far in school or in business as their abilities would normally justify. Finally, many of the most important national concerns have been expressed in Southern accents. Despite the bitterness of professional Bostonians, no president has worked harder than Lyndon Johnson for the general welfare, and his efforts have been eloquently supported by those of Martin Luther King and Ralph Abernathy. Nor does the change in administration greatly alter the realities of the situation. Despite the hate-mongering of such putative liberals as Nelson Rockefeller, it seems clear that President Nixon has abandoned the bloody shirt as the Republican emblem and has decided to accept Southerners as members of the human race and citizens deserving the respect customarily extended to those from other regions.

II

So now, in looking at the speech of the South against the background of other varieties of English—United States, Canadian, British and Commonwealth—we may begin by deflating a few old myths, some related particularly to Southern speech, but most of them with far wider implications.

The *uniformity* of Southern speech is grossly exaggerated. Many of our friends from further North speak of *"the* Southern accent" as if it were something monolithic. Actually, within the territory where Southern traditions are important, there is evidence of at least three major speech types: (1) Southern proper, the speech of the old plantation country; (2) South Midland, the speech of the Southern uplands, ultimately affiliated with that of Western Pennsylvania; and (3) North

*A version of this paper was presented at the Institute for Southern Culture, Longwood College, Farmville, Virginia, April 1966.

Midland, the speech of Pennsylvania and its immediate dependencies. Within these regional patterns one finds at least nine clearly marked areas of consequence in the pre-Revolutionary South alone and a number of minor areas;[1] even a preliminary examination shows more than half a dozen areas in Louisiana and Texas; when the returns are in we can expect to find at least thirty important sub-varieties of Southern speech, to say nothing of reflexes of foreign language settlements of European origin and the semi-creolized dialect of the Gullah Negroes. Truly, as Hans Kurath has repeatedly remarked, the South has the greatest diversity of speech forms to be found in English-speaking North America, with the possible exception of Newfoundland.

The origins of Southern dialects are also generally misunderstood. Many casual observers assert that the warm climate is responsible for a languid drawl. But even if a drawl were a general characteristic of Southern speech—as it is not—those who believe in the effects of hot climate would be confounded by the rapid-fire dialogue of the Bengali in eastern India. Similarly, the nasality of Southern upland speech cannot be explained by either excessive rainfall or excessive dryness —and both explanations have been offered. More prosaic causes—social forces—are responsible.

Nor are there *physiological* reasons. Though many laymen will assert that there are racial differences in speech, independent of region or education, the solid evidence is all on the other side. In controlled tests, Chicago middle-class whites have consistently identified as the voice of a rural uneducated Negro that of an urban educated Southern-born white—and Southerners are no more accurate.[2] Educated Negroes in Charleston sound much more like the Pinckneys and Rutledges than either group sounds like the uneducated of either race. Concededly, centuries of separate and unequal opportunities have left the average Southern Negro with a larger residue of folk pronunciations and non-standard grammatical forms; but where investigators have interviewed Negroes and Whites in the same community, with equivalent education and income, there is no consistent difference. In a few situations the values are even reversed: before 1954, West Virginia State College had an elite Negro student

[1] See particularly Hans Kurath, *A Word Geography of the Eastern U.S.*, Ann Arbor, University of Michigan Press, 1949. For a summary of scholarship see "Dialects," Chapter 7, Section 4, of H. L. Mencken, *The American Language*, one-volume abridged edition, edited by Raven I. McDavid, Jr., with the assistance of David W. Maurer, New York, Alfred A. Knopf, Inc., 1963.

[2] These findings will be found in *Communication Barriers for the Culturally Deprived*, a cooperative research project of the University of Chicago and the Illinois Institute of Technology, H.E.W. Project CR-2107.

body—for the most part the children of highly skilled craftsmen and high-level service employees—and a distinguished faculty with degrees from such universities as Northwestern and Chicago. With desegregation, the school began to attract the disadvantaged from the mountains and has had a constant struggle to maintain standards in the face of increasing white enrollment.

It is thus no wonder that popular accounts of the features of Southern dialect should often be wide of the mark. What is referred to as "the Southern drawl" is probably not a feature of language *per se;* it is rather something else—a relatively greater length of strong-stressed syllables in comparison with weak-stressed ones. For example, in the American Middle West, the first syllable of *highness* will be perhaps twice as long as the last; in much of the South it will be three or four times as long. But even in the South it is far from universal. It does not appear in Charleston speech, nor in Gullah—and even where it occurs, the tempo may be far from languid; the effect of drawl may be created by lengthening the strong-stressed syllables and shortening the weak-stressed ones, while the overall tempo remains rapid. The loss of post-vocalic /-r/ in *barn, beard* and the like—traditionally associated with "Southern speech"—is also far from universal in the South; its distribution is complex, part regional and part social. And the so-called "broad *a*" [ɑ] in *half, past, dance* and *tomatoes* is normal for only a small number of Southerners, even among the oldest and best families.

III

We are thus driven away from our folk beliefs toward the same forces that have created dialect differences elsewhere and at other times.

The most important cause is the pattern of settlement.

Immigrants to a new area bring their speech with them. Students of German dialects still take as their starting point the settlements of Germanic tribes in the Fifth and Sixth Centuries and label certain features of present-day German as Franconian or Alemannic in origin. In the same way it is often possible to identify an American dialect feature with early settlements, say, from East Anglia or Northern Ireland. Since the impact of languages other than English is greatest in the areas where those languages were spoken, one can expect a high incidence of Spanish loans in West Texas, of French loans in Southern Louisiana, of German loans in the Shenandoah Valley and on the Yadkin, and of Africanisms in the Sea Islands.

Similarly, speech forms are normally transmitted along major routes of migration and communication. Features of Parisian speech have followed the Rhone to the Mediterranean; features of Pittsburgh speech have moved down the Ohio into the Mississippi Valley. Conversely, a barrier to migration may become a dialect boundary: the Blue Ridge prevented expansion of the Virginia Piedmont in the Eighteenth Century, and today there is no sharper dialect boundary in the English-speaking world. Not only linguistic traits but other cultural ones are affected by such boundaries. Notice that the Virginia Piedmont prevailingly has the small Southern haystack built around a center pole; the Shenandoah generally has the long Pennsylvania rick or the square stack without a center pole. In vocabulary, in pronunciation, in haystack shapes, in folk songs, in all aspects of traditional life the influence of the old geographic barrier is still felt.

Ancient political boundaries sometimes become dialect boundaries. In the Rhineland, as Leonard Bloomfield has pointed out, linguistic differences often follow the boundaries of medieval German principalities that were liquidated by Napoleon. In the United States, where political boundaries have rarely constituted a barrier to the movements of people or goods, state lines are much less important; nonetheless, *county site* is common in Georgia as a synonym for *county seat,* but unknown in South Carolina. And if two adjacent states differ in the quality of their educational systems, the political boundary may mark the limits of linguistic features; time and and again, Pennsylvania will lack old-fashioned pronunciations or grammatical features that are very common in Maryland and the states further south. The schoolmasters of Pennsylvania simply did a more thorough job.

Where a city or a cluster of cities becomes an important cultural focus, its speech forms will spread into the surrounding area and even beyond. The Fall Line cities of the Virginia Piedmont—Fredericksburg-Falmouth, Richmond and Petersburg—have dominated Virginia speech; and the pronunciations of their first families have been emulated in Winchester, in Roanoke, and even in Charleston, West Virginia. In South Carolina, Charleston has played a role similar to that of Richmond and its sister cities in Virginia. In the Gulf States and Mississippi Valley the plantation pronunciation of [ɜɪ] in *bird* and the like (a pronunciation strongly resembling what was once common in Metropolitan New York, but lacking the stigma of the latter) is found in southeastern Alabama and the Tennessee Valley (but not around Birmingham), in New Orleans and in Vicksburg— to cite a few instances. Has this radiated from Montgomery or from New Orleans or both?

Finally, the social structure of an area will determine where the sharpest social distinctions in language happen to lie. In the Old South there was a sharp difference between the "old families" and the rest of the population; in Virginia, when the original surveys for the Atlas were conducted, only in this group did one find the "broad *a*" in *dance* or the /æ/ vowel of *patch* in *catch,* instead of the more common /ɛ/ of *fetch.* In inland communities the class markers in language were most likely to be those associated with education, notably the consistent use of the standard preterites and participles of irregular verbs: *I saw, did, ran* and the like.

IV

If we take the Southern evidence from the first stage of the Linguistic Atlas project, and extrapolate for areas yet uninvestigated, we find a few clear patterns. For our practical purposes we will consider the territorial South as consisting of the fifteen slave states of 1860, plus Oklahoma.[3] Our conclusions are surest for the area from the Mason-Dixon line to the Ocmulgee and northeastern Florida, and almost as sure for Kentucky.

Along the northern boundary we find considerable influence of the North Midland region—the area settled by the westward expansion of Pennsylvania. West Virginia north of the Kanawha watershed is North Midland, though without a focus to balance against the influence of the Pittsburgh area; its most characteristic feature to outlanders is the intrusive /r/ in *wash, push, bushel, judge, mush.* Further east, the Pennsylvania German area and the Delaware Valley with the cultural focus at Philadelphia have long influenced parts of Maryland and Virginia. There are offshoots of the Pennsylvania settlements in both central Maryland and the Shenandoah Valley. In Delaware there is a major speech boundary between Wilmington and the more rural southern part of the state; the strength of this boundary suggests that Wilmington has been a cultural satellite of Philadelphia since before the Revolution. Baltimore, a latecomer as Atlantic Seaboard communities go, had a well defined core of old Southern families, but soon came under the influence of Philadelphia. Today, with industrialization, its ties to the North Midland are growing stronger, those to the South growing weaker. This tendency was evident even as early as the 1930's, when for practical

[3] Most of the field work in the pre-Revolutionary South, as far west as the Ocmulgee in Georgia, was done in the two periods 1933-9 and 1945-8; that in Kentucky, mostly 1952-5; in Oklahoma 1958-62. Louisiana has been investigated, less professionally, by the students of C. M. Wise, mostly 1933-48. Texas vocabulary was fairly well investigated by the students of E. Bagby Atwood; its pronunciation less systematically, though there have been several first-rate studies. Field work in Missouri began in 1966. Elsewhere, we have largely vocabulary evidence collected by correspondence, but very reliable so far as it goes, thanks to the high standards of the investigator, Gordon Wood of Southern Illinois University.

purposes the regional boundary ran through the city, but younger and better educated speakers favored North Midland forms. Postvocalic /-r/ was pronounced; *horse* and *hoarse* were homonyms; *whip* and the like began with /w-/, not with /hw-/.

The South Midland region also derives from Pennsylvania, but less directly. In the middle of the Eighteenth Century, when the Ulster Scots in Pennsylvania reached the Alleghenies and found further progress westward blocked by the French and their Indian allies, they turned southwest into the Shenandoah. Some of them recrossed the Blue Ridge and followed the eastern slopes into the Piedmont of the Carolinas and Georgia; others descended the Clinch and Holston to the neighborhood of Knoxville and beyond; still others followed the Kanawha into the Ohio Valley. In the beginning, these Ulstermen were strongly opposed to the institutions and mores of the Plantation South; they were independent subsistence farmers, with little use for money crops or chattel slavery; their traditions are reflected by the migration of the Lincolns into the free land north of the Ohio, by the fission of West Virginia from the parent state and by the continuing political cleavage between planter and mountaineer in nearly every part of the South. The picture is obscured, however, by other facts of cultural and political history: in all of the South, as cotton became profitable and the decay of chattel slavery was arrested, money crop agriculture spread into the upper Piedmont and the rich bottomlands of the inland rivers; local government fell into the hands of those who accommodated themselves to the interests of the plantation economy; local autonomy was suppressed behind a facade of "states rights" and "the Solid South." Despite the extent of the South Midland settlements—from Harper's Ferry to San Antonio —it was not until after the Confederate War that the region developed cultural foci comparable to Philadelphia and Pittsburgh in the North Midland. Louisville, Lexington, Nashville, Memphis were outposts of the cultural values enunciated in Richmond, Charleston, Savannah, Montgomery and New Orleans. Linguistically, the South Midland has been passive until recent years, receptive to speech forms from outside foci—occasionally the North Midland but more generally the planting and mercantile coastal South. The prevalent loss of postvocalic /-r/ in the uplands among younger and more sophisticated speakers—as in *park your car*—is a case in point: in my boyhood in Greenville, S. C., this loss was characteristic of young people of better families in the city; outside the city, the small farmers, mountaineers and textile workers retained the /-r/ essentially unimpaired. The receptivity of the South Midland to plantation speech-forms has led to debate among scholars as to whether it belongs dialectally with the Midland or the South.[4] In either event, its transitional quality is undeniable.

Passive though the South Midland is in comparison with the South, it has its own subdivisions. At least three of these have been identified along the Atlantic Seaboard: (1) The Shenandoah Valley, (2) Southern West Virginia, with Southwestern Virginia and Eastern Kentucky, (3) the Carolina and Georgia mountains. Each has a few characteristic features, though—as with the South Midland in general—features not shared with other areas are fewer than one might expect.

The Shenandoah Valley was historically a route of diffusion of Midland settlers from Pennsylvania into the Southern uplands. Few words mark this route: *flannel cake* 'pancake,' focusing in Philadelphia and extending to the head of the Valley; *family pie* 'cobbler,' beginning in the Shenandoah and spreading into the Carolina Piedmont.

West Virginia from the Kanawha south, along with southwestern Virginia and the easternmost counties of Kentucky, has a few peculiar words of its own. Perhaps the most characteristic is *hobby* or *hobby bread*, to designate a small handshaped loaf of cornbread, smaller than the traditional *pone*, and generally baked three to an oven or skillet. Less widespread in West Virginia, but extending through the Carolina mountains, is *redworm*, a regional term for earthworm. A few mountain terms extend toward the seacoast, along the valleys of the Yadkin-Peedee and the Cape Fear, with the speech of mountain Ulstermen and Cape Fear Highlanders for once reinforcing each other. Among these words are *bighouse* for the living room and *fireboard* for the mantelpiece. Yet none of these South Midland areas is well defined; all are under pressure from both the older plantation centers and the newer cities.

The areas of the South proper have been much more distinctive than those of the South Midland, because (as noted) every focal community lay in the plantation area; plantation families that prospered with the plantations set the prestige patterns.

Throughout the South there are a few words of general currency. One of the most typical—if somewhat less frequently heard today, in a generation of technological change—is *lightwood* /laitəd/ (homonymous with the plantation pronunciation of *lightered*) for fatty pine

---

[4] On the basis of vocabulary, Kurath *(Word Geography)* considered it a part of the Midland, conceded that pronunciation features might group it with the South. In discussing the affiliations of Texas dialects, E. Bagby Atwood grouped Southern Coastal and South Midland together as *General Southern;* see *The Regional Vocabularly of Texas,* Austin, The University of Texas Press, 1962.

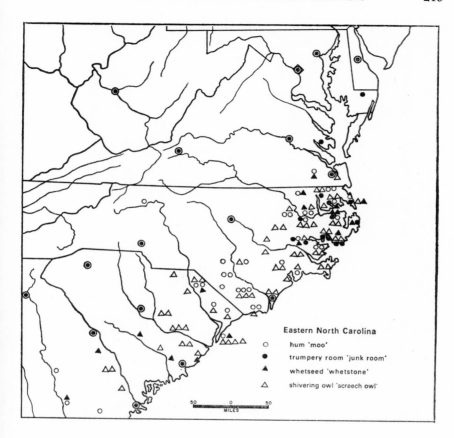

Eastern North Carolina

○　　hum 'moo'

●　　trumpery room 'junk room'

▲　　whetseed 'whetstone'

△　　shivering owl 'screech owl'

kindling. But even within the South there are a few well-defined belts. Along the coast below the Fall Line, the dragon fly is *mosquito hawk,* a clingstone peach is a *press peach,* and *budget, bulge, bulk* have the vowel of *cut*; above the Fall Line, we find, respectively, *snake doctor, plum peach* and the vowel of *put*.

The two strongest focal areas in the Old South, the Virginia Piedmont and the Charleston area, have several things in common. In pronunciation, the two areas share with Canadian speech striking alternations of the diphthongs /ai/ and /au/ according to the phonetic environment, with a strongly centralized variety occuring before voiceless consonants, as in *ice* and *house*. A few vocabulary items are also shared, such as *corn house* for corncrib and *croker sack* for burlap bag. In other respects, however, the two areas are sharply different: Virginia has the Africanism *goober* for peanut; South Carolina has *pinder*: Virginians call spoonbread *batterbread*—a term unknown in South Carolina; conversely *mutton corn* for the more common *roast-*

ing ears is a South Carolina term unfamiliar to Virginians. Such traditional Virginia pronunciations as /ə'frɛd/ for *afraid* and /hʊm/ for *home* are not found in Charleston, whose peculiar ingliding /e/ and /o/, as in *date* and *boat,* sound as exotic in Richmond as in Dubuque.

In contrast to focal areas like the Virginia Piedmont and the South Carolina Low-Country, the Old South has its relic areas, lacking influential centers to make their words and pronunciations fashionable; as a result their characteristic speech forms are chiefly retained by the older and less sophisticated, with others taking on the usage of the Virginia Piedmont, the South in general, or the nation as a whole.

One of the most striking relic areas has been Chesapeake Bay, heavily indented with bays and tidal rivers that have inhibited communication until the last two decades. Here we find *cow pound* for the more common *cow lot, caps* for *corn shucks, cornstack* for *corn crib, baseborn (child)* for *bastard, mongst-ye* instead of *you-all* as the polite plural, and the archaic *housen* for *houses.* Eastern North Carolina, caught between the two adjacent mountains of conceit, tenuously preserves *shivering owl* for *screech owl* and *hum* as a synonym for *moo; trumpery room* (instead of the Virginia *lumber room* or the more common *junk room*) and *whetseed* for *whetstone,* are practically confined to the shores of Albemarle Sound. Further south, there are relics of German settlement around Salisbury, North Carolina, and Newberry, South Carolina—with survivals of *rainworm* for *earthworm* and *smearcase* for *cottage cheese.* The Ulster Scot settlement around Kingstree, South Carolina, has kept the Northern Irish *chay!* as a call to cows. The descendants of the Salzburgers in the Savannah Valley still use *cripple* to designate the delicacy known in Philadelphia as *scrapple*—the term apparently coming from a South German word meaning drippings. The Savannah Valley also uses *stoop* for *porch,* especially an unroofed one; since *stoop* is traditionally derived from Dutch and associated with the Hudson Valley, its occurrence along the Savannah—where there was no Holland Dutch settlement—so far is inexplicable. Perhaps the term was brought South by the architects who designed the mansions of the Savannah well-to-do—houses with more than a casual resemblance to the brownstones of New York City. Further south, with their territory undefined, we encounter *gopher* designating a kind of burrowing turtle and *prairie* designating a damp meadowland—their oldest meanings in North American English, if somewhat overshadowed by what they refer to in the Upper Mississippi Valley.

Although there is little evidence to distinguish the speech of

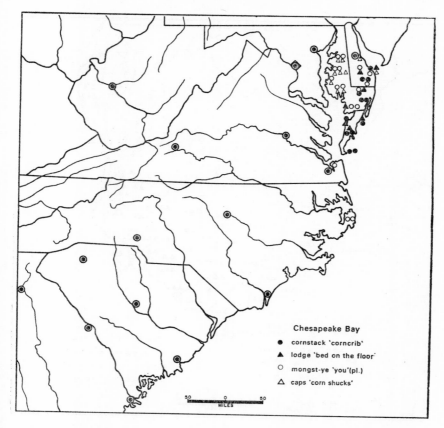

Chesapeake Bay

● cornstack 'corncrib'

▲ lodge 'bed on the floor'

○ mongst-ye 'you'(pl.)

△ caps 'corn shucks'

Southern Negroes from that of Southern Whites with comparable social advantages, there is one striking exception: the Gullah country of the South Carolina-Georgia coast. In this area, large numbers of slaves were imported in a relatively short time to work such money crops as indigo, rice and Sea Island cotton; endemic malaria discouraged white settlers, and encouraged long summer absences on the part of the few who lived there. Slavery, peonage, swamps and tidal rivers discouraged movement. For these reasons many speech forms of probable African origin are still established in these communities, though hardly known inland; in the same area, of course, the forces of geographical and cultural isolation also preserved old and humble speech forms that the slaves acquired from the whites among whom they worked.[5]

[5] See Lorenzo D. Turner, *Africanisms in The Gullah Dialect,* Chicago, The University of Chicago Press, 1949. Analogous phenomena in Louisiana Negro-French have been discussed by many observers, notably Raleigh Morgan.

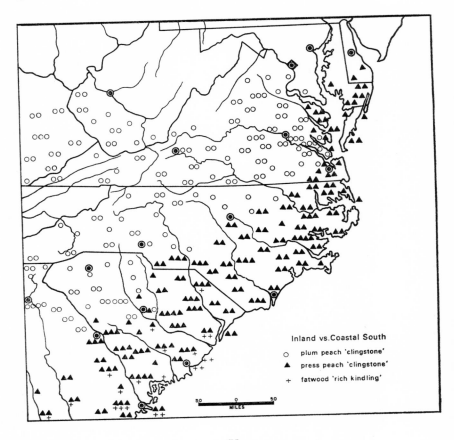

Inland vs. Coastal South

○   plum peach 'clingstone'

▲   press peach 'clingstone'

+   fatwood 'rich kindling'

V

To this point we speak on the basis of systematic evidence elicited in personal interviews by trained investigators. Once we cross the Appalachians, however, we are without this kind of evidence so far, save for Kentucky and Oklahoma and a few local studies. Nevertheless, the evidence we have is sufficient for an observer to make certain general observations on the patterns of Southern dialects before the age of mass-production industry and the subsequent age of automation.

In the New South, as in the old, social differences in language were more sharply marked than in the regions to the North. Status was determined by family background, education and wealth, with family at least ostensibly the most important—since the older families dominated the economy and had most of the opportunities for education and other indices of cultural prestige. Many schools designed for the less affluent soon became oriented to the dominant system of values; typical was Sweet Briar, originally founded to educate Vir-

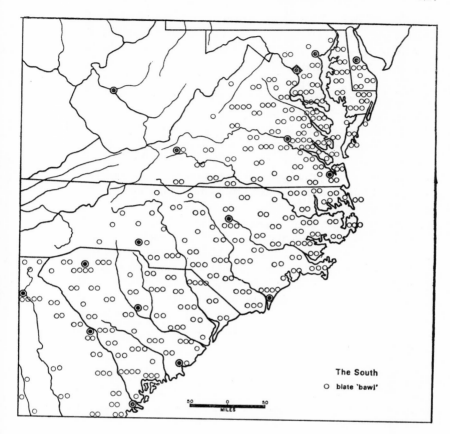

The South
O blate 'bawl'

MILES

ginia mountain girls, but by the 1920's popularly regarded as an advanced finishing school. The outsiders who built up new fortunes by skill or luck or a convenient lack of scruples adjusted so skillfully to the prevailing patterns of prestige that the community often forgot their humble beginnings—even in the first generation of prominence.[6] And the common economic ruin following the Confederate War only emphasized the inalienable advantages of family and culture, as contrasted with the ephemeral status of wealth.

As the South expanded westward, Southern society continued to be dominated by the planters and merchants. When cotton culture expanded in the early Nineteenth Century, the plantation system—and with it, a relatively large slave population—spread into rich upland areas. Some of the original South Midland small farmers rose into the planter class; others were pushed into the unproductive hills

[6] A not atypical example is given in W. J. Cash, *The Mind of the South*, New York, Alfred A. Knopf, Inc., 1940.

and pine barrens, crossed the Ohio into territory where slavery was forbidden (the Lincolns are the most notable representatives), or pushed further west. The social distinction between the planter and the redneck was fundamental in Southern society; the planters, a small minority, manipulated the political attitudes of the region for at least a generation after Reconstruction, and by such political contrivances as the creation of new counties with disproportionate representation kept at least a veto on significant legislative change until the recent decisions of the Federal courts.

But the planter group of the inland South was far more diverse than its coastal counterpart. A few of the older families, like the Hamptons and Hugers, either added new plantations in the Mississippi Valley to their older holdings along the coast or transferred the bulk of their operations from exhausted soil to new. They found, however, a local planter group—mostly French—already established and were soon augmented by the successful entrepreneurs who had made wealth on the frontier—as gory and violent as any of the later manifestations of the American tradition of the Wild West. As a consequence of this mobility, many features originally associated with the South Midland found their way into plantation speech, even in those areas most heavily settled from the plantation belt of the Old South.

The westward dialectal expansion of the Old South is a crazy quilt if compared to the orderly and well marked belts of coastal plain, Piedmont and mountains that we find along the Atlantic. Even in eastern Georgia the pattern begins to be confused, with the plantation areas expanding inland largely between the Savannah and the Ogeechee, and then sweeping west across the Piedmont; however, barely thirty miles west of Brunswick and St. Marys we encounter swamps, wiregrass and piney woods, settled by marginal farmers. Cherokees and Creeks long blocked expansion into the lower valleys of the Chattahoochee and Flint, which were first settled by land-hungry uplanders rather than by the westward extension of plantation holdings. The fertile bottomlands of the Mississippi and its tributaries produced an intricate interlacing of plantation and small farming areas, with the respective domination by Southern and South Midland features. To take one characteristic example, the Black Belt of Alabama, the lower Mississippi Valley, and the Tennessee Valley towns as far upriver as Athens and Decatur show the loss of /r/ coloring in *barn, beard* and *bird*—and often in the last the diphthong associated with older New York City speech; but the hill country around Birmingham and the pinelands of eastern Mississippi exhibit an /r/ as strong as anything to be found in the Middle West. A similar crazy-quilt pattern would not be unlikely in Arkansas and Missouri.

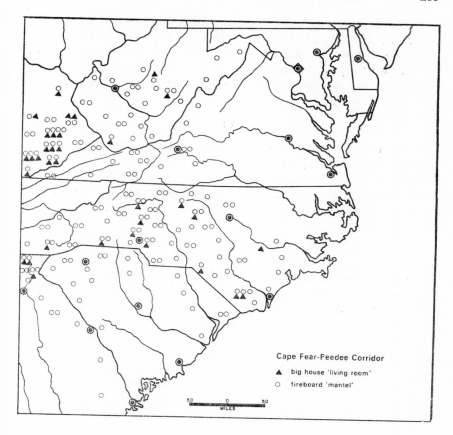

Cape Fear-Feedee Corridor

▲ big house 'living room'
○ fireboard 'mantel'

The territorial expansion of the South, of course, was not conducted solely by Southerners and South Midlanders. Pennsylvanians, Yan-
kees and York Staters pushed into Missouri; in combination with the
German exiles and the mountaineers who had always opposed slavery,
they were able to keep the *Show Me State* in the Union—though at
the price of local feuds that started Jesse James on his short career
as an outlaw and on his longer one as the first juvenile delinquent to
become a folk hero. And though the American Indians—except in
Oklahoma—were largely brushed aside, two other groups maintained
their identity, and indeed modified the invading Anglo-American
culture: the Spanish-Americans of Texas and the French of Louisiana. Loans from these two groups, in fact, mark respectively the two
principal focal areas of the Gulf States: the hacienda country of the
Southwest and the plantation area of Southern Louisiana, with its
metropolitan focus at New Orleans. Since these patterns persist in
the vocabulary despite the cultural changes of the last fifty years, it

is likely that they will also be found in pronunciation and even in grammar. Other probable focal areas in the New South—though the extent of their influence has not yet been determined—are the Kentucky Bluegrass, Metropolitan St. Louis, Memphis, the Nashville Basin and the Montgomery-Mobile axis in Southern Alabama.

VI

Since dialect patterns are rarely static, particularly in times when the population is rapidly growing, we should have expected this outline of Southern dialect patterns to have been modified over the past generation by the simple passage of time. But modification has been accelerated by a number of fundamental economic and social changes whose impact is likely to be even greater in the future.

The three principal forces operating in American society to create a different dialect situation from that to be found in Europe have been industrialization, urbanization, and general education. For a long time these forces were less active in the South than in other regions. In comparison with the other parts of the United States, the Southern regions have been the most predominantly agricultural (with a large proportion of small, marginal farms), the most predominantly rural, the least literate and sophisticated. Although in all of these respects the South as a whole is still behind the rest of the nation, the discrepancy is far less than it used to be. In industry and education the best Southern achievements rank with the best in other regions, though they are much less numerous.

Industrialization began in the 1830's, when such leaders as William Gregg developed cotton mills to provide employment for poor whites crowded off the land by the competition of slave labor and the low fertility of subsistence farms; to Gregg is due the unhappy tradition of Southern textiles as the most segregated and least unionized American industry. But it was not till after Reconstruction that the era of textile expansion began. Throughout the Piedmont of the South Atlantic States, almost every county seat and many smaller places became ringed with cotton mills, whose operatives—in company villages, with company stores, company schools and company churches —became a *de facto* third race in the pattern of segregation. Drawn from the pine barrens, the sandhills, the mountains and other areas of marginal farming, the textile workers swelled the population of urban areas; though their speech had little prestige, they altered the structure of urban society in such a way that through the educational opportunities of their children and grandchildren they would inevitably affect the patterns of local cultivated speech.

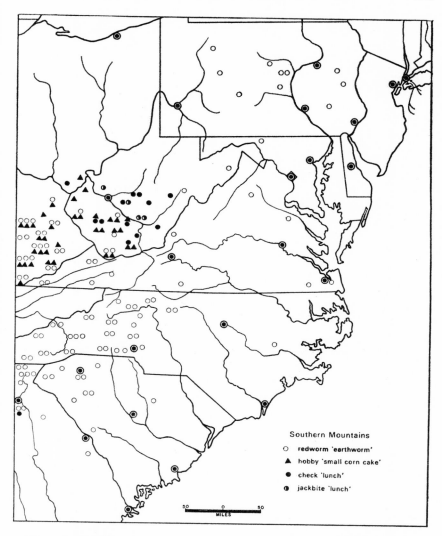

Southern Mountains

○ redworm 'earthworm'
▲ hobby 'small corn cake'
● check 'lunch'
◐ jackbite 'lunch'

50   0   50
MILES

Though textiles was the first industry to become established in the South, it was not alone. Tobacco manufacturing and coal mining soon followed—both, like textiles, employing relatively low-skilled labor at the outset and suffering disproportionately from economic cycles. But more sophisticated industries ultimately developed—steel, paper, shipbuilding, aircraft manufacturing among them. Especially on the Gulf coast, large fields of oil and gas brought rapid industrialization, centering first on refining and then on petrochemicals. And the tendency of giant corporations to decentralize only hastened the industrialization of the South.

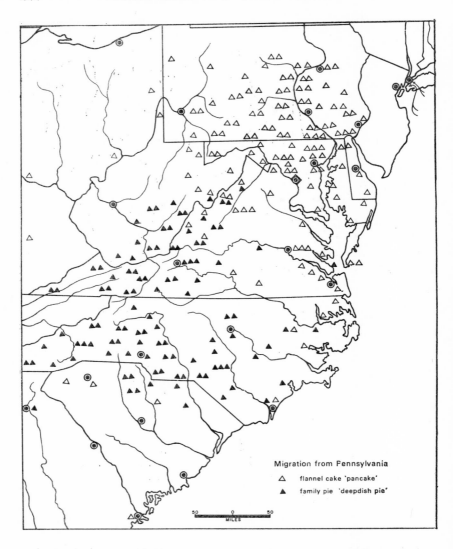

Migration from Pennsylvania

△   flannel cake 'pancake'

▲   family pie 'deepdish pie'

Industrialization requires the easy movement of raw materials to the factory and of finished products to the consumer. The industrializing South eagerly improved its means of transportation— railroads, roads, waterways. Moreover, since the distribution of industrial products is most efficiently handled through larger centers, industrialization inevitably led to the growth of cities. The urbanization of the South was also furthered by the general mechanization of agriculture and by the specific decline in cotton growing and the rise of timber cropping and cattle-raising, which required fewer hands and sent large numbers to the towns. The stores and services—from groceries to gin-mills—that sprang up to supply the mill workers and handle industrial products absorbed much of the labor surplus; some of the new arrivals quickly moved into the growing middle class, which was also swelled by newcomers from other regions. The expansion of Southern cities has been uneven; but this has been true in other regions as well. Some, despite their size, have remained little more than overgrown mill villages; some—like the Texas metropolises— have ostentatiously displayed great wealth and a reactionary social philosophy; a few, notably Atlanta, have walked open-eyed into the Twentieth Century and developed a character of their own. But throughout the South the typical cultural leader everywhere is now not the planter but the urban businessman, often not a Southerner except by adoption.

For the industrialization and urbanization of the South could not have been accomplished on Southern resources alone. With plentiful natural resources and a large labor supply, the region had a short-age of capital and of management talent. Although a few giant cor-porations were developed by Southern capital and leadership to the point where they could compete successfully on the national scene, most Southern industries soon passed into the control of Eastern capital; the vast majority of Southern factories are now owned by national corporations, and managed by representatives from the cen-tral organization.

This side of the change in Southern population is often overlooked. Everyone knows that hundreds of thousands of Southern Negroes have moved North — so that there are now more Negroes in the Chicago metropolitan area than in all of South Carolina. In Cleveland, Detroit, Philadelphia, New York, Negroes from the South and their chil-dren are a large part of the population; in such cities they are also one of the major economic problems since the demand for unskilled labor is declining and many of them lack the training for the new clerical and technical jobs that automation is creating. We are all aware that many poor whites have also gone North—to the assembly lines of Detroit, the rubber shops of Akron and the airplane factories of Dayton—and have created their share of social problems. We are also aware that within the South there has been a flow of both races from the country to the city—to Louisville and Little Rock, to Mem-phis and Birmingham and Atlanta. If we think of Northern migration southward, we are likely to think of the resort traffic and retirement colonies that have made the southern half of Florida an exclave of the Middle Atlantic States and the Middle West. We forget the more diffuse—and for that reason, probably the more influential— migration of plant superintendents, bank cashiers, store managers,

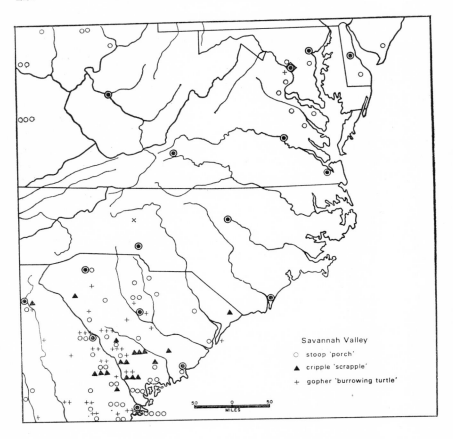

Savannah Valley

○ stoop 'porch'

▲ cripple 'scrapple'

+ gopher 'burrowing turtle'

industrial chemists, tool and die makers, and now of college professors, as the needs of the South outran local supplies and new opportunities made positions competitive with those available in other regions.[7]

[7] The development of Washington has been atypical, reflecting two disparate trends. Originally it was a small Southern town, and the lower echelons of government service held a disproportionate number of Southerners. Beginning with the 1930's, however, the expansion of government activities has drawn into the metropolitan area large numbers of Middle Westerners and Easterners to fill professional, technical, administrative and policy-making positions; in the same period, the extension of equal opportunities to Negroes and the desegregation of the public schools have attracted many Negroes from the South. As middle class whites—especially families with children—have fled to the suburbs, a peculiar situation has developed. In the suburbs the speech patterns are mixed, but with something other than the local Southern cultivated standard beginning to predominate; in the city proper, Negroes constitute about 55% of the population, over 90% of the school enrollment, and the cultivated speech of local middle class Negroes (itself strongly akin to local cultivated white speech) has been largely swamped by the new immigrants.

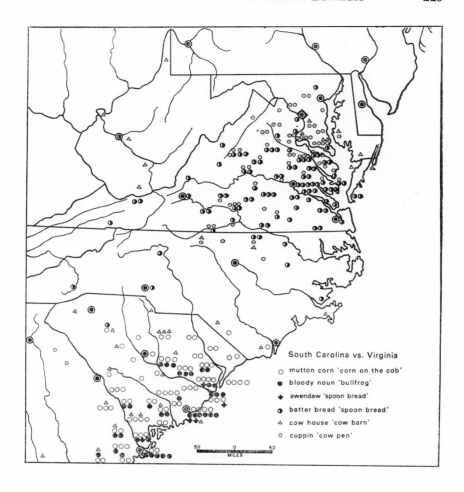

South Carolina vs. Virginia

○ mutton corn 'corn on the cob'
◐ bloody noun 'bullfrog'
✦ awendaw 'spoon bread'
◑ batter bread 'spoon bread'
△ cow house 'cow barn'
○ cuppin 'cow pen'

This has been most noticeable as the quality of Southern education has improved. Not unfittingly, some of the first steps were taken by the Reconstruction governments; the constitution of 1868 was the first one that committed South Carolina to general education. The ensuing century has seen the South, by and large, contributing to education a much larger proportion of its wealth than other regions—though the discrepancy in resources to tax meant that expenditures per pupil in Mississippi were nowhere near what they have been in Ohio or California. Progress has not been easy, as nostalgia, fundamentalism and petty politics have often hamstrung the best designed programs. But no one can deny that the general quality of Southern education has improved, at all levels. If the Johns Hopkins, the first real graduate university in the United States, failed to keep its preeminence (and in any event it is situated in a city whose Southern affilia-tions are rather weak), Duke is now unquestionably in the first rank today, and from Charlottesville to Austin, from Miami to Louisville, the better institutions have as high standards and as cosmopolitan an atmosphere as anyone could desire. As with indus-trialization and urbanization, education has advanced unevenly in the South, as indeed in other regions. But this development, too, will have a profound effect on Southern speechways.

The combined force of these developments promises to affect Southern speech in several ways.

First of all, the balance of population and wealth has shifted ir-reversibly from the plantation. The textile and tobacco centers of the Piedmont—increasingly diversified—centers of heavy industry like Birmingham, petrochemical foci like Baton Rouge, and the varie-gated industrial complexes like Atlanta and Louisville and Houston have reduced many of the old Southern towns to backwaters, sur-viving on the custom of Florida-bound tourists. Where seaports flourish—as Norfolk and Savannah and New Orleans—it is because they have exploited their geographical advantages to facilitate industrialization.

With industrialization and urbanization, wealth can be expected to replace family as a force for social prestige; since most of the new managerial class—whether Southerners or not—come from outside the plantation area, the influence of plantation speech will be diluted. Industrialization and urbanization will of course speed the disap-pearance of the more local terms in the vocabulary, especially those associated with the mule-powered farm. Not all the readers of this article can tell a *froe* from a *hamestring*, and I suspect all are less likely to make *curds* at home than to buy *cottage cheese* at the supermarket.

As higher education becomes more general, a smaller proportion of those attending college will be the children and grandchildren of college graduates. In this way the influence of the old elite will be further attenuated, and the characteristics of educated Southern speech will become somewhat different. Since the majority of the white population of the South is found in areas where the South Midland influence is strong, the enlargement of the ranks of the educated is bound to increase the importance of the South Midland component of Southern speech, at the expense of coastal Southern. Education will also tend to eliminate such folk grammatical forms as *div* or *seed,* and such pronunciations as /dif/ for *deaf* or /waundid/ for *wounded.* It is probable, given the prevailing attitude in American schools, that many Southerners will adopt the fashion of full rather

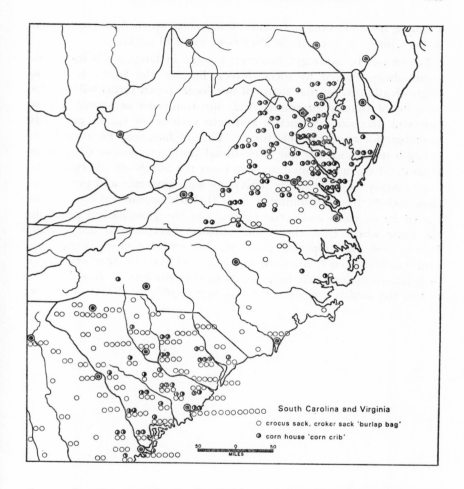

South Carolina and Virginia

O crocus sack, croker sack 'burlap bag'
◑ corn house 'corn crib'

50   50
MILES

than reduced vowels in final syllables, so that *Tuesday* and *borrow* will come to have final /-e/ and /-o/ respectively. And even educated Charlestonians may come to avoid *ain't* in polite conversation with their equals.

Some of this change is already under way. As early as 1946 I noticed that upland vowels were common among native Savannians; in 1949, I found that Knoxvillians were losing the distinction between *horse* and *hoarse,* between *merry* and *marry* and *Mary*. Seven years ago, I discovered that the younger speakers in the Kanawha Valley were pronouncing *tube* and *due* and *new* as /tub/, /du/ and /nu/ in the fashion of Northern West Virginia. In 1965, in a sample of recordings from high school students in Charleston I found little of the traditional pronunciation of *date* and *boat;* and the daughter of a couple from Gloucester County, but grown up in Arlington, spoke to me without a trace of the Piedmont *out* and *night*.

Let us not be nostalgic, however; change in language is inevitable —and always moved by social forces. Besides, the South is still so linguistically diverse that many of our local speech forms will survive in spite of outside pressures. And our traditions of speech are so powerful that some distinctive Southern varieties of speech are likely to endure for the forseeable future. This, in fact, may be a source of strength toward solving our educational problems; unlike Chicago or Detroit, where uneducated arrivals from the South—of whatever race —are sharply set off from the natives by both grammar and pronunciation, each Southern community finds its basic pronunciation patterns shared by all races and social classes, and the grammatical problems the same where educational and cultural backgrounds are similar. We do not need separate programs for separate groups—only one program intelligently designed and effectively taught. Our knowledge of Southern dialects may help Southern communities to show how the rest of the nation can solve the language problems of the classroom.

THE CONTRIBUTORS

BOWER ALY ("The Fourth of July Revisited") is Professor of Speech at the University of Oregon. He was at the University of Missouri from 1930-1957 and has taught at Columbia University, C.C.N.Y., University of Wisconsin, Louisiana State University, and the University of Hawaii. Among his major publications is *The Rhetoric of Alexander Hamilton*. He is a former president of the Speech Association of America (1944) and a former editor of *The Quarterly Journal of Speech* (1951-53). Dr. Aly is one of the country's leading contributors to the literature on American rhetoric and public address.

JOHN W. BLACK ("Interconsonantal Differences") is Professor of Speech and Hearing Sciences at the Ohio State University. He has taught at Adrian College, Kenyon College and the University of Minnesota. Among his many honors are his Fulbright Research Professorship to Italy (1954-1955), his Regents Professorship, awarded 1966 by the Ohio Board of Regents, and special honors conferred by both the American Speech and Hearing Association and the Speech Association of America. He was president of the Speech Association of America (1966), editor of *Speech Monographs* (1958-59), and vice-president of the American Speech and Hearing Association (1964). He is a leading contributor to the areas of experimental and linguistic phonetics.

ARTHUR J. BRONSTEIN (one of the co-editors) is Professor of Speech and Co-ordinator of the Interdepartmental Program in Linguistics at Herbert H. Lehman College of the City University of New York and the Executive Officer of the Doctoral Program in Speech at the City University of New York Graduate Center. He has taught at Ohio University, the University of Hawaii, and Queens College and was Fulbright Professor in English Linguistics at Tel-Aviv University 1967-68. He is the author of *The Pronunciation of American English* (1960) and the co-author of *Your Speech and Voice* (with B. F. Jacoby). His published papers and reviews have appeared in such journals as *American Speech,* the *Journal of Speech and Hearing Disorders, The Quarterly Journal of Speech and Speech Monographs.* He has acted as pronunciation consultant for the *American College Dictionary, Collier's Encyclopedia,* and the *Random House Dictionary of the English Language.*

HILDA B. FISHER ("Research in Developmental Phonology") is Associate Professor of Communicative Disorders at Northwestern University, where she has taught since 1949. Among her major publications are *Improving Voice and Articulation* (1966). Her essays have appeared in *The Quarterly Journal of Speech* and the *Journal of Speech and Hearing Research.*

HUBERT C. HEFFNER ("Rhetoric and Poetic in Mimetic Drama") is Distinguished Professor of Dramatic Literature at Indiana University. He is a Fellow and Past President of the American Educational Theatre Association and served a term as the editor of the *Educational Theatre Journal*. His publications include *Davy Crockett and other Plays, Modern Theatre Practice* (with S. Selden and H. D. Sellman). His *The Nature of Drama* is now in its fourth edition.

WESLEY D. HERVEY ("An Alphabet for the Hawaiians") has recently become Associate Professor of Speech at the University of Oregon after serving on the Faculty at the University of Hawaii since 1957. Prior to that, he was at the University of Wisconsin. His specialized interests, as revealed by his publications, are in the area of Hawaiian speech and language.

ARCHIBALD A. HILL ("How Does Rhythmic Prose Work?") is Professor of English and Linguistics at the University of Texas. He has served as President of the Linguistic Society of America (1969) after long service as its Executive Secretary. His publications include *Introduction to Linguistic Structure* and numerous articles in the major linguistic journals. He is a leading contributor to the area of general linguistics.

ILSE LEHISTE ("The Quest for Phonetic Reality") is Professor of Linguistics and Chairman of the department at the Ohio State University. She had taught at the University of Cologne, U.C.L.A., and the University of Michigan. She is the Director of the 1970 Summer Institute of Linguistics. She has published numerous monographs, articles, and reviews in the major linguistic journals. Her *Suprasegmentals* is currently in press. (MIT press)

RAVEN I. McDAVID, JR. ("Changing Patterns of Southern Dialects") is Professor of English and Linguistics at the University of Chicago. He has been associated with the Linguistic Atlas of the United States and Canada since 1941 and has been editor of *The Linguistic Atlas of the Middle and South Atlantic States* since 1964. His publications include *The Pronunciation of English in the Atlantic States* (with Hans Kurath), the chapter on "American English Dialects" for W. Nelson Francis' *The Structure of American English*. He has edited, with the assistance of David W. Maurer, Mencken's *The American Language* (1963). He is a leading scholar of and contributor to the study of American dialectology, with an especial interest in the dialects of the southern United States.

LUCIA C. MORGAN ("The Status of /r/ Among North Carolina Speakers") was Associate Professor in the Speech Division of the Department of English at the University of North Carolina at Chapel Hill. She had also taught at Louisiana State University. Her publications include the *Progressive Phonetic Workbook* (1948, with C. M. Wise) and *The Voice and Diction Drillbook for Students in Speech* (1950). Her special interests were the dialects of North Carolina.

JOHN B. NEWMAN ("Sound, Syntax, and Sense—and Meaning") is Professor of Communication Arts and Sciences at Queens College of The City University of New York. His publications have appeared in *The Quarterly Journal of Speech, ETC., Speech Monographs, The Journal of Communication*, and other journals.

GORDON E. PETERSON ("Units in Phonology") was Professor of Communication Sciences and Electrical Engineering at the University of Michigan. He was the Director of the Communication Science Laboratory and Chairman of the Graduate Program of Communication Science there. His extensive publications have appeared in the *Journal of the Acoustical Society of America*, the *Journal of Speech and Hearing Research, and Language and Speech.* He was, before his recent death, a leading contributor to the literature of speech science.

KENNETH L. PIKE ("Five Poems") is Professor of Linguistics at the University of Michigan and the President of the Summer Institute of Linguistics, Inc. He has lectured in major universities throughout the United States and in many other countries. His publications include *Phonetics, Phonemics, The Intonation of American English,* and *Language in Relation to a Unified Theory of a Structure of Human Behavior.* His papers have appeared in the major linguistic journals. He is a major contributor to the field of general linguistics. He has served as President of The Linguistics Society of America (1961).

CLAUDE L. SHAVER (one of the co-editors) is Distinguished Professor of Speech and Chairman of the interdisciplinary program in linguistics at Louisiana State University. He has taught at the University of Hawaii and the University of Alaska and was a Smith-Mundt visiting professor to Hong Kong. His special academic interests include both linguistics and theatre. His publications have appeared in such journals as *The Quarterly Journal of Speech,* and the *Educational Theatre Journal.*

JUNE E. SHOUP ("Units in Phonology") is Director of the Speech Communication Research Laboratory, Santa Barbara, California and Adjunct Associate Professor of Linguistics at the University of Southern California. She was previously associated with the Communication Sciences Laboratory at the University of Michigan. Her publications include "A Physiological Theory of Phonetics" and "The Elements of Acoustic Phonetic Theory," both with Gordon E. Peterson. Both appeared in the *Journal of Speech and Hearing Research.*

CHERYL JUDITH STEVENS designed the dust jacket for this volume. She is a graduate of Louisiana State University and knew Claude M. Wise for the last twenty years of his life. Her special interests are in art and theatre.

Cj STEVENS ("Ergo Sum") (one of the co-editors) is Professor of Speech and Chairman of the Department of Speech and Theatre at Herbert H. Lehman College of the City University of New York. He has taught at the University of Kansas City, Shepherd State College, Hunter College, Universidad Autónomo del Estado de México, and Louisiana State University. He has served Georgetown University overseas (in Ankara, Turkey) as Director of the Intensive English Language Program. His publications have appeared in such journals as *The Quarterly Journal of Speech, Speech Monographs,* and *American Speech.*

SHIGERU TAKEBAYASHI ("A Comparative Study of Japanese and English Consonant Phonemes") is an Assistant Professor of Phonetics and English in the Humanities Section of Tokyo University of Foreign Studies. His special interests are English and Japanese linguistics. He is an editor of the recently issued *Japanese-English Dictionary* (Tokyo, 1968).

KARL R. WALLACE ("A Modern View of Delivery") is Professor of Speech at the University of Massachusetts. He has taught at the University of Virginia and at the University of Illinois where he was Chairman of the Department of Speech from 1959-1968. His publications include *Francis Bacon on Communication and Rhetoric* (1943), *Francis Bacon on the Nature of Man* (1967), *Oral Communication* (co-author with D. Bryant, now in its third edition) and *Fundamentals of Public Speaking* (co-author with D. Bryant, now in its fourth edition). He was editor-in-chief of *The History of Speech Education in America* (1954). He is a leading contributor to the literature of rhetoric and public address.

HARRY S. WISE, M.D., M.P.H. ("Two Anthropological Studies in Speech") is Director of the Norfolk City Health Department. He directed the Speech Center at the University of Witwatersrand and has taught at Colorado State College and Hunter College. He served as a graduate fellow in the Massachusetts Eye and Ear Hospital and at the University of Washington. He has served as medical illustrator for Kantner and West's *Phonetics,* Gray and Wise's *Bases of Speech,* and Wise's *Applied Phonetics and Introduction to Phonetics.* He is the co-author of a *Manual for Group Auricular Training* (Borden General Army Hospital) and he has served as Public Health Officer in such places as Washington, D.C., the states of New York, Arizona, Washington, and Louisiana, and in Vietnam. His first two degrees were in Speech at Louisiana State University. His publications are predominantly in medical journals. He is Claude M. Wise's oldest son.

SELECTED BIBLIOGRAPHY – C. M. WISE

This list represents the more important publications of C. M. Wise in the professional area together with a brief supplementary bibliography of plays and short stories. For a more complete list see *Southern Speech Journal,* XXXIV, No. 3, or *Louisiana Speaks,* Spring, 1966.

BOOKS

Dramatics for School and Community (Cincinnati: Steward Kidd Co., 1923), 147 pp.

A Book of Dramatic Costume, with Edith Dabney (Crofts, 1930), 163 pp.

The Bases of Speech, with Giles W. Gray, 1st edition, 1934, 439 pp.; 2nd edition, 1946, 610 pp.; 3rd edition, 1959, 562 pp. (Harper and Row).

Foundations of Speech, with James H. McBurney, Louis A. Mallory, Charles R. Strother, William J. Temple, and J. M. O'Neill, ed. (Prentice-Hall, Inc., 1941), 499 pp.

Modern Speech, with Gladys L. Borchers (Harcourt, Brace, 1947), 522 pp.

A Progressive Phonetic Workbook for Students in Speech, with Lucia Morgan, 1st edition, 1948, 68 pp.; 2nd edition, 1967, 93 pp. (William C. Brown).

Dramatic Costume for Children, with Edith Dabney (St. Louis: Educational Publishers, 1949), 80 pp.

Applied Phonetics (Prentice-Hall, Inc., 1957), 546 pp.

Introduction to Phonetics (Prentice-Hall, Inc., 1958), 251 pp.

Patterns of English: A Book of Pattern Practices for Chinese Students, with Bertha Hensman, Jack Hobbs (London and Hong Kong: Longmans, Green & Co., 1966).

BOOK CONTRIBUTIONS

"Pronunciation," in *Elements of Speech,* 2nd ed., by James M. O'Neill and Andrew T. Weaver (Longmans, Green and Co., 1933), Chapter X, pp. 170-212.

"Thesis and Antithesis in the Evolution of English Linguistics," *In Honour of Daniel Jones,* edited by David Abercrombie, D. B. Fry, P. A. D. MacCarthy, N. C. Scott, and J. L. M. Trim (Longmans, Green, 1964), pp. 206-215.

"Transcription in Normalized Southern Speech," *Phonetic Readings in American Speech,* by James F. Bender and Victor A. Fields (Pitman Publishing Corp., 1939), p. 52.

"Militarism and Pacifism Among Phonemes in American English," *Proceedings of the Third International Congress of Phonetic Sciences,* (Ghent, Belgium, 1939), 42-47.

"A Comparison of Certain Features of British and American Pronunciation," *Proceedings of the Second International Congress of Phonetic Sciences, London, 1935.* (Cambridge University Press, 1936), 285-291.

"Acoustic Structure of English Diphthongs and Semi-Vowels vis-á-vis Their Phonemic Symbolization," *Proceedings of the Fifth International Congress of Phonetic Sciences* (Basel and New York: S. Karger, 1965) 589-593.

"The Operation of the Principle of Assimilation in Graphemics," *Study of Sounds,* IX (Tokyo: The Phonetic Society of Japan, 1961), 23-32.

ARTICLES

"After the Uvular—What?" *American Speech,* IX (April, 1934), 157-158.

"Benjamin Franklin as a Phonetician," *Speech Monographs,* XV (1948), 99-120.

"Chest Resonance," *Quarterly Journal of Speech,* XVIII (June, 1932), 446-452.

" 'Chiefess'—A Hawaiian Word," *American Speech,* XXVI (May, 1951), 116-121.

"Common Errors in Our Daily Speech," *Southern Speech Journal,* II (October, 1936), 1-8.

"Departments of Speech—A Point of View," *Southern Speech Journal,* XX (Fall, 1954), 1-6.

"The Dialect Atlas of Louisiana—A Report of Progress," *Studies in Linguistics,* Vol. 3, No. 2, 1945, pp. 37-42.

" 'Different(ly) Than' Becomes a Model of Style," *American Speech,* XXII (October, 1947), 237.

"dɪfθɔŋgaɪzeɪʃən əv o ənd a ɪn ðə mɔsko daɪələkt əv rʌʃən," *Le Maitre Phonetique,* No. 94 (July-Dec., 1950), 28-29.

"Directions in Linguistics," with Ruth Hirsch, *Quarterly Journal of Speech,* XXXIX (April, 1953), 225-231.

"Establishing a State Course of Study in Speech," *Southern Speech Journal,* VIII (September, 1942), 24-25.

"The Evolution of Hawaiian Orthography," with Wesley Hervey, *Quarterly Journal of Speech,* XXXVIII (October, 1952), 211-325.

"Intelligibility of Whispering in a Tone Language," with Lily Pao-Hu Chong, *The Journal of Speech and Hearing Disorders,* XXII (September, 1957), 335-338.

"Is Nasal Resonance Actually Nasal-Pharyngeal Resonance?" *Le Maitre Phonetique,* No. 89 (Jan.-June, 1948), 4-5.

"The Language Problems of German-Speaking Refugees and English-Speaking Invaders," with Morris Cohen, *Quarterly Journal of Speech,* XXX (December, 1944), 402-406.

"Lanier's Theories as to the Relation of Music and Verse," *Southern Speech Journal,* XI (March, 1946), 97-100.

"A Letter from Daniel Jones," *Southern Speech Journal,* XVIII (December, 1952), 81-86.

"Louisiana Speech Under Many Flags," *Southern Speech Journal,* IV (March, 1939), 8-13.

"Negro Dialect," *Quarterly Journal of Speech,* XIX (November, 1933), 522-528.

"On Wilbur Gilman's 'Unity in Diversity,'" *Quarterly Journal of Speech,* XXXVIII (October, 1952), 337-338.

"Phonetic Transcriptions: West Central Arkansas," *Quarterly Journal of Speech,* XXXV (April, 1949), 228.

"Retrospect and Prospect," *Southern Speech Journal,* VIII (March, 1943), 105-108.

"Russian and English Speech Sounds," *Journal of Speech and Hearing Disorders.* 14 (December, 1949), 322-344.

"A Shakespeare Cipher in the Bible," *Southern Speech Journal,* XXIV (Summer, 1961), 261-270.

"Some English Problem Sounds for Cantonese Students," *Speech Teacher,* XII (March, 1963), 92-104.

"Some 'Problem' Sounds in English for Cantonese Students," *English Bulletin,* IV (June, 1962), Hong Kong: Education Dept.

"The Southern American Diphthong [aɪ]," *Southern Speech Journal,* XIX (May, 1954), 304-312.

"The Southern American Drawl," *Le Maitre Phonetique,* No. 44 (October-December, 1933), 69-71.

"Southern American Speech," *American Speech,* VIII (April, 1933), 37-43.

"Speaking Instruction in College Military Units: In the South," *Quarterly Journal of Speech,* XXIX (December, 1943), 419-423.

"A Specimen of Louisiana French-English, or 'Cajan.'" *American Speech,* VIII (Oct., 1933), 63-64.

"The Structure of Tragedy," *The New Asia College Academic Journal* (Hong Kong: New Asia College), IV (September, 1962), 39-46.

SUPPLEMENTARY BIBLIOGRAPHY—PLAYS AND SHORT STORIES

"The State of Riverbank," a short story under the pseudonym of Roman Laim, *Scribner's Magazine,* LXXXIII March 1928), 291-303.

"The Calabash of Paka's," *Paradise of the Pacific,* December, 1950.

"Lelani and Word of Command," story in three parts, *Paradise of the Pacific,* Part I, Vol. 66, No. 6 (June, 1954); Part II, Vol. 66, No. 7 (July 1954); Part III, Vol. 66, No. 8 (August 1954).

Boy Blue, a play in one-act, under the pseudonym of Roman Laim (Row, Peterson, 1928).

A Friend at Court, a play in one-act (Row, Peterson, 1931).

Roman Holiday, a play in three acts, under pseudonym of Roman Laim (Row, Peterson, 1928, 1931).

Editor, *The Thalian Guild Series of Plays* (Samuel French, 1927), 4 volumes.

Editor, *The Gateway Series of Tested Plays* (Row, Peterson, 1928 *passim*), 51 vols.

The Yearbook of Short Plays, First Series, Editor with Lee Owen Snook (Row Peterson, 1931).